Quantum Algorithms and Their Applications in Cryptology

Cryptography has long been an essential tool in safeguarding digital communication and securing sensitive information. As technology has progressed, so has the complexity of the methods used to protect our data. In the wake of quantum computing's rise, traditional cryptographic systems face serious challenges, demanding a new understanding of how quantum algorithms could both undermine and enhance security.

Chapter 1 deals with the Basics of Cryptography lays the groundwork by introducing classical cryptography, tracing its evolution from ancient ciphers to modern cryptosystems.

In Chapter 2, readers are introduced to Quantum Algorithms, the principles of quantum mechanics relevant to computing, including qubits, superposition, and entanglement.

Chapter 3 focuses on Shor's algorithm, a landmark quantum algorithm that threatens the security of widely used public-key cryptosystems like RSA and ECC.

In Chapter 4, Grover's Algorithm is examined in the context of brute-force attacks on symmetric key cryptography.

Chapter 5, focuses on Simon's Algorithm and its role in breaking cryptographic primitives through structure exploitation.

In Chapter 6, a broader discussion about Cryptographic Implications of Quantum Computing is given on how quantum computing affects modern cryptographic systems.

Finally, in Chapter 7, the future of cryptography in the quantum era is discussed.

Quantum Algorithms and Their Applications in Cryptology

A Practical Approach

Bhupendra Singh, Mohankumar Mylsamy and
Thamaraimanalan Thangarajan

CRC Press
Taylor & Francis Group
Boca Raton London New York

CRC Press is an imprint of the
Taylor & Francis Group, an **informa** business

Designed cover image: Shutterstock

First edition published 2026
by CRC Press
2385 NW Executive Center Drive, Suite 320, Boca Raton FL 33431

and by CRC Press
4 Park Square, Milton Park, Abingdon, Oxon, OX14 4RN

CRC Press is an imprint of Taylor & Francis Group, LLC

ISBN: 978-1-032-99817-6 (hbk)
ISBN: 978-1-032-99852-7 (pbk)
ISBN: 978-1-003-60633-8 (ebk)

DOI: 10.1201/9781003606338

Typeset in Nimbus Roman font
by KnowledgeWorks Global Ltd.

Publisher's note: This book has been prepared from camera-ready copy provided by the authors.

Dedication

This book is dedicated to all the researchers, educators, and innovators who strive to shape the future of quantum technology and make the world a better place.

Contents

SECTION I Basics of Cryptography

SECTION II An Introduction to Quantum Algorithms

SECTION III   Shor's Algorithm: Factoring and Cryptanalysis

SECTION IV   Grover's Algorithm: Quantum Search

SECTION V   Simon's Algorithm: Collision Finding

SECTION VI   *Cryptographic Implications of Quantum Computing*

SECTION VII   *Future Trends and Applications*

Preface

Cryptography has long been an essential tool in safeguarding digital communication and securing sensitive information. As technology has progressed, so has the complexity of the methods used to protect our data. In the wake of quantum computing's rise, traditional cryptographic systems face serious challenges, demanding a new understanding of how quantum algorithms could both undermine and enhance security.

Chapter 1 deals with the Basics of Cryptography lays the groundwork by introducing classical cryptography, tracing its evolution from ancient ciphers to modern cryptosystems. It provides foundational concepts such as stream and block ciphers and distinguishes between symmetric and asymmetric key systems, setting the stage for deeper cryptographic analysis in later chapters.

In Chapter 2, readers are introduced to Quantum Algorithms, the principles of quantum mechanics relevant to computing, including qubits, superposition, and entanglement. The chapter draws distinctions between classical and quantum computation and introduces key quantum algorithms and gates—forming the conceptual basis for understanding quantum cryptanalysis.

Chapter 3 focuses on Shor's algorithm, a landmark quantum algorithm that threatens the security of widely used public-key cryptosystems like Rivest-Shamir-Adleman (RSA) and Elliptic Curve Cryptography (ECC). Readers explore its theoretical foundation, circuit implementation, and resource estimation, including practical experiments using IBM Qiskit.

In Chapter 4, Grover's algorithm is examined in the context of brute-force attacks on symmetric key cryptography. The chapter includes a detailed cryptanalysis of the simplified Grain cipher using Grover's technique, and presents experimental results and quantum resource estimates for various attack scenarios.

Chapter 5 focusing on Simon's Algorithm and its role in breaking cryptographic primitives through structure exploitation. It details the application of Simon's algorithm to stream ciphers like Grain-128a, with thorough circuit design, implementation strategies, and test case evaluations.

In Chapter 6, a broader discussion about Cryptographic Implications of Quantum Computing is given on how quantum computing affects modern cryptographic systems. It explains the vulnerabilities of RSA, ECC, AES, and other algorithms under quantum threats and underscores the urgent need for transitioning to quantum-resistant alternatives.

Finally, in Chapter 7, the future of cryptography in the quantum era is discussed. It introduces Mosca's Theorem for risk forecasting and presents a taxonomy of quantum-safe cryptographic primitives. Topics include quantum key distribution (QKD), post-quantum cryptography (PQC), countermeasures, standardization, and infrastructure readiness for quantum networks.

The book is written for anyone with an interest in the intersection of cryptography and quantum computing. Whether you're a student, a professional, or just someone curious about how quantum algorithms will impact security, this book will provide you with a comprehensive understanding of the topic.

The authors would like to express sincere gratitude to the following organizations and individuals for their valuable contributions and support during the preparation of this book:

The **Directorate of Extramural Research & Intellectual Property Rights (DER&IPR)**, DRDO, for their continuous guidance and encouragement throughout the project.

Centre for Artificial Intelligence & Robotics (CAIR), for providing the necessary resources and technical expertise.

The **Management** and **Principal** of **Sri Eshwar College of Engineering, Coimbatore**, for their support in facilitating the work and providing a conducive environment for research and development.

Their unwavering support has been instrumental in the successful completion of this work.

Acknowledgments

The first author would like to acknowledge the motivation received from Shri T S Raghavan, Dr S S Bedi, Shri Sanjay Burman former director CAIR DRDO, Shri K Ravi Sankar, Dr P K Saxena former director SAG DRDO, Dr G Athithan former DG(MCC) DRDO, Dr Subrata Rakshit former DG(TM) DRDO, Dr U K Singh former director CAIR DRDO, Ms Suma Varughese DG(MCC) DRDO, Shri L C Mangal DG(TM) DRDO, Dr Rituraj Kumar director CAIR DRDO, Dr N R Pillai director SAG DRDO, Dr S K Pal, Prof Sugata Gangopadhyay IIT Roorkee, Prof V Vetrival IIT Madras, Prof Ashok ji Gupta IIT(BHU), Prof Anshuman Karmakar, IIT Kanpur, Prof Bimal Kumar Roy, Prof Subhamoy Maitra ISI Kolkata, Prof Arpita Maitra TCG CREST Kolkata, Prof Veni Madhavan, Prof Om Prakash IIT Patna, Prof Manoj Mishra IIT Roorkee, Prof Somitra Kumar Sanadhya IIT Jodhpur, Prof Bimal Mondal IIT Jodhpur, Prof Kuntal Som IIT Jodhpur, Prof Ratikanta Behera IISc Bangalore, Prof Shashank Singh IISER Bhopal, Prof Neeraj Shukla IIT Indore, Prof P K Singh Allahabad University, Prof Sahadeo Padhye, MNNIT Allahabad, and Prof Atul Chaturvedi AH Kanpur.

First author also would like to thank his colleagues. His heartfelt thanks to Pankaj Pandey, Ashish Tiwari, Lexy Alexander, Alok Mishra, Royal Pradhan, Santosh, Ankit, Jimmy, Ms V P Persia and Ms Anshu Bharadwaj. Thanks to Dr Indivar Gupta, Dr Dhananjoy Dey, Dr Yogesh Kumar, Dr P R Mishra, Dr Girish Pandey, and Dr Santu Sardar.

The second and third authors would like to express their sincere gratitude to Dr Bhupendra Singh, Centre for Artificial Intelligence and Robotics (CAIR), DRDO, for his invaluable guidance, support, and encouragement throughout the development of this work. His insights and mentorship have been very helpful in shaping the direction and quality of this textbook.

We also extend our heartfelt thanks to Shri. R. Mohanram, Chairman, Shri. R. Rajaram, Director, and Dr Sudha Mohanram, Principal of Sri Eshwar College of Engineering, for their unwavering support and for providing us with the platform and opportunity to pursue this academic endeavor. Their collective contributions have been vital to the successful completion of this textbook, and we are deeply appreciative of their commitment to excellence in education and research.

Authors

Bhupendra Singh is an alumnus of Allahabad University, IIT Madras, and Masaryk University, Brno, Czech Republic. He joined DRDO as a Scientist-B in 2005 and is currently working as a Scientist-F at the same organization. He is the project director of a project of national importance. His areas of research include the design and analysis of symmetric key cryptographic algorithms, the design and analysis of quantum-safe symmetric and asymmetric key cryptographic algorithms, the analysis of quantum random number generators, and construction of cryptographically significant Boolean functions and S-Boxes. He was a panelist at VAIBHAV-2020 in the Quantum Technology Vertical, organized by the PMO. His team won the second prize of Rs. 2.5 lakhs at the International Quantum Science and Technology Hackathon 2022, organized by the Office of the Principal Scientific Advisor, Government of India. Singh has been an elected executive committee member of the Cryptology Research Society of India since 2015. He has filed three patents and holds one copyright in the area of cybersecurity and quantum algorithms.

Mohankumar Mylsamy obtained his Ph.D. degree in Information and Communication Engineering from Anna University, Chennai, Tamil Nadu, India in 2020, received the M.E. degree in Information and Communication Engineering from Anna University of Technology, Coimbatore, India, in 2010; currently he is working as an Associate Professor in the Department of Electronics and Communication Engineering, Sri Eshwar College of Engineering, Coimbatore, Tamil Nadu, India. He served as principal investigator for a funded project from DRDO, focusing on Quantum Simulator and Cryptography algorithms. He is a life member of professional societies including ISTE and IAENG. His research interests include Wireless Sensor Networks, VLSI design, Image processing, and Quantum Computing.

Thamaraimanalan Thangarajan holds a Ph.D. in Information and Communication Engineering, awarded by Anna University, Chennai, India. With a remarkable 15 years of teaching and 13 years of research experience, his expertise spans various domains, notably Quantum Computing and Cryptography. He currently serves as an Associate Professor at Sri Eshwar College of Engineering, Coimbatore, Tamil Nadu, India. He served as Co-Principal Investigator of a DRDO funded project, focusing on Quantum Simulator and quantum cryptanalysis of asymmetric and symmetric key cryptographic algorithms. He has published several research papers in renowned international journals and presented his work at prestigious conferences, contributing significantly to advancements in his field of expertise. He is a member of professional societies including IEEE (Senior Member), ISTE, IETE, and IAENG. His research interests encompass quantum computing, artificial intelligence, machine learning, the Internet of Things (IoT), Low power VLSI design, and Wireless Sensor Networks.

Section I

Basics of Cryptography

1 Basics of Cryptography

"Every secret creates a potential failure point."

— Bruce Schneier

SUMMARY

This chapter provides a comprehensive overview of cryptography, beginning with its historical development and evolution, from ancient cryptography to the modern era, and extending to the challenges and advancements in post-quantum cryptography. It introduces stream ciphers, covering their types, advantages, and disadvantages, followed by a detailed look at the encryption and decryption processes involved. The chapter also explores asymmetric key cryptography, with an emphasis on Rivest-Shamir-Adleman (RSA), ElGamal, and Elliptic Curve Cryptography (ECC). Finally, it discusses symmetric key cryptography, particularly focusing on the Grain family of ciphers, including Grain v1, Grain-128, and Grain-128a.

1.1 INTRODUCTION

Cryptography, in general, is the practice and study of techniques for secure communication in the presence of adversarial behavior. It's like creating a secret message that others can't understand unless they have the special key to decode it. People use cryptography to keep data like messages, passwords, and financial details safe from hackers or anyone trying to access them without permission [1].

Derived from the Greek words meaning "hidden writing", cryptography involves encrypting information to ensure only the intended recipient can understand it. The practice of sending secret messages dates back to ancient civilizations and has been a vital tool throughout history. Today, cryptography is a cornerstone of cybersecurity, safeguarding personal communications, authenticating documents, securing online payment data, and protecting classified government information [2].

1.2 HISTORICAL DEVELOPMENT OF CRYPTOLOGY

Although cryptography has been used for thousands of years to cover secret messages, its formal study as both a science and an art began only about 1949. Cryptography, in its earliest forms, dates back to ancient civilizations like the Egyptians, Greeks, and Romans. One of the earliest known examples is the Caesar cipher, used by Julius Caesar around 60 BCE. However, modern cryptography, as we understand it today, began to take shape in the early 20th century with the development of mathematical techniques and more sophisticated encryption methods [3].

DOI: 10.1201/9781003606338-1

The earliest known use of cryptography dates back to around 1900 BC, found in an inscription in the tomb of the Egyptian nobleman Khnumhotep II. This inscription included unusual pictograph symbols substituted for standard ones. While the purpose wasn't to mask the message, it seems to have been an attempt to alter its appearance, perhaps to make it more formal or prestigious. Though not truly secret writing, it represents one of the first examples of text transformation. Evidence of cryptographic techniques has been observed in many early civilizations. For instance, in ancient India, Kautilya's Arthashastra, a foundational text on governance, discusses intelligence and mentions spies using "secret writing", which is a fascinating ancestor to modern covert operations [4].

Around 100 BC, Julius Caesar famously employed a form of encryption to send secret messages to his generals during wartime. This method, known today as the Caesar cipher, is one of the most widely referenced historical ciphers in academic discussions. A cipher refers to a method or algorithm used for encrypting or decrypting the ciphertext. In the Caesar cipher, each character in the original message (called plaintext) is replaced with a different character to create an encrypted message (called ciphertext). Caesar's version specifically involved shifting each letter by three places in the alphabet. For example, the letter "A" became "C," "B" became "D," and so on. When the alphabet reached its end, it wrapped around, so "Y" shifted to "A" as shown in Figure 1.1. It's clear that the security of such ciphers relies more on keeping the method secret rather than the encryption key itself. Once the technique becomes known, decoding the messages becomes straightforward [5].

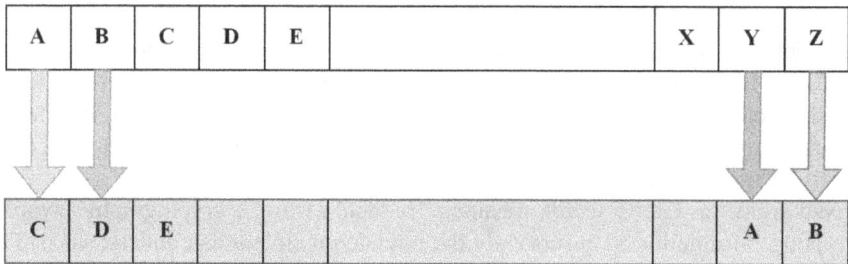

Figure 1.1 Model of Caesar cipher

In the 16th century, Vigenère introduced a cipher that was one of the first to use an encryption key. In one version of his method, the encryption key was repeated to match the length of the message. As depicted in Figure 1.2, the ciphertext was generated by combining each character of the message with the corresponding character of the key using modulo 26 arithmetic. (Modulo, or mod, is a function which returns the remainder value when a number is divided by another number.) Although Vigenère's cipher could also be broken, it was notable for introducing the concept of encryption keys. Unlike the Caesar cipher, where secrecy relied on hiding the method, Vigenère's cipher emphasized protecting the key to ensure message confidentiality, even though its implementation had flaws [6].

As technology became increasingly electric, Edward Hebern developed an electro-mechanical device known as the Hebern rotor machine. This machine

Key	C	R	Y	P	T	O	C	R	Y	P	T	O	C	R	Y	P	T	O	C
+Mod 26																			
Plaintext	W	E	L	C	O	M	E	T	O	Q	U	A	N	T	U	M	E	R	A
Ciphertext	Z	W	K	S	I	B	H	L	N	G	O	P	Q	L	T	C	Y	G	D

Figure 1.2 Model of Vigenère's cipher

featured a single rotor containing a secret key embedded within a rotating disk. The key defined a substitution table, and each press of a keyboard key produced a corresponding ciphertext character. With every keypress, the disk rotated one notch, altering the substitution table for the next character. However, this system was eventually broken by analyzing the frequency of letters [7].

Later, at the end of World War I, German engineer Arthur Scherbius invented the Enigma machine, which became widely used by German forces during World War II. Unlike Hebern's rotor machine, the Enigma used multiple rotors, such as three, four, or more than that rotated at varying rates with each keypress, creating a highly complex substitution system. The key to the Enigma machine as shown in Figure 1.3 was the initial rotor settings. Despite its sophistication, the Enigma cipher was eventually deciphered by Polish cryptographers, who passed their findings to British codebreakers. The British further developed methods to determine the daily keys, significantly aiding the Allied war effort [8].

Until World War II, cryptography was primarily used for military purposes, mainly to safeguard classified military information. However, after the War, it began to gain commercial importance as businesses sought ways to protect their data from competitors. In the early 1970s, IBM recognized the growing demand for encryption from its customers. In response, the company formed a "crypto group" led by Horst Feistel, which developed a cipher named Lucifer [9]. In 1973, the National Bureau of Standards (now known as NIST) in the United States issued a call for proposals for a block cipher to serve as a national encryption standard. This move reflected their realization that many commercial products lacked adequate cryptographic security. IBM's Lucifer was ultimately chosen and became known as Data Encryption Standard (DES).

By 1997, advances in computing power exposed a significant weakness in DES, its small key size, which made it vulnerable to exhaustive search attacks or brute force attack [10]. Recognizing the need for stronger encryption, NIST issued another request for proposals in 1997 to develop a new block cipher. After evaluating 50 submissions, NIST selected Rijndael in 2000 and adopted it as Advanced Encryption Standard (AES). Today, AES is a widely used and trusted standard for symmetric key encryption [11].

Figure 1.3   Enigma machine

1.2.1 A BRIEF HISTORY OF CRYPTOGRAPHY: THE EVOLUTION OF SENDING SECRET MESSAGES

Cryptosystems typically start with plaintext, an unencrypted message, which is transformed into ciphertext, an encrypted form using one or more encryption keys. This ciphertext is then transmitted to the intended recipient. If intercepted, the ciphertext remains meaningless without the proper decryption key, provided the encryption method is strong. The rightful recipient, with the correct key, can decrypt the message back into its original form [12].

1.2.2 ANCIENT CRYPTOGRAPHY TO TILL DATE

Cryptography has evolved significantly over millennia, transitioning from basic techniques of message concealment to modern cryptographic algorithms. Here's a summary of cryptographic development across time as follows.

1.2.2.1 Ancient Era

Egyptian Hieroglyphics (1900 BCE):
   Egyptian hieroglyphics, dating back to around 1900 BCE, were a system of pictorial symbols used for writing and recording information. While not a cipher in the modern sense, certain symbols or combinations of hieroglyphs were used to encode messages or hidden meanings, especially in religious and royal contexts. Hieroglyphics played a key role in Egyptian communication, with some texts involving symbolic or metaphorical encoding to convey deeper meanings [6].

Mesopotamian Ciphers (c. 1500 BCE):
   Mesopotamian ciphers, dating back to around 1500 BCE, represent some of the earliest examples of cryptographic techniques. These ciphers were primarily used

for securing communications, often in the form of encoded messages carved on clay tablets. The ciphers typically involved simple substitution methods, where symbols or characters were replaced with others to obscure the original message. The use of ciphers in ancient Mesopotamia was likely linked to both administrative needs and military communications, marking an early application of cryptographic methods in society [13].

Scytale Cipher (Sparta, c. 600 BCE):

The Scytale cipher, used in Sparta around 600 BCE, is a transposition cipher that involved wrapping a strip of parchment around a cylindrical object. The message was written across the wrapped strip, and when unwrapped, the text appeared scrambled. Only those with a matching cylinder could decode the message. This simple yet effective cipher was used primarily for military communication [14].

Atbash Cipher (Hebrew, c. 500 BCE):

The Atbash cipher, originating around 500 BCE in Hebrew, is a simple substitution cipher where the first letter of the alphabet is substituted with the last, the second with the second-last, and so on. This method was used for encoding Hebrew texts, particularly for creating encrypted messages or for providing cryptic interpretations of religious texts [15].

Caesar Cipher (Rome, c. 50 BCE):

The Caesar cipher, used around 50 BCE in ancient Rome, is a substitution cipher where each letter in the plaintext is shifted by a fixed number of positions in the alphabet. Named after Julius Caesar, who used it to protect military messages, the cipher is one of the earliest and simplest forms of encryption, offering a basic level of security by shifting letters [16, 17].

Ancient Indian Cryptology (300 BCE):

India has a rich history of cryptography that dates back thousands of years, with several unique cryptographic methods emerging in ancient times. While there were no formalized systems of cryptography as we understand today, early Indian cryptographers used various techniques for encryption and securing messages, particularly in military and royal communication [17].

1. **Kautilya's Arthashastra (3rd Century BCE):** One of the earliest references to cryptography in India comes from the Arthashastra, a treatise on statecraft, military strategy, and economics written by Kautilya (Chanakya) in the 3rd century BCE. The text mentions the use of ciphers for secure communication and is one of the earliest known instances where cryptography is discussed in the context of espionage and statecraft [4].

   Kautilya describes several methods of cryptography:

   Substitution Ciphers: One of the methods mentioned is the substitution cipher, where letters of the alphabet are substituted with other symbols or letters.

This early reference to substitution ciphers aligns with later cipher techniques like the Caesar cipher.

Use of Indirection: He also discusses using indirect communication, where the true message might be hidden within a larger body of text or disguised using a cipher.

2. **The Use of Codes in Indian Literature** Ancient Indian literature and religious texts also contained encoded messages. One such example is the Mahabharata, where hidden meanings and messages were often embedded in the text, requiring deciphering or interpretation. In the Sanskrit language, the use of poetic meters (known as Chandas) often had encoded meanings. The Brahmi script, one of the earliest scripts used in India, is also believed to have contained encrypted elements in some of its forms [18].

3. **The "Shabda" Cipher (Word-based Ciphers):** Ancient Indian cryptography also involved word-based ciphers, known as Shabda Ciphers, where words or phrases would be substituted with other meanings or symbols. This form of encoding often used synonyms, antonyms, or references to objects, gods, or symbols that had a particular significance. A text would look like a normal phrase or story but would carry a hidden message if interpreted correctly [19].

4. **Cipher Systems in Indian Kingdoms:** Indian kings and military strategists were known to have used cryptographic methods to safeguard their communications. This is evident in the military treatises from ancient and medieval India, where cryptographic methods were vital in maintaining secrecy, especially in the case of espionage. The Chola dynasty, for instance, is believed to have used forms of encryption for military communications [20].

5. **The Use of Ciphertext in the Indian Subcontinent:** Cipher texts, especially those using substitution methods, were sometimes used in royal courts for confidential matters. Royal decrees and private communications between rulers and courtiers may have been encrypted using simple ciphers, though the exact details of these ciphers are not always well documented.

6. **Indians and the Concept of "Encryption":** While the term "encryption" wasn't used in ancient India, the concept of securing information through transformation and manipulation of text was well understood. The Kautilya Arthashastra and other texts show that encryption was often used for military, political, and royal purposes. A variety of simple substitution ciphers, like the Caesar cipher, which shifts letters in the alphabet, could have been used, as well as methods of using polyalphabetic or homophonic ciphers, which were more advanced forms of encryption.

7. **Early Examples of Cryptographic Practices in India:**

Brahmi Script: The Brahmi script, one of the earliest scripts used in India, had some cryptographic properties. Some of the inscriptions in this script have led scholars to believe that encryption was employed to hide secret messages or encode religious texts [19].

Asokan Edicts: King Ashoka's edicts (circa 3rd century BCE) found on pillars and rocks across India are written in Kharosthi and Brahmi scripts. Though not strictly ciphers, some scholars argue that the edicts' meanings were encoded or contained hidden instructions that required interpretation beyond the visible text.

8. **Ancient Indian Ciphers in Modern Cryptography:** Though ancient Indian cryptography did not develop into a formal system or survive in detailed records, its influence on the development of encryption can be recognized in modern cryptographic methods. The techniques described by Kautilya and others align with those used in modern encryption, such as substitution ciphers, polyalphabetic ciphers, and even the application of basic cryptanalysis principles [20].

1.2.2.2 Middle Ages

Arabic Cipher (c. 800 CE):
Arabic cryptography, emerging around 800 CE, played a significant role in the development of cryptographic techniques during the Islamic Golden Age. Arab scholars, such as Al-Kindi, are credited with pioneering methods like frequency analysis to break simple ciphers. They expanded on earlier encryption methods, including the use of substitution ciphers, and made advancements that laid the groundwork for modern cryptographic concepts. Their work in cryptanalysis, particularly the study of letter frequencies, greatly influenced the evolution of cryptography [21].

Vigenère Cipher (c. 1500 CE):
The Vigenère cipher, developed around 1500 CE, is a polyalphabetic substitution cipher that uses a keyword to determine the shift for each letter in the plaintext. Unlike simple ciphers like the Caesar cipher, the Vigenère cipher applies a different shift for each letter, making it more secure and harder to break. The keyword is repeated to match the length of the message, and each letter of the plaintext is shifted based on the corresponding letter of the keyword [22].

Cipher Disks (1400s CE):
Cipher disks, developed in the 1400s CE, were a mechanical tool used for encryption and decryption. A cipher disk typically consisted of two rotating disks, each inscribed with the alphabet. By aligning the disks in various ways, a letter from the plaintext could be substituted with a letter from the corresponding position on the other disk. This method allowed for easier encryption compared to manually writing out substitution ciphers and provided a more efficient way of encrypting messages. Cipher disks were widely used in the Renaissance period for securing communications [23].

Playfair Cipher (1854 CE):
The Playfair cipher, introduced in 1854 by Charles Wheatstone and popularized by Lord Playfair, is a digraph substitution cipher. It encrypts pairs of letters (digraphs) rather than individual letters. A 5×5 matrix of letters is used, where each pair of plaintext letters is substituted with letters from the matrix based on

specific rules. The cipher was notable for being more secure than simple substitution ciphers, as it removed the predictability of single-letter frequency analysis. It was used primarily by the British military during the late 19th and early 20th centuries [24].

1.2.2.3 Modern Cryptography

Claude Shannon's Information Theory (1949):
Claude Shannon's Information Theory, introduced in 1949, revolutionized cryptography and communication. Shannon's work established the mathematical foundations of information transmission, encryption, and data compression. He defined key concepts like entropy (measuring information content) and redundancy and introduced the idea of "perfect secrecy" with his one-time pad model. this groundbreaking study, "A Mathematical Theory of Communication", laid the groundwork for modern cryptography, demonstrating how encryption systems could be analyzed and optimized for security [25].

Data Encryption Standard (DES, 1970s):
The DES, developed in the 1970s, was a symmetric key encryption algorithm standardized by the U.S. National Bureau of Standards (now NIST). It uses a 56-bit key and a Feistel structure to encrypt data in 64-bit blocks through 16 rounds of substitution and permutation. DES became widely adopted for securing sensitive data but was eventually deemed insecure due to advances in computing power, which made brute-force attacks feasible. It was later replaced by stronger algorithms like Diffie-Hellman (1976) [26] and AES [27].

Public Key Cryptography (RSA, 1978):
This cryptography is introduced with the RSA algorithm in 1978 by Ron Rivest, Adi Shamir, and Leonard Adleman, revolutionized public key encryption. RSA uses a pair of keys: a public key for encryption and a private key for decryption. It is based on the computational difficulty of factoring large numbers, making it secure for data transmission and digital signatures. RSA became the foundation of modern cryptography, enabling secure communication over untrusted networks like the internet [28].

Advanced Encryption Standard (AES, 2001):
The AES, adopted in 2001 by NIST, is a symmetric key encryption algorithm designed to replace DES. Developed by Vincent Rijmen and Joan Daemen, AES uses a block size of 128 bits and supports key sizes of 128, 192, or 256 bits. It operates through multiple rounds of substitution, permutation, and mixing, providing strong security and efficiency. AES is widely used globally to secure data in applications such as online transactions, wireless communications, and data storage [27].

Elliptic Curve Cryptography (ECC, 1986):
Elliptic Curve Cryptography (ECC), introduced in 1986 by Neal Koblitz and Victor Miller, is a form of public key cryptography based on the mathematics of elliptic curves over finite fields. ECC offers strong security with smaller key sizes compared to RSA, making it more efficient for devices with limited computational power and bandwidth. Its applications include secure messaging, digital signatures, and key exchange protocols, playing a vital role in modern cryptographic systems like TLS/SSL and blockchain technologies [29].

1.2.2.4   Post-Quantum Cryptography (PQC), (Present and Future)

Code based PQC (1978):
Code-based cryptography is one of the PQC methods and is based on error-correcting codes, particularly binary linear codes. The most well-known code-based cryptosystem is the McEliece cryptosystem. The McEliece cryptosystem is a public key encryption algorithm based on the hardness of decoding a random linear code. It is considered resistant to attacks by cryptographically relevant large quantum computers (CRLQC) [30].

Quantum Cryptography (1984):
Quantum cryptography, introduced in 1984 with the BB84 protocol by Charles Bennett and Gilles Brassard, leverages the principles of quantum mechanics to achieve secure communication. BB84 uses quantum properties like the no-cloning theorem and quantum superposition to enable quantum key distribution (QKD), ensuring that any eavesdropping on the transmission disturbs the system and can be detected. Quantum cryptography offers unprecedented security, as it relies on the laws of physics rather than computational assumptions, making it resistant to both classical and quantum attacks [31].

Lattice-based (2010s):
Lattice-based and hash-based cryptographic schemes, emerging prominently in the 2010s, are key components of PQC, designed to resist quantum attacks.

Lattice-based cryptography relies on the complexity of solving lattice problems, such as the Shortest Vector Problem (SVP), which are hard even for quantum computers. It offers efficient encryption, digital signatures, and key exchange protocols [32].

Hash-based schemes (2010s): Hash-based cryptography uses cryptographic hash functions for security, primarily in digital signatures. Schemes like XMSS (eXtended Merkle Signature Scheme) are quantum-resistant and rely on the strength of hash functions rather than number-theoretic assumptions [33].

Both approaches are critical in developing secure systems for the post-quantum era.

Cryptography Today (2024):
Cryptography in 2024 continues to evolve to address modern challenges, including the rise of quantum computing, increasing data privacy demands, and the expansion of the Internet of Things (IoT). PQC, with algorithms resistant to quantum attacks, is a major focus, as organizations prepare for the quantum era. Techniques like homomorphic encryption enable computations on encrypted data without decryption, enhancing privacy in cloud computing. Additionally, lightweight cryptography ensures secure communication for resource-constrained devices in IoT. Blockchain technology, zero-knowledge proofs, and advancements in secure multi-party computation further drive innovation, making cryptography essential for secure digital systems in a hyper-connected world [34].

1.3 INTRODUCTION TO STREAM CIPHERS

Stream ciphers are a class of encryption algorithms that operate on data one bit or byte at a time, producing a stream of ciphertext corresponding to a stream of plaintext. Unlike block ciphers, which encrypt fixed-size blocks of data, stream ciphers work by generating a pseudorandom key stream, which is then combined with the plaintext using a simple operation, typically XOR (exclusive OR). The key stream is usually generated from a secret key and an initialization vector (IV) to ensure that the encryption remains unpredictable. Stream ciphers are highly efficient and suitable for applications where data needs to be encrypted in real-time or in continuous flows, such as secure communications or video streaming. They are typically faster and more resource-efficient than block ciphers, making them ideal for environments with constrained computational resources or limited bandwidth. However, stream ciphers require careful management of keys and IVs to prevent vulnerabilities. Reusing the same key stream for multiple messages can lead to catastrophic security breaches. Well-known stream ciphers include RC4 (historically) and Salsa20/ChaCha20, which are commonly used in protocols like TLS and SSH. Despite their efficiency, stream ciphers can be susceptible to certain types of attacks, particularly if the key stream is predictable or improperly implemented [35, 36].

Stream ciphers can be broadly categorized into two main types: synchronous stream ciphers and self-synchronizing stream ciphers. The Stream cipher representation is shown in Figure 1.4. These types differ in how the key stream is generated and how they synchronize with the plaintext during encryption and decryption.

1.3.1 SYNCHRONOUS STREAM CIPHERS

In synchronous stream ciphers, the key stream is generated independently of the plaintext or ciphertext. The key stream is produced using a secret key and an initialization vector (IV) and is combined with the plaintext (or ciphertext) bit by bit,

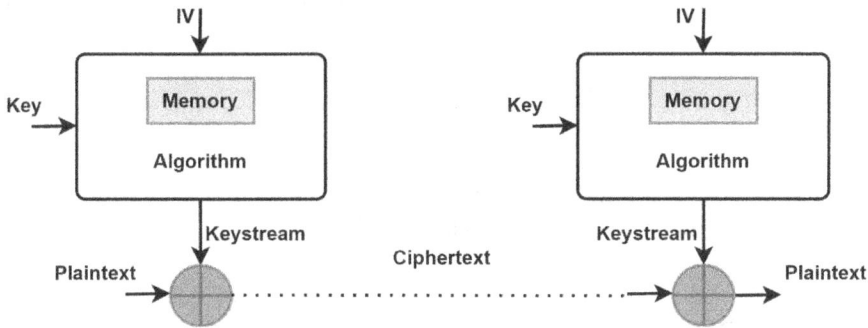

Figure 1.4 Stream ciphers

typically via an XOR operation. The encryption and decryption processes are independent of the message data, which means that both sender and receiver must stay synchronized to ensure the correct decryption.

Examples: RC4: One of the most famous (now considered insecure) stream ciphers, used in protocols like SSL/TLS and WEP. Salsa20 and ChaCha20: Secure and modern stream ciphers, widely used in cryptographic protocols like TLS and SSH.

1.3.2 SELF-SYNCHRONIZING STREAM CIPHERS

In self-synchronizing stream ciphers, the key stream is generated in such a way that it depends on both the previous ciphertext and the secret key. This means that if part of the ciphertext is lost or corrupted, the cipher can "resynchronize" after a certain number of bits without needing the complete previous ciphertext.

Examples: A block cipher in cipher feedback mode and a lightweight stream cipher designed for resource-constrained environments, like IoT devices.

1.3.3 ADVANTAGES OF STREAM CIPHERS

Efficiency: Stream ciphers are typically faster and more efficient than block ciphers, especially for encrypting long streams of data. They operate bit-by-bit or byte-by-byte, making them ideal for real-time or high-speed encryption applications (e.g., streaming video, voice communication).

Low Overhead: Since they encrypt data incrementally (one bit or byte at a time), stream ciphers have lower memory and computational requirements, which is valuable for devices with limited processing power, such as embedded systems or IoT devices.

Flexible Length: Stream ciphers can encrypt data of any length, unlike block ciphers which require padding to fill out data to a fixed block size. This flexibility makes stream ciphers suitable for streaming data or when the data length is unpredictable.

No Padding: Stream ciphers do not require padding as block ciphers do. This can reduce overhead and simplify the encryption process for certain types of data.

Real-Time Encryption: Stream ciphers are well-suited for scenarios where data is being transmitted in real-time, such as in video streaming or VoIP, where low latency is important.

1.3.4 DISADVANTAGES OF STREAM CIPHERS

Key Management Issues: Stream ciphers rely on a pseudo random key stream, which must be unique for each session or message. Reusing the same key stream for multiple messages (key reuse) can result in catastrophic security vulnerabilities, such as key stream reuse attacks. Proper key and IV management is crucial.

Susceptibility to Errors: A single bit error in the cipher text can propagate throughout the decryption process. If the key stream is not synchronized properly, it can cause the entire message to be corrupted or lead to incorrect decryption.

Vulnerability to Key Stream Predictability: If the algorithm used to generate the key stream is weak or predictable, it can be easily broken by attackers. For example, older stream ciphers like RC4 have been shown to have vulnerabilities that make them insecure against modern cryptanalytic attacks.

Security Risks with Poor Implementation: Stream ciphers are sensitive to implementation flaws. Weaknesses such as improper handling of initialization vectors (IVs) or key management errors can compromise the security of the stream cipher.

Limited Strength in the Face of Known-Plaintext Attacks: In some stream ciphers, attackers may exploit known-plain text attacks if they have access to both cipher text and corresponding plaintext. These types of attacks are harder to defend against in poorly designed stream ciphers.

1.4 OVERVIEW OF THE ENCRYPTION AND DECRYPTION PROCESS IN STREAM CIPHERS

Stream ciphers encrypt and decrypt data by processing plaintext (or ciphertext) bit-by-bit or byte-by-byte, using a pseudo-random key stream generated from a secret key. The process is designed for speed and efficiency, making stream ciphers ideal for real-time communication and data streaming. The encryption and decryption processes in stream ciphers follow a similar structure but occur in opposite directions.

1.4.1   ENCRYPTION PROCESS IN STREAM CIPHERS

Key Stream Generation: The core of stream cipher operation lies in generating a pseudorandom key stream (also called the key stream). This key stream is created using a secret key (and possibly an initialization vector, IV). The key stream should be unpredictable and ideally never repeat to ensure security. The key stream is generated independently of the plaintext, often using a cryptographic primitives such as a linear feedback shift register (LFSR), Boolean function, S-boxes or a more modern function like Salsa20 or ChaCha20 and Forero.

XOR operation: Once the key stream is generated, it is combined with the plaintext. This is typically done using the XOR (exclusive OR) operation:

$$\text{Ciphertext} = \text{Plaintext} \oplus \text{Keystream}$$

The truth table for the XOR gate is:

A	B	$A \oplus B$
0	0	0
0	1	1
1	0	1
1	1	0

Transmission of Ciphertext: The resulting ciphertext is then transmitted over the communication channel. This ciphertext looks like random noise to anyone who intercepts it, as long as the keystream is kept secret.

Each bit (or byte) of the plaintext is XORed with the corresponding bit (or byte) of the key stream. The XOR operation ensures that the ciphertext is unrecognizable and appears random, making it hard for attackers to discern the original plaintext without the keystream.

1.4.2   DECRYPTION PROCESS IN STREAM CIPHERS

Key Stream Generation (Same as Encryption): The decryption process begins similarly to the encryption process: the receiver uses the same secret key and initialization vector (IV) (if used) to regenerate the same keystream that was used during encryption. It is crucial that both the sender and the receiver have synchronized keystreams for decryption to work correctly.

XOR Operation (Same as Encryption): The receiver then applies the XOR operation to the ciphertext and the keystream:

$$\text{Plaintext} = \text{Ciphertext} \oplus \text{Keystream}$$

Since XOR is a symmetric operation, applying the same keystream that was used for encryption will recover the original plaintext.

For example, if:
$$\text{Ciphertext} = \text{Plaintext} \oplus \text{Keystream}$$
then,
$$\text{Plaintext} = \text{Ciphertext} \oplus \text{Keystream}$$
This results in the original plaintext being restored.

Use of Plaintext: After decryption, the original plaintext is recovered and can be processed or displayed as needed.

1.5 INTRODUCTION TO ASYMMETRIC KEY CRYPTOGRAPHY

Before the advent of asymmetric key cryptography, symmetric cryptographic methods dominated. In symmetric cryptography, the sender and receiver share the same secret key for encryption and decryption. This model, while efficient, posed a critical challenge: securely distributing keys to both parties. In large networks, this problem became increasingly complex and prone to interception [37]. In 1976, Whitfield Diffie and Martin Hellman introduced the concept of public-key cryptography, revolutionizing the field of cryptography [26]. Their work laid the foundation for secure key exchange without prior trust. Shortly after, the RSA algorithm was developed by Rivest, Shamir, and Adleman, which became the first practical implementation of asymmetric cryptography.

Asymmetric key cryptography, often termed as public-key cryptography, is a transformative innovation in the field of digital security, providing a key for secure communication and data exchange. Unlike symmetric key cryptography, which relies on a single shared key, asymmetric cryptography uses a pair of keys: a public key, openly distributed for encryption or signature verification, and a private key, securely held for decryption or signature creation. This dual-key mechanism eliminates the need for pre-established trust or secure key exchange, overcoming a significant limitation of earlier cryptographic methods. It enables secure communication over untrusted networks such as the internet, forming the foundation of modern digital security. Asymmetric key cryptography powers critical technologies like digital signatures, which authenticate data and ensure its integrity; secure online transactions, which protect sensitive financial information; and digital identity verification, which establishes trust in online interactions. Furthermore, it plays a pivotal role in blockchain systems by securing transactions and ensuring the authenticity of decentralized ledgers. Its applications extend to secure email systems like PGP, virtual private networks (VPNs) for safeguarding online privacy, and protocols like SSL/TLS, which underpin secure web communications. Beyond enhancing cybersecurity, asymmetric key cryptography has significantly contributed to the growth of e-commerce, remote work, and global collaboration by establishing trust across digital platforms. However, the advent of quantum computing presents a new challenge, as quantum algorithms like Shor's could potentially break traditional asymmetric systems by efficiently solving the mathematical problems on which they are based. To address this threat, researchers are developing quantum-resistant cryptographic algorithms, ensuring that asymmetric key cryptography continues to secure the digital landscape. As a cornerstone of modern cryptography, asymmetric systems remain indispensable in building a safe, trustworthy, and interconnected world [38].

Asymmetric cryptography relies on the mathematical relationship between two keys:

1. **Public Key:** Used for encryption or signature verification and can be freely shared.
2. **Private Key:** Used for decryption or signature creation and must be kept secret.

The security of these systems depends on the computational difficulty of certain mathematical problems, such as prime factorization (RSA) or the Elliptic Curve Discrete Logarithm Problem (ECDLP). Figure 1.5 shows different keys are used for encryption and decryption process.

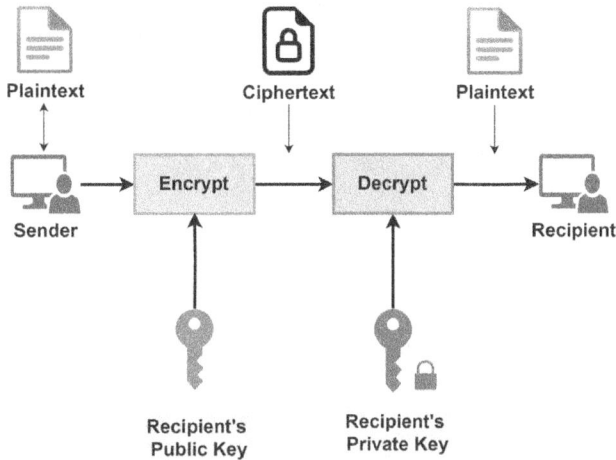

Figure 1.5   Asymmetric key cryptography

Key Generation Process

Key generation typically involves:

1. Selecting a large random number (or numbers).
2. Applying a mathematical function to derive the keys.
3. Ensuring the keys meet security criteria, such as sufficient entropy and uniqueness.

Encryption and Decryption Process

1. **Encryption:** The sender encrypts a plaintext message using the recipient's public key. This ensures that only the recipient can decrypt the message.

2. **Decryption:** The recipient uses their private key to decrypt the ciphertext, recovering the original message.

1.5.1 RIVEST SHAMIR ADLEMAN (RSA)

RSA is a well-known public-key or asymmetric cryptographic algorithm as shown in Figure 1.6. It protects sensitive data through encryption and decryption using a private and public key pair. First introduced in 1977 by Ron Rivest, Adi Shamir, and Leonard Adleman of the Massachusetts Institute of Technology, RSA is named after their last initials. RSA utilizes a private and public key pair. The private key is kept secret and known only to the creator of the key pair, while the public key is available to anyone. In RSA, either the public key or the private key can be used for encryption, and the other key is used for decryption. This is the main advantage of RSA [39].

Sender   Plaintext   Ciphertext   Decrypted Plaintext   Recipient

Public Key   Private Key

Figure 1.6 Process of RSA algorithm

RSA is one of the most widely used encryption mechanisms worldwide. However, the computational complexity of RSA makes it a relatively less efficient and resource-heavy algorithm. Hence, it is not suitable for encrypting large messages or files.

RSA is based on factorizing large integers. First, two large prime numbers must be chosen for the key pair. The prime numbers must be selected randomly and with a substantial difference between them. For example, consider the two chosen prime numbers as p and q. Then, the algorithm calculates their product, denoted by:

$$n = p \times q$$

The values of p and q should be kept secret, while n, is the modulus value. Next, the Euler's totient function is calculated using p and q, and the integer e, whose value is used as the public exponent, is selected. Then the next step is calculating the value of d, which is used as the private exponent. The public key is the pair (n, e), while the private key is the pair (n, d).

Encryption: When encrypting a plaintext, the sender uses the public key (n, e) of the recipient to compute the ciphertext, where the ciphertext C is given by:

$$C = m^e \bmod \times n$$

where m indicates the plaintext message.

Decryption: When decrypting an RSA encrypted message, the recipient uses their private key (n, d) to compute the plaintext message, where the plaintext message m is given by:

$$m = C^d \bmod \times n$$

APPLICATIONS AND USE CASES OF RSA

RSA is used in several information security and cryptography applications. Some of the most widely used applications include:

1. Digital signatures
2. Digital certificates
3. Secure communication protocols
4. Secure key exchange of cryptographic system

The RSA algorithm is difficult to crack, provided that it adheres to the recommendations. Several vulnerabilities in RSA have been discovered over the past few years. These vulnerabilities are:

1. Side-channel attacks
2. Inadequate key length
3. Weaknesses in prime numbers (Pseudoprime)
4. Lost or stolen keys
5. Fault-based attacks

MITIGATING RSA VULNERABILITIES

There are several things you can do to mitigate RSA vulnerabilities:

1. Use a strong prime number generator to ensure that the prime numbers are unpredictable and cannot be easily guessed by an attacker.
2. Avoid using weak prime numbers, such as small primes or primes too close to each other.
3. Use a minimum length of 2048 bits for the RSA key.
4. Take necessary actions to protect against fault-based attacks, such as using tamper-resistant hardware.
5. Manage and secure the RSA keys properly using techniques like regular key rotation and different keys for different applications.
6. Keep the RSA algorithm up to date by regularly monitoring for vulnerabilities and updates.

1.5.2   ELGAMMAL PUBLIC-KEY ENCRYPTION

ElGamal cryptography works in three stages:

1. Key Generation
2. ElGamal Encryption
3. ElGamal Decryption

Figure 1.7 shows the process of ElGamal Cryptography.

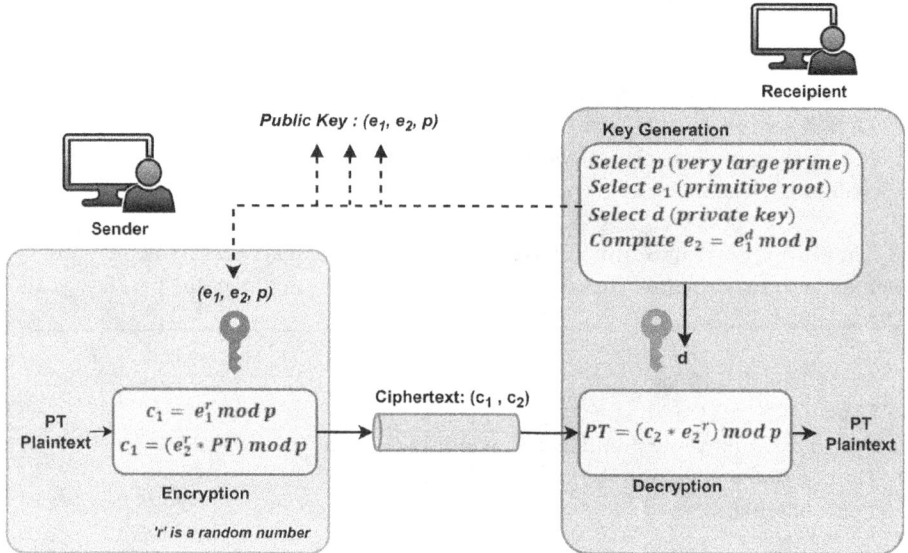

Figure 1.7   ElGamal cryptography process

A. ELGAMAL KEY GENERATION:

Select a large prime number p
Select encryption key e_1 to be a primitive root modulo p
Select decryption key d such that $1 \leq d \leq p - 2$
Select encryption key e_2 such that

$$e_2 = e_1^d \mod p$$

Form the public key as the set (e_1, e_2, p) to be announced publicly
Private key d is kept secret.

B. ELGAMAL ENCRYPTION:

Select a random number r

Compute the first part of the ciphertext c_1:

$$c_1 = e_1^r \mod p$$

Compute the second part of the ciphertext c_2:

$$c_2 = (e_2^r \cdot \text{PT}) \mod p$$

where PT is the plaintext message.

C. ELGAMAL DECRYPTION:

$$\text{PT} = (c_2 \cdot (c_1^{-r})) \mod p$$

where c_1 and c_2 are the ciphertext parts.

EXAMPLE 1: ELGAMAL ENCRYPTION AND DECRYPTION

Let us consider the following parameters:

Plaintext $M = 7$
Encryption key $e_1 = 2$
Private key $d = 3$
Random number $r = 4$
Prime number $p = 11$

STEP 1: KEY GENERATION

First, let's go through the key generation process.

Select a large prime number p: In this case, $p = 11$, which is a small prime number for demonstration purposes. In real-world applications, p should be a large prime number, typically at least 1024 bits long, to ensure security.

Ensure $p - 1$ has a large prime factor: Here, $p - 1 = 10$, and the prime factorization of 10 is 2×5, which is simple for demonstration but not secure for real applications. For stronger security, the prime number p should be chosen such that $p - 1$ has a large prime factor.

Select encryption key e_1: The encryption key $e_1 = 2$ is chosen to be a primitive root modulo $p = 11$. This is an arbitrary choice in this example. In general, e_1 should be a primitive root modulo p, meaning that $e_1^r \mod p$ should generate all values in the set $\{1, 2, \ldots, p - 1\}$.

Select the decryption key d: The decryption key is $d = 3$, which is selected such that $1 \leq d \leq p - 2$.

Compute e_2:

$$e_2 = e_1^d \mod p$$

Substituting the values:

$$e_2 = 2^3 \mod 11 = 8 \mod 11 = 8$$

So, the second part of the public key is $e_2 = 8$.
Form the public key: The public key is the set (e_1, e_2, p), which in this case is:

$$(e_1, e_2, p) = (2, 8, 11)$$

The private key is $d = 3$, and it is kept secret.

STEP 2: ENCRYPTION

Now, let's proceed to encrypt the plaintext $M = 7$.

Select a random number r: In this example, $r = 4$.
Compute the first part of the ciphertext c_1:

$$c_1 = e_1^r \mod p$$

Substituting the values:

$$c_1 = 2^4 \mod 11 = 16 \mod 11 = 5$$

So, $c_1 = 5$.
Compute the second part of the ciphertext c_2:

$$c_2 = (e_2^r \cdot \text{PT}) \mod p$$

Substituting the values:
$$c_2 = (8^4 \cdot 7) \mod 11$$

First, calculate $8^4 \mod 11$. To do this step-by-step:

$$8^2 = 64 \mod 11 = 9 \quad (\text{since } 64 \div 11 = 5 \text{ remainder } 9)$$

Now, calculate $8^4 \mod 11$:

$$8^4 = (8^2)^2 = 9^2 = 81 \mod 11 = 4 \quad (\text{since } 81 \div 11 = 7 \text{ remainder } 4)$$

Now, calculate c_2:

$$c_2 = (4 \cdot 7) \mod 11 = 28 \mod 11 = 6$$

So, $c_2 = 6$.

STEP 3: DECRYPTION

Now, let's decrypt the ciphertext $(c_1, c_2) = (5, 6)$.

Compute c_1^{p-1-d} mod p. We need to calculate:

$$c_1^{p-1-d} \mod p = c_1^{-r} \mod p$$

Substituting the values $p = 11$, $d = 3$, and $c_1 = 5$:

$$c_1^{p-1-d} = 5^{11-1-3} = 5^7 \mod 11$$

Now, let's compute 5^7 mod 11:

$$5^2 = 25 \mod 11 = 3$$

$$5^4 = (5^2)^2 = 3^2 = 9 \mod 11$$
$$5^6 = 5^4 \cdot 5^2 = 9 \cdot 3 = 27 \mod 11 = 5$$
$$5^7 = 5^6 \cdot 5 = 5 \cdot 5 = 25 \mod 11 = 3$$

So, 5^7 mod $11 = 3$.
Calculate the plaintext (PT):

$$PT = (c_2 \cdot (c_1^{p-1-d})) \mod p = (6 \cdot 3) \mod 11$$

$$PT = 18 \mod 11 = 7$$

Thus, the decrypted plaintext is 7, which matches the original message $M = 7$.

1.5.3 ELLIPTIC CURVE CRYPTOGRAPHY

In the year 1985, Neal Koblitz and Victor S. Miller independently leveraged elliptic curves over finite fields for public key cryptography. The motivation behind this was the reduction in the key size compared to conventional public key cryptography. The smaller key size helps in key management and reduces the resource requirement in hardware implementations. Lenstra also used elliptic curves to factor a positive integer.

In ECC, the design and analysis of cryptographic primitives are carried out using elliptic curves. The elliptic curve cryptographic primitives are more efficient than traditional public key cryptographic primitives. Like other public-key cryptosystems, the security of elliptic curve cryptosystems is also based on hard mathematical problems [40].

ELLIPTIC CURVES

An elliptic curve equation is given as:

$$E : y^2 = x^3 + ax^2 + bx + c,$$

where a, b, c are elements over a finite field $\mathbb{F}$ of characteristic not equal to 2. Points $A = (x_1, y_1)$ and $B = (x_2, y_2)$ that satisfy the equation are called points on the elliptic curve. The set of all such points, along with the **point at infinity**, form an additive group.

DISCRETE LOGARITHMS FOR ELLIPTIC CURVES

Suppose we have two points A and B on an elliptic curve E and $A = gB$ for some integer g. Finding g is known as the **discrete logarithm problem** for elliptic curves. Most public key cryptographic primitives in ECC are constructed based on the hardness of this problem.

REPRESENTING MESSAGES AS POINTS ON ELLIPTIC CURVES

Before performing any cryptographic operation on a message, it must be represented as a point on the underlying algebraic structure. In most cryptographic systems, the mapping of the message is straightforward. However, in ECC, this is not the case. To use ECC, an efficient method for mapping a message onto a point on an elliptic curve is necessary. Since the operations are performed over elliptic curve points, encoding the message is a non-trivial task.

PUBLIC KEY ENCRYPTION OVER ELLIPTIC CURVES

Public key encryption has the following constituents:

1. Key generation algorithm
2. Encryption algorithm
3. Decryption algorithm

ECC-based public key encryption shares these same constituents. In ECC, these operations are performed over elliptic curve points. Public key encryption using ECC can be constructed by instantiating the ElGamal framework with an elliptic curve group. Such systems are based on the hardness of the elliptic curve discrete logarithm problem.

DIGITAL SIGNATURES OVER ELLIPTIC CURVES

Digital signatures consist of the following components:

1. Key generation algorithm
2. Signing algorithm

3. Verification algorithm

ECC-based digital signature schemes follow the same structure, with operations executed over elliptic curve points. These can also be constructed by instantiating the ElGamal framework with an elliptic curve group, relying on the hardness of the elliptic curve discrete logarithm problem [41].

ADOPTION AND FUTURE OUTLOOK

In 2004, NIST and the NSA endorsed the use of ECC with 384-bit keys for top secret communications. ECC began to see widespread use after 2005. However, due to advancements in quantum computing, ECC is expected to be replaced by post-quantum cryptographic algorithms in the future.

1.6 INTRODUCTION TO SYMMETRIC KEY CRYPTOGRAPHY

Symmetric key cryptography is a method where the same key is used to encrypt and decrypt data. Both the sender and the receiver need to have the secret key to send and receive messages securely. This type of encryption is fast and efficient, making it good for handling large amounts of data. However, the biggest challenge is keeping the key safe, because if someone else gets the key, they can easily read the encrypted messages. The key must be shared securely between the two parties to ensure privacy and security.

The rise of computers in the mid-20th century marked a transformative phase in symmetric key cryptography, enabling the shift from mechanical to digital encryption. In 1977, the DES became the first widely adopted symmetric encryption standard, developed by IBM and endorsed by the U.S. government. Despite its popularity, DES's 56-bit key length proved vulnerable to brute-force attacks as computational power grew. This led to extensions like Triple DES (3DES) and eventually to the AES in 2001, chosen through an open competition by NIST. AES, with its 128, 192, and 256 bit key options, became the gold standard due to its balance of security, efficiency, and versatility.

In parallel, lightweight symmetric ciphers such as the Grain family and RC4 were developed for performance-critical environments, especially with the rise of IoT and embedded systems. As the digital landscape evolved, symmetric key cryptography adapted to meet emerging threats, including the looming challenge of quantum computing, which threatens to weaken traditional algorithms. Modern research focuses on optimizing symmetric key encryption for minimal resource usage and designing quantum-resistant alternatives to ensure its enduring relevance. From ancient hand-ciphers to today's advanced digital algorithms, symmetric key cryptography has continually evolved to protect data in an ever-changing technological world.

Symmetric key cryptography, also known as secret-key or private-key cryptography or one-key cryptography, is a foundational cryptographic technique where a single key is used for both encryption and decryption of data. The core concept involves securely sharing a secret key between the sender and the recipient prior to communication. This key must remain confidential, as its compromise allows adversaries to decrypt intercepted messages. Symmetric algorithms are typically categorized into two types: block ciphers, which encrypt data in fixed-size blocks (e.g., AES, DES), and stream ciphers, which encrypt data one bit or byte at a time (e.g., RC4, Grain). These algorithms are known for their efficiency and are commonly used in environments requiring high-speed processing, such as securing data in transit over the internet (e.g., TLS/SSL) or encrypting stored data (e.g., file encryption). While symmetric key cryptography is computationally efficient and suitable for large-scale data encryption, it faces challenges in key distribution and management, especially in large networks, since each pair of users requires a unique key. Modern implementations often combine symmetric cryptography with asymmetric techniques to resolve these limitations, such as in hybrid encryption systems [42].

Process of Symmetric Key Cryptography

Symmetric key cryptography works by using a single, shared secret key for both encryption and decryption processes. Here's how it generally works:

1. **Key Generation:** A secret key is generated. This key is shared securely between the sender and the recipient before communication begins. It must be kept confidential, as anyone with access to the key can decrypt the data under the assumption that algorithm details is known.
2. **Encryption:** The sender uses the shared secret key along with an encryption algorithm (e.g., AES or DES) to transform plaintext (original readable data) into ciphertext (encrypted, unreadable data). The encryption algorithm follows a set of mathematical rules that take the plaintext and the secret key as inputs to produce ciphertext. The process of symmetric key cryptography is depicted in Figure 1.8.
3. **Transmission:** The encrypted ciphertext is then transmitted to the recipient over a communication channel, which may be insecure (e.g., over the internet). The key is not transmitted during this phase, as it must be kept private.
4. **Decryption:** Upon receiving the ciphertext, the recipient uses the same secret key and the corresponding decryption algorithm (which is essentially the reverse of the encryption process) to transform the ciphertext back into plaintext.
5. **Security Considerations:** The security of symmetric key cryptography relies entirely on the secrecy of the key. If an adversary gains access to the key, they can easily decrypt the data. One of the main challenges is securely distributing and managing the key, especially in large-scale systems where many users need to communicate with each other. Typically, symmetric encryption is used for encrypting large volumes of data, while asymmetric encryption (using public and private key pairs) is used for securely sharing the symmetric key in the first place.

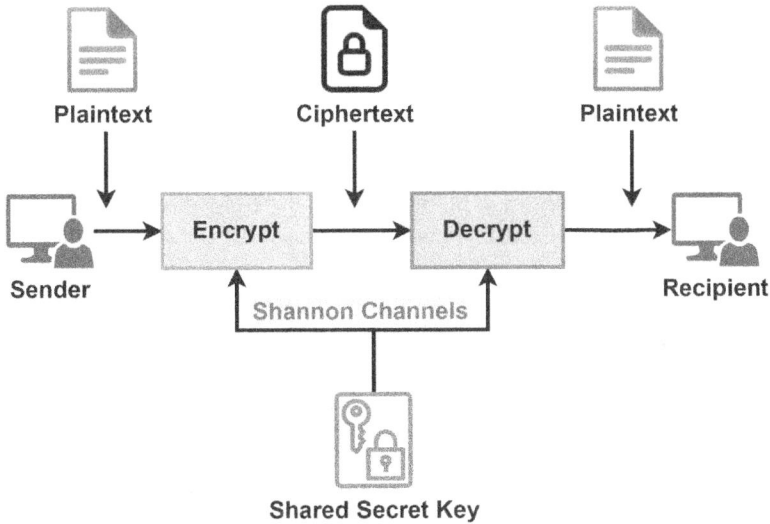

Figure 1.8 Process of symmetric key cryptography

1.6.1 CIPHERS OF GRAIN FAMILY

The *Grain family* of stream ciphers is a class of lightweight cryptographic algorithms designed for efficient hardware implementation in resource-constrained environments such as IoT devices and embedded systems. Grain ciphers operate on the principle of generating keystream bits using Linear Feedback Shift Registers (LFSRs) and Non-Linear Feedback Shift Registers (NFSRs), combined with non-linear output functions. The family includes variants like **Grain v1**, **Grain-128**, and **Grain-128a**, each optimized for specific security levels and application requirements [43].

Grain-128a, for instance, enhances the design by supporting optional authentication, making it suitable for securing both data confidentiality and integrity. These ciphers are favored for their small footprint and high speed but face vulnerabilities in the context of quantum computing. For example, Grover's algorithm can effectively reduce their key search complexity, raising the need for quantum-resistant alternatives. Despite these challenges, the Grain family remains a cornerstone in lightweight cryptography, particularly in constrained environments.

1.6.1.1 Grain v1

Grain v1 is a stream cipher designed to provide both high security and efficient performance, making it suitable for hardware and software implementations. It was developed as part of the eStream project, which aimed to evaluate and standardize stream ciphers for widespread use in cryptographic applications. Grain v1 is particularly known for its simplicity, speed, and small footprint, making it ideal for environments with constrained resources, such as embedded systems and devices with limited processing power.

Key Features of Grain v1

Stream Cipher: Grain v1 generates a pseudo-random stream of bits (keystream), which is then XORed with the plaintext to produce ciphertext. The same key is used to decrypt the ciphertext back into plaintext, as is typical with symmetric key encryption.

Internal Structure: Grain v1 operates using a combination of two main components:

Non-linear Feedback Shift Register (NLFSR): Provides the randomness necessary for keystream generation. It is initialized with a 160-bit key and an 80-bit initialization vector (IV).

Linear Feedback Shift Register (LFSR): Provides additional randomness and integrates with the NLFSR to generate high-quality keystream. Both feedback registers work together efficiently.

Key and IV Setup: Grain v1 is initialized with a 160-bit secret key and an 80-bit IV. The key is used to set up the internal state of the cipher, and the IV ensures that the same key can be used with different inputs without producing the same keystream.

Keystream Generation: The keystream is generated by the interaction of the NLFSR and LFSR. The output bits are combined to form the keystream, which is then XORed with the plaintext to produce ciphertext.

Speed and Efficiency: Grain v1 is designed with efficiency in mind, especially for applications requiring high throughput and minimal resource usage. It is known for its simplicity in both hardware and software implementations.

Security: Grain v1 provides a high level of security, resistant to various cryptanalysis techniques such as linear and differential cryptanalysis. However, its security depends on the proper management of the key and IV, particularly ensuring that the same key-IV pair is not reused.

1.6.1.2   Grain-128

Grain-128 is an enhanced version of Grain v1, designed to offer greater security and performance while maintaining the lightweight and efficient characteristics of its predecessor. It was developed as part of the eStream project and is tailored for applications requiring high security but limited computational resources [44].

Key Features of Grain-128

Stream Cipher: Grain-128 is a stream cipher that encrypts data bit-by-bit using a keystream generated from a secret key and an initialization vector (IV).

Key and IV Size:

Key: Grain-128 uses a 128-bit secret key.

IV: It uses a 128-bit IV, which increases the randomness and state space compared to the 80-bit IV of Grain v1.

Internal Structure: Grain-128 uses a combination of two main components for keystream generation:

Non-Linear Feedback Shift Register (NLFSR): Produces pseudo-random values that are critical for keystream generation.

Linear Feedback Shift Register (LFSR): Works alongside the NLFSR to ensure security and randomness in the keystream.

Keystream Generation: The interaction between the NLFSR and LFSR produces a stream of pseudo-random bits, which are XORed with the plaintext to produce ciphertext.

Security:

Grain-128 resists attacks such as linear and differential cryptanalysis due to the combination of the nonlinear NLFSR and linear LFSR.

The 128-bit key size offers robust security against modern brute-force attacks.

Performance: Grain-128 is optimized for low-latency encryption, making it suitable for embedded systems and real-time communication systems.

Applications of Grain-128

Embedded Systems: It is ideal for low-power embedded devices, such as IoT devices, sensors, and wearables.

Real-Time Communication: Grain-128 is well-suited for secure wireless communications and secure data transmission in constrained environments.

Cryptographic Standards: Grain-128 is considered for use in applications requiring lightweight cryptography, such as wireless standards and military-grade encryption for resource-constrained systems.

1.6.1.3 Grain-128a

Grain-128a is a variant of Grain-128 designed to improve resistance to attacks, enhance performance, and offer better flexibility. It retains the basic structure of Grain-128 while improving security [45].

Key Features of Grain-128a

Grain-128a is an **authenticated encryption stream cipher**. It generates a pseudo-random keystream, which is XORed with the plaintext for encryption. Unlike its predecessor (Grain-128), it includes **message authentication**, ensuring both confidentiality and integrity.

Key and IV Size

Uses a **128-bit key** and a **128-bit initialization vector (IV)**, providing strong security against brute-force attacks.

Different IVs ensure unique ciphertexts even with the same key.

Improved Security

Resists **differential cryptanalysis** and **linear cryptanalysis** due to modifications in its internal structure.

Features optimized **LFSR (Linear Feedback Shift Register)** and **NLFSR (Non-Linear Feedback Shift Register)** to enhance security while maintaining high performance.

Keystream Generation

The keystream is derived from the combined operation of **LFSR and NLFSR**.

The improved design increases resistance to state recovery and reverse-engineering attacks.

Authentication and Tag Generation

Unlike traditional stream ciphers, Grain-128a provides **message authentication** via an authentication tag.

The **tag is generated during encryption** and ensures integrity, protecting against message tampering.

The authentication process is tightly integrated with keystream generation, minimizing additional computational overhead.

Efficiency

Highly efficient in both **hardware and software**, making it ideal for **low-latency encryption** and **real-time applications**.

Suitable for lightweight cryptographic applications, including **IoT** and **embedded systems**.

Applications of Grain-128a

Embedded Systems: Grain-128a is particularly suited for embedded systems, such as IoT devices, smart cards, and sensors.

Wireless Communication: It is suitable for secure wireless communication standards where low power and high efficiency are required.

Military and Industrial Applications: Grain-128a is ideal for applications in secure communications, remote sensing, and other industrial uses.

REFERENCES

1. Abood, O. G., & Guirguis, S. K. (2018). A survey on cryptography algorithms. *International Journal of Scientific and Research Publications, 8*(7), 495–516.
2. Dooley, J. F. (2018). History of cryptography and cryptanalysis. In *history of computing*. Springer International Publishing.
3. Sams, E. (1985). Cryptanalysis and historical research. *Archivaria,* Vol No. 21, 87–97.
4. Singh, B. (2020). Kautilya's Arthashastra. *International Journal of Applied Social Sciences, 7*(11–12), 595–600.

5. Patni, P. (2013). A poly-alphabetic approach to Caesar cipher algorithm. *International Journal of Computer Science and Information Technologies, 4*(6), 954–959.
6. Darnell, J. C. (2020). Ancient Egyptian cryptography: Graphic hermeneutics. *Enigmatic Writing in the Egyptian New Kingdom I: Revealing, Transforming, and Display in Egyptian Hieroglyphs, ZÄS Beihefte, 12,* 7–48.
7. Nurcahya, S. D., & Nazelliana, D. (2024). Message security in classical cryptography using the Vigenere cipher method. *International Journal Software Engineering and Computer Science (IJSECS), 4*(1), 350–357.
8. Deavours, C. A. (1977). Analysis of the Hebern cryptograph using isomorphs. *Cryptologia, 1*(2), 167–185.
9. Khan, D. (1967). *The codebreakers: The story of secret writing* (pp. 503–510). Weidenfeld and Nicholson.
10. Schneier, B. (2007). *Applied cryptography: Protocols, algorithms, and source code in C.* John Wiley & Sons.
11. Standard, D. E. (1999). Data encryption standard. *Federal Information Processing Standards Publication, 112,* 3.
12. Stinson, D. R. (2005). *Cryptography: Theory and practice.* Chapman and Hall/CRC.
13. Mollin, R. A. (2005). *Codes: The guide to secrecy from ancient to modern times.* Chapman and Hall/CRC.
14. Kartalopoulos, S. V. (2006). A primer on cryptography in communications. *IEEE Communications Magazine, 44*(4), 146–151.
15. Leighton, A. C. (1969). Secret communication among the Greeks and Romans. *Technology and Culture, 10*(2), 139–154.
16. Rubin, F. (2022). Secret key cryptography: Ciphers, from simple to unbreakable. Simon and Schuster.
17. Goyal, K., & Kinger, S. (2013). Modified Caesar Cipher for better security enhancement. *International Journal of Computer Applications, 73*(3), 26–31.
18. Upadhyaya, P. A. (2024). *ManusCrypt: Designed for mankind–anthropocentric information security.* CRC Press.
19. Kaur, S., & Sagar, B. B. (2023). Efficient scalable template-matching technique for ancient Brahmi Script image. *Computers, Materials & Continua, 75*(1).
20. Shandilya, S. K., Datta, A., & Nagar, A. K. (2023). *A nature-inspired spproach to cryptology.* Springer.
21. Al-Kadit, I. A. (1992). Origins of cryptology: The Arab contributions. *Cryptologia, 16*(2), 97–126.
22. Rubinstein-Salzedo, S. (2018). The Vigenere cipher. In *Cryptography,* Springer Undergraduate Mathematics Series. Springer, Cham, 41–54.
23. Crowley, P. (2001). Mercy: A fast large block cipher for disk sector encryption. In *Fast software encryption: 7th international workshop, FSE 2000 New York, NY, USA, April 10–12, 2000 Proceedings 7* (pp. 49–63). Springer Berlin Heidelberg.
24. Dunin, E., Ekhall, M., Hamidullin, K., Kopal, N., Lasry, G., & Schmeh, K. (2022). How we set new world records in breaking Playfair ciphertexts. *Cryptologia, 46*(4), 302–322.
25. Abou Jaoude, A. (2017). The paradigm of complex probability and Claude Shannon's information theory. *Systems Science & Control Engineering, 5*(1), 380–425.
26. Diffie, W., Hellman, M. E., & Ellis, J. (1976, June). Public key cryptography. In *IEEE International Symposium on Information Theory.*
27. Rijmen, V., & Daemen, J. (2001). Advanced encryption standard. In *Proceedings of federal information processing standards publications, National Institute of Standards and Technology*, pp. 19–22.

28. Imam, R., Areeb, Q. M., Alturki, A., & Anwer, F. (2021). Systematic and critical review of RSA based public key cryptographic schemes: Past and present status. *IEEE Access, 9*, 155949–155976.
29. Hankerson, D., & Menezes, A. (2021). Elliptic curve cryptography. In *Encyclopedia of cryptography, security and privacy* (pp. 1–2). Springer Berlin Heidelberg.
30. Balamurugan, C., Singh, K., Ganesan, G., & Rajarajan, M. (2021). Post-quantum and code-based cryptography—Some prospective research directions. *Cryptography, 5*(4), 38.
31. Pirandola, S., Andersen, U. L., Banchi, L., Berta, M., Bunandar, D., Colbeck, R., ... & Wallden, P. (2020). Advances in quantum cryptography. *Advances in Optics and Photonics, 12*(4), 1012–1236.
32. Micciancio, D., & Regev, O. (2009). Lattice-based cryptography. In *Post-quantum cryptography* (pp. 147–191). Springer Berlin Heidelberg.
33. Srivastava, V., Baksi, A., & Debnath, S. K. (2023). An overview of hash based signatures. *Cryptology ePrint Archive.*
34. Chahar, S. (2025). Exploring the future trends of cryptography. In *Next generation mechanisms for data encryption* (pp. 234–257). CRC Press.
35. Rueppel, R. A. (2012). *Analysis and design of stream ciphers.* Springer Science & Business Media.
36. Cusick, T. W., Ding, C., & Renvall, A. R. (2004). *Stream ciphers and number theory* (Vol. 66). Gulf Professional Publishing.
37. Delfs, H., Knebl, H., & Knebl, H. (2002). *Introduction to cryptography* (Vol. 2). Springer.
38. Banoth, R., & Regar, R. (2023). Asymmetric key cryptography. In *Classical and modern cryptography for beginners* (pp. 109–165). Springer Nature Switzerland.
39. Milanov, E. (2009). *The RSA algorithm* (pp. 1–11). RSA Laboratories.
40. Trappe, W., & Washington, L. C. (2008). *Introduction to cryptography with coding theory,* (2nd Ed.). Pearson.
41. Washington, L. C. (2008). *Elliptic curves: Number theory and cryptography*, Chapman & Hall/CRC.
42. Delfs, H., Knebl, H., Delfs, H., & Knebl, H. (2015). *Symmetric-key cryptography.* Introduction to cryptography: Principles and applications (pp. 11–48) Springer, Berlin, Heidelberg.
43. Kumar, S., & Wollinger, T. (2006). Fundamentals of symmetric cryptography. In *Embedded security in cars: Securing current and future automotive IT applications* (pp. 125–143). Springer Berlin Heidelberg.
44. Banik, S., Maitra, S., & Sarkar, S. (2012, September). A differential fault attack on the grain family of stream ciphers. In *International workshop on cryptographic hardware and embedded systems* (pp. 122–139). Springer Berlin Heidelberg.
45. Berzati, A., Canovas, C., Castagnos, G., Debraize, B., Goubin, L., Gouget, A., ... & Salgado, S. (2009, July). Fault analysis of GRAIN-128. In *2009 IEEE international workshop on hardware-oriented security and trust* (pp. 7–14). IEEE.
46. Joan, D., & Vincent, R. (2002). The design of Rijndael: AES-the advanced encryption standard. *Information Security and Cryptography, 196,* 1–253
47. Katkuri, S. (2024). Need of encryption legislation: Protecting India's digital realm and beyond. *Indian Journal of Public Administration, 70*(3), 562–578.
48. Tsiounis, Y., & Yung, M. (1998, February). On the security of ElGamal based encryption. In *International Workshop on Public Key Cryptography* (pp. 117–134). Springer Berlin Heidelberg.
49. Stallings, W. (2013). Digital signature algorithms. *Cryptologia, 37*(4), 311–327.

Section II

An Introduction to Quantum Algorithms

2 An Introduction to Quantum Algorithms

"If you think you understand quantum mechanics, you don't understand quantum mechanics."

— Richard Feynman

SUMMARY

This chapter provides an introduction to quantum algorithms, starting with the fundamentals of quantum computing. It covers the basics of quantum mechanics, the potential for quantum speedup, and the challenges and limitations of quantum computing. The chapter also highlights the key differences between classical and quantum computing, focusing on concepts such as bits and qubits, quantum measurement, superposition, and qubit properties, with a detailed explanation of qubit states on the Bloch sphere. Additionally, it explores quantum gates and algorithms, including single-qubit and multiple-qubit gates, the Quantum Fourier Transform (QFT), and important quantum algorithms such as Shor's algorithm for factoring, Grover's algorithm for searching, and Simon's algorithm for collision finding.

2.1 FUNDAMENTALS OF QUANTUM COMPUTING

Quantum computing is an emerging field of computation that influences the principles of quantum mechanics to process information in fundamentally different ways than classical computers. While classical computers use bits to represent data as either 0 or 1, quantum computers use quantum bits, or qubits, which can represent both 0 and 1 simultaneously, using the phenomenon known as quantum superposition. Quantum computing promises to revolutionize industries by solving complex problems faster than classical computers ever could. Tasks that would take thousands of years for classical computers could be done much faster using quantum algorithms. This chapter introduces the fundamental concepts of quantum computing, its potential, the key principles that differentiate it from classical computing, and an introduction to quantum algorithms [1, 2].

2.1.1 THE BASICS OF QUANTUM MECHANICS

To understand quantum computing, it's important to have a basic grasp of quantum mechanics. While classical mechanics describes the behavior of everyday objects,

DOI: 10.1201/9781003606338-2

quantum mechanics governs the behavior of particles at the smallest scales atoms, electrons, and photons [3]. Some of the key principles of quantum mechanics that quantum computers depend on are the following:

Quantum superposition: In classical computing, a bit can only exist in one of two states, 0 or 1. However, in quantum computing, a qubit can be in a superposition of both 0 and 1 at the same time. This allows quantum computers to perform multiple calculations simultaneously, offering exponential speedup in certain cases.

Quantum entanglement: When qubits become entangled, the state of one qubit is directly linked to the state of another, even if they are far apart. This phenomenon enables qubits to work together in a way that classical bits cannot, creating powerful correlations between qubits that help quantum algorithms solve complex problems.

2.1.2   QUANTUM SPEEDUP AND ITS POTENTIAL

Quantum computing holds the promise of solving problems that are currently unsolvable or too time-consuming for classical computers. One of the most famous examples is Shor's algorithm, which can factor large numbers exponentially faster than classical algorithms. This has profound implications for cryptography, as many encryption schemes rely on the difficulty of factoring large numbers. Shor's algorithm achieves this by utilizing quantum parallelism and the QFT to find the periodicity of a function, enabling the factorization process to be performed in polynomial time, rather than the exponential time required by classical methods [4].

Another important quantum algorithm is Grover's algorithm, which speeds up unstructured search problems by a factor of about two. While this is not as powerful as the exponential speedup from Shor's algorithm, it still provides a clear advantage over classical search methods. Grover's algorithm uses amplitude amplification to increase the probability of finding the correct solution in an unsorted database, reducing the search time from $O(N)$ to $O(\sqrt{N})$. This quadratic speedup can be highly beneficial for various applications, including database search and optimization problems, demonstrating the significant potential of quantum computing. Both Shor's and Grover's algorithms highlight the transformative power of quantum computing, providing the way for advancements in fields such as cryptography, data search, and optimization [5].

2.1.3   CHALLENGES AND LIMITATIONS OF QUANTUM COMPUTING

Despite its vast potential, quantum computing faces numerous challenges:

Decoherence and Noise: *Decoherence* refers to the process by which a quantum system loses its quantum properties due to interactions with its surrounding environment. This loss of coherence disrupts the delicate quantum states of qubits, making it difficult to maintain the superposition and entanglement necessary for quantum computations. Quantum computers are highly sensitive to their environment, and small disturbances can cause them to lose their quantum properties. Maintaining the quantum state of qubits long enough to perform calculations is one of the biggest hurdles [6]. *Noise* in quantum systems encompasses various types of errors and disturbances that can affect qubits during computations. These disturbances can come from several sources, including thermal fluctuations, electromagnetic interference, and imperfections in the quantum hardware itself. Even the slightest perturbations can introduce errors in quantum computations, leading to incorrect results. Due to the extreme sensitivity of quantum states, noise must be minimized and managed effectively [7].

Error Correction: It is a critical area of research in quantum computing due to the inherent fragility of qubits. Unlike classical bits, qubits are highly susceptible to errors caused by environmental noise, imperfections in the quantum hardware, and other forms of interference. These errors can disrupt the delicate quantum states necessary for accurate computations, making the development of robust error correction methods essential for the reliability, scalability and performance of quantum computers [8].

Hardware Limitations: Building a scalable quantum computer requires sophisticated hardware capable of manipulating and measuring quantum states with extreme precision. Current quantum computers, known as Noisy Intermediate-Scale Quantum (NISQ) devices, are in the early stages and are not yet capable of solving large-scale practical problems. These devices face significant challenges such as high error rates, short coherence times, and the need for cryogenic environments. Overcoming these hardware limitations involves improving qubit designs, implementing robust quantum error correction methods, and developing advanced fabrication techniques [10].

2.1.4   THE FUTURE OF QUANTUM COMPUTING

Quantum computing is still in its infancy, with significant progress needed before it can reach its full potential. However, the possibilities it presents are vast. Applications of quantum computing range from cryptography and optimization to machine learning and drug discovery. Researchers are actively working on developing more stable and efficient quantum computers, improving quantum algorithms, and exploring quantum-resistant encryption methods for a future where quantum computers might be widely accessible [11].

2.2 DIFFERENCE BETWEEN CLASSICAL AND QUANTUM COMPUTING

Classical and quantum computing represent two fundamentally different approaches to processing information, each with unique characteristics, capabilities, and applications. Understanding these differences is crucial for grasping the potential impact of quantum technology on various fields [12] (Table 2.1).

Table 2.1: Classical vs quantum computing

Parameters	Classical computing	Quantum computing
Basic Units of Information	The fundamental unit of information in classical computing is the bit, which can be either 0 or 1. This binary representation allows classical computers to perform operations using deterministic algorithms based on Boolean logic.	Quantum computing employs quantum bits (qubits), which can exist in multiple states simultaneously due to the principles of quantum superposition. A qubit can be 0, 1, or both at the same time, allowing for a richer representation of information than classical bits.
Information Processing	Classical computers process information sequentially, executing one operation at a time. This linear processing is governed by classical physics and relies on transistors and logic gates to perform computations.	Quantum computers influence quantum mechanics to perform calculations in parallel across multiple states. This capability allows them to explore numerous solutions simultaneously, potentially leading to exponential speedups for certain types of problems.
Nature of Computation	Operations are based on classical physics principles, utilizing deterministic algorithms that yield predictable outcomes. These computers excel in tasks that require straightforward logic operations and are widely used in everyday applications.	Quantum computation harnesses phenomena such as quantum superposition and quantum entanglement. This enables quantum computers to solve complex problems probabilistically and explore multiple solutions concurrently, which is particularly advantageous for optimization and cryptographic tasks.

Parameters	Classical Computing	Quantum Computing
Algorithmic Approach	Algorithms in classical computing are designed for sequential processing and deterministic results. They typically involve a series of well-defined steps that lead to a specific outcome.	Quantum algorithms take advantage of quantum properties like quantum superposition and quantum entanglement. These algorithms can process vast amounts of data simultaneously, making them suitable for solving problems such as integer factorization much more efficiently than classical counterparts.
Error Correction	Well-established error correction techniques ensure data integrity in classical systems. These methods are effective due to the predictable nature of bits.	Quantum systems face significant challenges related to qubit coherence and error rates caused by environmental noise. Advanced quantum error correction methods are necessary to maintain accuracy in computations.
Speed and Scalability	The computational power of classical computers increases linearly with the number of bits or transistors. While they can perform parallel processing, their overall speed is limited by physical constraints such as clock rates.	The power of quantum computers increases exponentially with the addition of qubits. Each additional qubit doubles the number of possible states, allowing for vastly more complex computations than classical systems can handle.

2.2.1 CONCEPT OF BIT AND QUBIT

Bit: Bits, which can be either 0 or 1, are used by digital computers to store and process data. Anything with two different configurations, one denoted by "0" and the other by "1" can be considered a bit physically. There could be two different and recognizable options for the system. The lack or presence of an electrical signal, which encodes "0" and "1", respectively, is how bits are represented in contemporary computing and communications.

Qubit: Quantum information is physically carried by qubits, which are the quantum counterparts of classical bits. A qubit's quantum state can be expressed in terms of two basis states, denoted by $|0\rangle$ and $|1\rangle$. This notation is called *ket* notation $|\rangle$, where *ket* refers to the column vector. The corresponding *bra* notation $\langle|$, denoted as $\langle 0|$ and $\langle 1|$, is used for the complex conjugate transpose. Together, the *bra* and *ket* notations form Dirac notation. These basis states are often represented as two-dimensional column vectors [13].

$$|0\rangle = \begin{pmatrix} 1 \\ 0 \end{pmatrix}, \quad |1\rangle = \begin{pmatrix} 0 \\ 1 \end{pmatrix}$$

A qubit can exist in one of two states or in a superposition of both simultaneously. In quantum computation, two distinguishable states of a system are required to represent a bit of data.

For example, consider an electron orbiting a single atom. The electron's *spin* can be in two states: "spin-up" ($|0\rangle$) and "spin-down" ($|1\rangle$). Similarly, in the context of atomic energy levels, the *ground state* energy level can be denoted as $|0\rangle$, while the *excited state* energy level is represented as $|1\rangle$.

2.2.1.1   Quantum Measurement

Measurement refers to the act of determining the state of a quantum system. Unlike classical measurement, which yields definite results, quantum measurement is inherently probabilistic. When a qubit (the quantum counterpart of a classical bit) is measured, it can collapse to either 0 or 1, depending on its superposition prior to measurement. This superposition allows qubits to represent multiple states simultaneously, a fundamental aspect that gives quantum computers their immense computational power. Quantum measurement is crucial for reading out results from quantum computations and for controlling and manipulating quantum systems. However, it poses significant challenges, such as decoherence, where the quantum system loses its coherent superposition due to interactions with the environment [14].

2.2.1.2   Superposition of Two States

The key difference between qubits and classical bits is that a qubit can exist in a *superposition* of the two states $|0\rangle$ and $|1\rangle$ [15]. For example, if α and β are the probability amplitudes of an electron being in the ground state (i.e., in $|0\rangle$) and the excited state (i.e., in $|1\rangle$), then the qubit's state can be expressed as a linear combination:

$$|\psi\rangle = \alpha|0\rangle + \beta|1\rangle$$

Here, α and β are complex numbers, and due to the normalization condition:

$$|\alpha|^2 + |\beta|^2 = 1$$

This normalization ensures that the total probability of all possible outcomes (in this case, being in either $|0\rangle$ or $|1\rangle$) sums to 1. Specifically, $|\alpha|^2$ represents the probability of measuring the qubit in the state $|0\rangle$, and $|\beta|^2$ represents the probability of measuring the qubit in the state $|1\rangle$. Therefore, when a qubit is measured, it will collapse to one of the two states, either $|0\rangle$ or $|1\rangle$, with corresponding probabilities.

Consider the quantum state:

$$|\Psi\rangle = \frac{1}{\sqrt{2}}|0\rangle + \frac{1}{\sqrt{2}}|1\rangle$$

$$|\Psi\rangle = \alpha|0\rangle + \beta|1\rangle = \frac{1}{\sqrt{2}}|0\rangle + \frac{1}{\sqrt{2}}|1\rangle$$

where $\alpha = \frac{1}{\sqrt{2}}$ and $\beta = \frac{1}{\sqrt{2}}$. The squared magnitudes of the probability amplitudes are:

$$|\alpha|^2 = \left|\frac{1}{\sqrt{2}}\right|^2 = \frac{1}{2}, \quad |\beta|^2 = \left|\frac{1}{\sqrt{2}}\right|^2 = \frac{1}{2}$$

Thus, the probabilities of measuring the qubit in the states $|0\rangle$ and $|1\rangle$ are both $\frac{1}{2}$. The normalization condition is satisfied:

$$|\alpha|^2 + |\beta|^2 = \frac{1}{2} + \frac{1}{2} = 1$$

This means that with a 50% probability, the qubit will be found in the $|0\rangle$ state, as well as in the $|1\rangle$ state, upon measurement. These superposed states are often referred to as *superposition states*, while $|0\rangle$ and $|1\rangle$ are known as *basis states*. Basis states are the fundamental states of the system, and any quantum state, including superposition states, can be represented as a linear combination of these basis states [16].

2.2.1.3   Properties of Qubits

1. **Qubits use discrete energy states**: Qubits typically make use of discrete energy states in physical particles such as electrons, photons, or atoms.
2. **Quantum superposition**: Qubits can exist in two quantum states, $|0\rangle$ and $|1\rangle$, or in a *superposition* of both states. This means a qubit can be in a linear combination of these states simultaneously.
3. **Quantum Interference**: Quantum interference is a key concept in quantum computing that leverages the unique properties of qubits. Unlike classical bits, which can only be 0 or 1, a qubit can be in both states at once, thanks to superposition. This means a 4-qubit register can represent all 16 possible numbers (from 0 to 15) at the same time, unlike a classical 4-bit register which can only hold one number at a time. Quantum interference happens when these superposed states interact, helping quantum computers to amplify the right answers and cancel out the wrong ones, making them incredibly powerful for solving complex problems [17].
4. **Measurement and State Collapse**:When a qubit is measured, it collapses to one of the two basis states, $|0\rangle$ or $|1\rangle$, with certain probabilities determined by the probability amplitudes. These probability amplitudes are complex numbers that

describe the likelihood of the qubit being in a particular state before measurement. The squared magnitude of the amplitude gives the actual probability of the qubit collapsing to that state. This probabilistic nature of quantum measurement is what makes quantum computing both powerful and fundamentally different from classical computing, as it allows for the exploration of many possible states simultaneously until the measurement forces a definite outcome [18]

5. **Quantum Entanglement**: It is a remarkable phenomenon in quantum mechanics, where qubits become so deeply interconnected that the state of one qubit instantaneously influences the state of another, no matter the distance separating them. This relationship means that measuring the state of one entangled qubit provides immediate knowledge about the state of its partner. Entanglement is essential for many quantum computing processes, including quantum teleportation and superdense coding, as it allows for the coordination and correlation of qubits across vast distances [19].

6. **Quantum Tunneling**: Quantum tunneling is a phenomenon where particles, such as qubits, can pass through energy barriers that would be insurmountable in classical physics. This occurs due to their wave-like properties, where the particle's wavefunction extends through the barrier, allowing it to appear on the other side despite lacking the classical energy needed to overcome it. This process is integral to technologies like quantum annealing, where it helps find solutions to complex optimization problems, and is also fundamental in the workings of modern electronic devices and nuclear fusion processes in stars. Quantum tunneling exemplifies the unique and often counterintuitive nature of quantum mechanics [20].

7. **Bloch Sphere Representation**: The state of a qubit can be visually represented using the *Bloch sphere*, which is a geometric representation that shows all possible states of a qubit on the surface of a sphere [21].

2.2.1.4   Representation of Qubits by Bloch Sphere (Single Qubit State)

The *Bloch sphere* is an abstract representation used to visualize pure single-qubit states as points on the surface of a unit sphere (Figure 2.1). The sphere has a unit radius, and the two poles of the sphere represent the computational basis states [22]:

The **North Pole** represents the state $|0\rangle$ (e.g., spin-up ↑).
The **South Pole** represents the state $|1\rangle$ (e.g., spin-down ↓).

All other points on the surface of the Bloch sphere represent *superposition states*, which are linear combinations of the $|0\rangle$ and $|1\rangle$ states. This spherical representation allows the state of a qubit to be expressed in spherical coordinates (r, θ, ϕ).

For a single qubit state, it is often written as:

$$|\psi\rangle = \cos\left(\frac{\theta}{2}\right)|0\rangle + e^{i\phi}\sin\left(\frac{\theta}{2}\right)|1\rangle \tag{2.1}$$

Where:

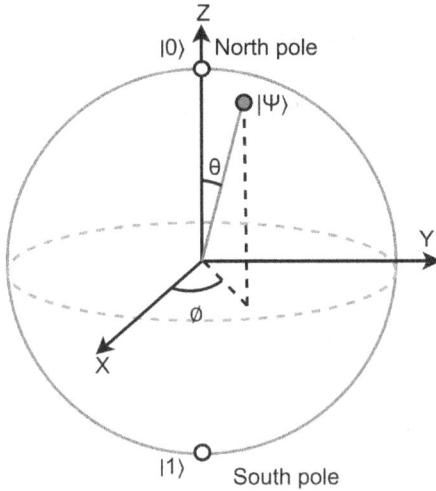

Figure 2.1   Bloch sphere

θ is the polar angle (from the North Pole),
ϕ is the azimuthal angle around the z-axis,
$r = 1$ because the qubit is in a pure state.

This representation allows one to visualize and manipulate the state of a qubit geometrically.

2.2.1.5   State of Qubit on the Bloch Sphere

The state of a qubit $|\psi\rangle$ on the Bloch sphere makes an angle θ with the z-axis, and its projection (azimuth) makes an angle ϕ with the x-axis, as shown in Figure 2.1. It is clear that $0 < \theta < \pi$ and $0 < \phi < 2\pi$.

2.2.1.6   Examples for Different θ and ϕ

CASE 1: $\theta = 0, \phi = 0$

Substituting $\theta = 0$ and $\phi = 0$ into equation (2.1), we get:

$$|\psi\rangle = \cos\left(\frac{0}{2}\right)|0\rangle + e^{i0}\sin\left(\frac{0}{2}\right)|1\rangle = 1 \cdot |0\rangle + 0 \cdot |1\rangle$$

Thus,

$$|\psi\rangle = |0\rangle$$

CASE 2: $\theta = \pi$, $\phi = 0$

Substituting $\theta = \pi$ and $\phi = 0$ into equation (2.1), we get:

$$|\psi\rangle = \cos\left(\frac{\pi}{2}\right)|0\rangle + e^{i0}\sin\left(\frac{\pi}{2}\right)|1\rangle = 0 \cdot |0\rangle + 1 \cdot |1\rangle$$

Thus,

$$|\psi\rangle = |1\rangle$$

CASE 3: $\theta = \frac{\pi}{2}$, $\phi = 0$

Substituting $\theta = \frac{\pi}{2}$ and $\phi = 0$ into equation (2.1), we get:

$$|\psi\rangle = \cos\left(\frac{\pi}{4}\right)|0\rangle + e^{i0}\sin\left(\frac{\pi}{4}\right)|1\rangle = \frac{1}{\sqrt{2}}|0\rangle + \frac{1}{\sqrt{2}}|1\rangle$$

Thus,

$$|\psi\rangle = \frac{1}{\sqrt{2}}|0\rangle + \frac{1}{\sqrt{2}}|1\rangle$$

CASE 4: $\theta = \frac{\pi}{2}$, $\phi = \pi$

Substituting $\theta = \frac{\pi}{2}$ and $\phi = \pi$ into equation (2.1), we get:

$$|\psi\rangle = \cos\left(\frac{\pi}{4}\right)|0\rangle + e^{i\pi}\sin\left(\frac{\pi}{4}\right)|1\rangle = \frac{1}{\sqrt{2}}|0\rangle - \frac{1}{\sqrt{2}}|1\rangle$$

Thus,

$$|\psi\rangle = \frac{1}{\sqrt{2}}|0\rangle - \frac{1}{\sqrt{2}}|1\rangle$$

The Bloch sphere provides a geometrical way to visualize and represent the state of a qubit.

2.2.2 COMPUTATIONAL BASIS – DIRAC NOTATION AND MATRIX OPERATIONS

Bra-Ket Notation

In quantum mechanics, states are represented using the Dirac notation [23]:

Ket vector $|\psi\rangle$: A column vector.
Bra vector $\langle\psi|$: A row vector, which is the conjugate transpose of the ket.

For example:

$$|0\rangle = \begin{pmatrix} 1 \\ 0 \end{pmatrix}, \quad |1\rangle = \begin{pmatrix} 0 \\ 1 \end{pmatrix}$$

and the corresponding bra vectors are:

$$\langle 0| = \begin{pmatrix} 1 & 0 \end{pmatrix}, \quad \langle 1| = \begin{pmatrix} 0 & 1 \end{pmatrix}.$$

OPERATORS AND MATRICES

Identity Operator:
The identity operator I leaves states unchanged:

$$I = \begin{bmatrix} 1 & 0 \\ 0 & 1 \end{bmatrix}.$$

$$I|0\rangle = |0\rangle, \quad I|1\rangle = |1\rangle.$$

Hermitian and Unitary Matrices:

A matrix A is **Hermitian** if $A^\dagger = A$.
A matrix U is **Unitary** if $U^\dagger U = I$.

2.2.3 INNER PRODUCT AND ORTHONORMALITY

Inner Product// The **inner product** helps measure the relationship between two vectors. In quantum mechanics and linear algebra, it determines how much one vector aligns with another.

For two quantum states $|u\rangle$ and $|v\rangle$, their inner product is given by:

$$\langle u|v\rangle = u_1^* v_1 + u_2^* v_2$$

where $*$ denotes the complex conjugate.

If $\langle u|v\rangle = 0$, the vectors are **orthogonal**, meaning they are independent or at a 90-degree angle in some sense.

ORTHOGONALITY AND ORTHONORMALITY

Two quantum states $|u\rangle$ and $|v\rangle$ are **orthogonal** if their inner product is zero [24]:

$$\langle u|v\rangle = 0.$$

Orthonormality means that:

1. Each vector has a unit length:

$$\langle 0|0\rangle = 1, \quad \langle 1|1\rangle = 1.$$

2. Different basis states are orthogonal:

$$\langle 0|1 \rangle = 0.$$

In quantum computing, **orthonormality** ensures that basis states like $|0\rangle$ and $|1\rangle$ are properly normalized and independent, which is essential for reliable quantum operations.

PAULI MATRICES

The **Pauli matrices** represent fundamental quantum operations (spin transformations and quantum gates). They are defined as [25]:

$$\sigma_x = \begin{bmatrix} 0 & 1 \\ 1 & 0 \end{bmatrix}, \quad \sigma_y = \begin{bmatrix} 0 & -i \\ i & 0 \end{bmatrix}, \quad \sigma_z = \begin{bmatrix} 1 & 0 \\ 0 & -1 \end{bmatrix}.$$

Pauli-X (Bit Flip Gate):

$$\sigma_x = \begin{bmatrix} 0 & 1 \\ 1 & 0 \end{bmatrix}$$

This swaps $|0\rangle$ and $|1\rangle$, similar to a classical NOT gate.

Pauli-Y:

$$\sigma_y = \begin{bmatrix} 0 & -i \\ i & 0 \end{bmatrix}$$

It introduces a phase shift along with swapping states.

Pauli-Z (Phase Flip Gate):

$$\sigma_z = \begin{bmatrix} 1 & 0 \\ 0 & -1 \end{bmatrix}$$

It changes the phase of $|1\rangle$ while leaving $|0\rangle$ unchanged.

These matrices are essential in quantum mechanics and quantum computing for manipulating qubits.

PROPERTIES OF PAULI MATRICES

Square of Pauli matrices:

$$\sigma_x^2 = \sigma_y^2 = \sigma_z^2 = I.$$

Hermitian Property:

$$\sigma_x^\dagger = \sigma_x, \quad \sigma_y^\dagger = \sigma_y, \quad \sigma_z^\dagger = \sigma_z.$$

Unitary Property:

$$\sigma_x^\dagger \sigma_x = I, \quad \sigma_y^\dagger \sigma_y = I, \quad \sigma_z^\dagger \sigma_z = I.$$

ACTION ON COMPUTATIONAL BASIS STATES

The Pauli matrices act on $|0\rangle$ and $|1\rangle$ as follows:

Pauli-X (σ_x) flips the states:

$$\sigma_x |0\rangle = |1\rangle, \quad \sigma_x |1\rangle = |0\rangle.$$

Pauli-Y introduces a phase factor:

$$\sigma_y |0\rangle = i|1\rangle, \quad \sigma_y |1\rangle = -i|0\rangle.$$

Pauli-Z changes the phase of $|1\rangle$:

$$\sigma_z |0\rangle = |0\rangle, \quad \sigma_z |1\rangle = -|1\rangle.$$

SUMMARY TABLE OF PAULI MATRICES ON COMPUTATIONAL BASIS STATES

Operation	Input $|0\rangle$	Result	Input $|1\rangle$	Result
σ_x	$|0\rangle$	$|1\rangle$	$|1\rangle$	$|0\rangle$
σ_y	$|0\rangle$	$i|1\rangle$	$|1\rangle$	$-i|0\rangle$
σ_z	$|0\rangle$	$|0\rangle$	$|1\rangle$	$-|1\rangle$

2.2.4   PROBABILITY AND MEASUREMENT

For a quantum state:

$$|\psi\rangle = \alpha |0\rangle + \beta |1\rangle,$$

the probability of measuring $|0\rangle$ or $|1\rangle$ is:

$$P(|0\rangle) = |\alpha|^2, \quad P(|1\rangle) = |\beta|^2.$$

The normalization condition ensures:

$$|\alpha|^2 + |\beta|^2 = 1.$$

2.2.4.1   Representation of Multiple Qubits

Two Qubits: Consider a system with two qubits. The two qubits can be in one of four possible basis states, represented as follows [27]:

$$|00\rangle, \quad |01\rangle, \quad |10\rangle, \quad |11\rangle$$

These basis states can be written as column vectors:

$$|00\rangle = \begin{pmatrix} 1 \\ 0 \\ 0 \\ 0 \end{pmatrix}, \quad |01\rangle = \begin{pmatrix} 0 \\ 1 \\ 0 \\ 0 \end{pmatrix}, \quad |10\rangle = \begin{pmatrix} 0 \\ 0 \\ 1 \\ 0 \end{pmatrix}, \quad |11\rangle = \begin{pmatrix} 0 \\ 0 \\ 0 \\ 1 \end{pmatrix}$$

The general state of a two-qubit system can be expressed as a linear combination (superposition) of these four states:

$$|\Psi\rangle = \alpha_{00}|00\rangle + \alpha_{01}|01\rangle + \alpha_{10}|10\rangle + \alpha_{11}|11\rangle$$

Here, $\alpha_{00}, \alpha_{01}, \alpha_{10}, \alpha_{11}$ are complex amplitudes, and the normalization condition is:

$$|\alpha_{00}|^2 + |\alpha_{01}|^2 + |\alpha_{10}|^2 + |\alpha_{11}|^2 = 1$$

Three Qubits: For a system with three qubits, there are eight possible basis states:

$$|000\rangle, |001\rangle, |010\rangle, |011\rangle, |100\rangle, |101\rangle, |110\rangle, |111\rangle$$

The general state for a three-qubit system is:

$$|\Psi\rangle = \alpha_{000}|000\rangle + \alpha_{001}|001\rangle + \alpha_{010}|010\rangle + \alpha_{011}|011\rangle$$
$$+ \alpha_{100}|100\rangle + \alpha_{101}|101\rangle + \alpha_{110}|110\rangle + \alpha_{111}|111\rangle$$

The normalization condition for this system is:

$$|\alpha_{000}|^2 + |\alpha_{001}|^2 + \cdots + |\alpha_{111}|^2 = 1$$

Generalization to N Qubits: For a system of N qubits, the number of possible basis states is 2^N, and each state is represented by a unique binary number from 0 to $2^N - 1$. The general state of an N-qubit system is:

$$|\Psi\rangle = \sum_{i=0}^{2^N-1} \alpha_i|i\rangle$$

where α_i are the complex amplitudes for each basis state $|i\rangle$, and the normalization condition is:

$$\sum_{i=0}^{2^N-1} |\alpha_i|^2 = 1$$

Thus, for N qubits, the superposition state involves 2^N complex amplitudes, and the system can be in any combination of these states simultaneously.

2.3 INTRODUCTION TO QUANTUM GATES AND QUANTUM ALGO-RITHMS

QUANTUM GATES

Quantum gates are the fundamental components of quantum circuits. They perform operations on qubits and are represented mathematically as unitary matrices. Unitarity ensures that quantum gates are reversible, a crucial property for quantum computing. Quantum gates differ from classical logic gates in that they operate on quantum states, enabling phenomena such as quantum superposition and quantum entanglement [28, 29].

KEY PROPERTIES OF QUANTUM GATES

1. **Unitarity:** The matrix representation of a quantum gate U satisfies $U^\dagger U = I$, where $U^\dagger$ is the conjugate transpose and I is the identity matrix.
2. **Reversibility:** All quantum operations are reversible due to their unitary nature.
3. **Probabilistic Measurement:** The output state of a quantum gate is probabilistic until measured, governed by the amplitudes of the state vector.

2.3.1 SINGLE-QUBIT GATES

Single-qubit gates operate on individual qubits. Below is a detailed explanation of common single-qubit gates, their mathematical representations, and their effects.

I. X-GATE (QUANTUM NOT GATE)

The X-gate performs a bit-flip operation, analogous to a classical NOT gate as shown in Figure 2.2.

Figure 2.2 X gate

Matrix Representation:

$$X = \begin{bmatrix} 0 & 1 \\ 1 & 0 \end{bmatrix}$$

Action on Computational Basis States:

$$X|0\rangle = |1\rangle, \quad X|1\rangle = |0\rangle$$

Action on a Superposed State: For a superposed state $|\psi\rangle = \alpha|0\rangle + \beta|1\rangle$:

$$X|\psi\rangle = \alpha|1\rangle + \beta|0\rangle$$

Use Case: The X-gate is used for flipping qubit states and forms the basis for constructing controlled operations such as the CNOT gate.

II. Y-GATE (PAULI-Y GATE)

The Y-gate combines a bit-flip and a phase-flip operation as shown in Figure 2.3.

$$\alpha|0\rangle + \beta|1\rangle \quad \boxed{Y} \quad i\alpha|1\rangle - i\beta|0\rangle$$

Figure 2.3   Y gate

Matrix Representation:

$$Y = \begin{bmatrix} 0 & -i \\ i & 0 \end{bmatrix}$$

Action on Computational Basis States:

$$Y|0\rangle = i|1\rangle, \quad Y|1\rangle = -i|0\rangle$$

Action on a Superposed State: For $|\psi\rangle = \alpha|0\rangle + \beta|1\rangle$:

$$Y|\psi\rangle = i\beta|0\rangle - i\alpha|1\rangle$$

Use Case: The Y-gate introduces a phase difference while flipping qubit states, making it useful in quantum algorithms requiring specific phase manipulations.

III. Z-GATE (PAULI-Z GATE)

The Z-gate flips the phase of the $|1\rangle$ state but leaves $|0\rangle$ unchanged as shown in Figure 2.4.

$$\alpha|0\rangle + \beta|1\rangle \quad \boxed{Z} \quad \alpha|0\rangle - \beta|1\rangle$$

Figure 2.4   Z gate

Matrix Representation:

$$Z = \begin{bmatrix} 1 & 0 \\ 0 & -1 \end{bmatrix}$$

Action on Computational Basis States:

$$Z|0\rangle = |0\rangle, \quad Z|1\rangle = -|1\rangle$$

Action on a Superposed State: For $|\psi\rangle = \alpha|0\rangle + \beta|1\rangle$:

$$Z|\psi\rangle = \alpha|0\rangle - \beta|1\rangle$$

Use Case: The Z-gate is often used in phase correction and is a building block for more complex gates such as the T-gate.

IV. HADAMARD GATE (H-GATE)

The Hadamard gate creates superposition as shown in Figure 2.5 and is crucial for many quantum algorithms.

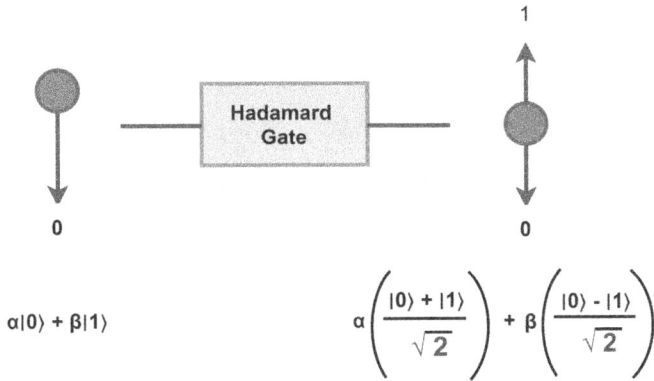

Figure 2.5 Hadamard gate

Matrix Representation:

$$H = \frac{1}{\sqrt{2}}\begin{bmatrix} 1 & 1 \\ 1 & -1 \end{bmatrix}$$

Action on Computational Basis States:

$$H|0\rangle = \frac{|0\rangle + |1\rangle}{\sqrt{2}}, \quad H|1\rangle = \frac{|0\rangle - |1\rangle}{\sqrt{2}}$$

Action on a Superposed State: For $|\psi\rangle = \alpha|0\rangle + \beta|1\rangle$:

$$H|\psi\rangle = \frac{\alpha+\beta}{\sqrt{2}}|0\rangle + \frac{\alpha-\beta}{\sqrt{2}}|1\rangle$$

Use Case: The H-gate is used to create superpositions, making it essential for quantum algorithms such as Grover's search and Shor's algorithm.

α|0⟩ + β|1⟩ ————————[**S**]———————— α|0⟩ + i β|1⟩

Figure 2.6   S gate

V. PHASE GATE (S-GATE)

The S-gate introduces a $\pi/2$ phase shift. The S gate representation is shown in Figure 2.6.

Matrix Representation:

$$S = \begin{bmatrix} 1 & 0 \\ 0 & i \end{bmatrix}$$

Action on Computational Basis States:

$$S|0\rangle = |0\rangle, \quad S|1\rangle = i|1\rangle$$

Action on a Superposed State: For $|\psi\rangle = \alpha|0\rangle + \beta|1\rangle$:

$$S|\psi\rangle = \alpha|0\rangle + i\beta|1\rangle$$

Use Case: The S-gate is commonly used in phase rotation operations and QFTs.

VI. T-GATE ($\pi/8$ GATE)

The T-gate introduces a $\pi/4$ phase shift. The T gate representation is shown in Figure 2.7.

α|0⟩ + β|1⟩ ————————[**T**]———————— α|0⟩ + e^{iπ/4} β|1⟩

Figure 2.7   T gate

Matrix Representation:

$$T = \begin{bmatrix} 1 & 0 \\ 0 & e^{i\pi/4} \end{bmatrix}$$

Action on Computational Basis States:

$$T|0\rangle = |0\rangle, \quad T|1\rangle = e^{i\pi/4}|1\rangle$$

Action on a Superposed State: For $|\psi\rangle = \alpha|0\rangle + \beta|1\rangle$:

$$T|\psi\rangle = \alpha|0\rangle + \beta e^{i\pi/4}|1\rangle$$

Use Case: The T-gate is a key component of universal quantum computing and is often used in conjunction with Clifford gates (*A Clifford gate is a quantum gate that maps Pauli operators to other Pauli operators through conjugation. Types include the Hadamard (H), Phase (S), and Controlled-NOT (CNOT) gates*).

2.3.2 MULTIPLE-QUBIT GATES

Quantum gates that operate on two or more qubits are called **multiple-qubit gates**. These gates involve both control and target qubits. The behavior of a multiple-qubit gate can be summarized as follows:

* The target qubit is altered only when the control qubit is in the state $|1\rangle$.
* The control qubit remains unaltered during the transformation.

For two qubits, the possible input states are:

$$|00\rangle, |01\rangle, |10\rangle, |11\rangle.$$

For three qubits, the possible input states are:

$$|000\rangle, |001\rangle, |010\rangle, |011\rangle, |100\rangle, |101\rangle, |110\rangle, |111\rangle.$$

I. CONTROLLED-NOT GATE (CNOT GATE)

The Controlled-NOT (CNOT) gate operates on two qubits:

The **control qubit** determines whether the operation occurs.
The **target qubit** is flipped (i.e., $|0\rangle \leftrightarrow |1\rangle$) if and only if the control qubit is $|1\rangle$.
The CNOT gate representation is shown in Figure 2.8.

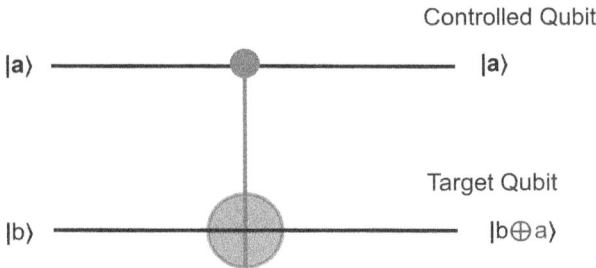

Figure 2.8 CNOT gate

Matrix Representation

The CNOT gate is represented by the following matrix:

$$\text{CNOT} = \begin{bmatrix} 1 & 0 & 0 & 0 \\ 0 & 1 & 0 & 0 \\ 0 & 0 & 0 & 1 \\ 0 & 0 & 1 & 0 \end{bmatrix}$$

Transformation Rule

The CNOT gate transforms the input state $|a,b\rangle$ as:

$$|a,b\rangle \to |a,b \oplus a\rangle,$$

where $\oplus$ represents addition modulo 2.

Action on Input States

$|00\rangle \to |00\rangle$ (control qubit is $|0\rangle$, no change).
$|01\rangle \to |01\rangle$ (control qubit is $|0\rangle$, no change).
$|10\rangle \to |11\rangle$ (control qubit is $|1\rangle$, target qubit flips).
$|11\rangle \to |10\rangle$ (control qubit is $|1\rangle$, target qubit flips).

Truth Table for CNOT Gate

Input	Output
$|00\rangle$	$|00\rangle$
$|01\rangle$	$|01\rangle$
$|10\rangle$	$|11\rangle$
$|11\rangle$	$|10\rangle$

II. SWAP GATE

The SWAP gate exchanges the states of two qubits. The SWAP gate representation and its operation is shown in Figures 2.9 and 2.10 respectively.

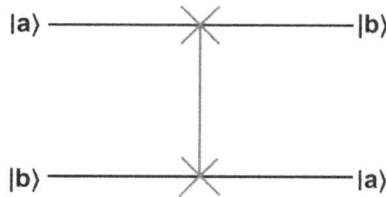

Figure 2.9 SWAP gate

$$|a,b\rangle \to |b,a\rangle.$$

Matrix Representation

$$SWAP = \begin{bmatrix} 1 & 0 & 0 & 0 \\ 0 & 0 & 1 & 0 \\ 0 & 1 & 0 & 0 \\ 0 & 0 & 0 & 1 \end{bmatrix}$$

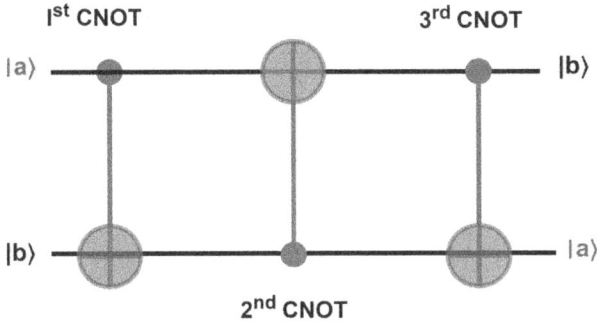

Figure 2.10   Operation of SWAP gate

Action on Input States $|a\rangle\,|b\rangle$:

- If the qubits are in state $|00\rangle$, they remain $|00\rangle$.
- If the qubits are in state $|01\rangle$, they become $|10\rangle$.
- If the qubits are in state $|10\rangle$, they become $|01\rangle$.
- If the qubits are in state $|11\rangle$, they remain $|11\rangle$.

Truth Table for SWAP Gate

Input	Output
$|00\rangle$	$|00\rangle$
$|01\rangle$	$|10\rangle$
$|10\rangle$	$|01\rangle$
$|11\rangle$	$|11\rangle$

III. CONTROLLED-Z GATE

The Controlled-Z (CZ) gate applies a Pauli-Z operation to the target qubit if the control qubit is $|1\rangle$. It does not alter the control qubit. The representation of controlled Z-gate is shown in Figure 2.11.

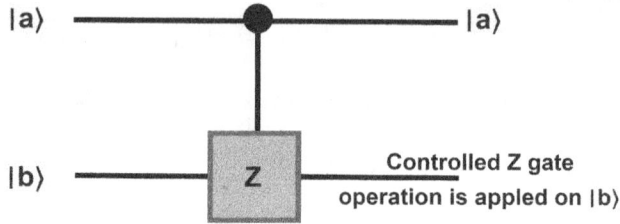

Figure 2.11   Controlled Z-gate

Matrix Representation

$$CZ = \begin{bmatrix} 1 & 0 & 0 & 0 \\ 0 & 1 & 0 & 0 \\ 0 & 0 & 1 & 0 \\ 0 & 0 & 0 & -1 \end{bmatrix}$$

Action on Input States

$|00\rangle \rightarrow |00\rangle$ (control qubit is $|0\rangle$, no change).
$|01\rangle \rightarrow |01\rangle$ (control qubit is $|0\rangle$, no change).
$|10\rangle \rightarrow |10\rangle$ (control qubit is $|1\rangle$, no change to target qubit).
$|11\rangle \rightarrow -|11\rangle$ (control qubit is $|1\rangle$, target qubit flipped in phase).

Truth Table for Controlled Z-Gate

Input	Output
$|00\rangle$	$|00\rangle$
$|01\rangle$	$|01\rangle$
$|10\rangle$	$|10\rangle$
$|11\rangle$	$-|11\rangle$

IV. TOFFOLI GATE (CCNOT GATE)

The Toffoli gate, or Controlled-Controlled-NOT gate, is a three-qubit gate:

It flips the target qubit if both control qubits are $|1\rangle$ and the control qubits remain unaltered.

The representation of CCNOT gate is shown in Figure 2.12.

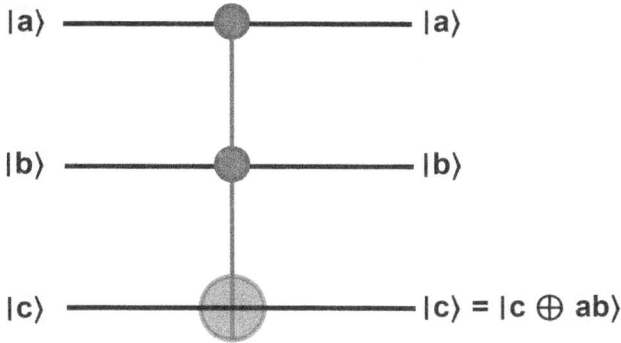

Figure 2.12 CCNOT gate

Matrix Representation

The Toffoli gate is represented as an 8×8 matrix, and its representation is:

$$CCNOT = \begin{bmatrix} 1 & 0 & 0 & 0 & 0 & 0 & 0 & 0 \\ 0 & 1 & 0 & 0 & 0 & 0 & 0 & 0 \\ 0 & 0 & 1 & 0 & 0 & 0 & 0 & 0 \\ 0 & 0 & 0 & 1 & 0 & 0 & 0 & 0 \\ 0 & 0 & 0 & 0 & 1 & 0 & 0 & 0 \\ 0 & 0 & 0 & 0 & 0 & 1 & 0 & 0 \\ 0 & 0 & 0 & 0 & 0 & 0 & 0 & 1 \\ 0 & 0 & 0 & 0 & 0 & 0 & 1 & 0 \end{bmatrix}$$

Truth Table for CCNOT Gate

Input	Output
$|000\rangle$	$|000\rangle$
$|001\rangle$	$|001\rangle$
$|010\rangle$	$|010\rangle$
$|011\rangle$	$|011\rangle$
$|100\rangle$	$|100\rangle$
$|101\rangle$	$|101\rangle$
$|110\rangle$	$|111\rangle$
$|111\rangle$	$|110\rangle$

2.3.3 QUANTUM FOURIER TRANSFORM (QFT)

In quantum computing, the QFT is a linear transformation on quantum bits and is the quantum analogue of the discrete Fourier transform. The QFT is a part of many quantum algorithms, notably Shor's algorithm for factoring and computing the discrete logarithm, the quantum phase estimation (QPE) algorithm for estimating the eigenvalues of a unitary operator, and algorithms for the hidden subgroup problem. The QFT was discovered by Don Coppersmith. With small modifications to the QFT, it can also be used for performing fast integer arithmetic operations such as addition and multiplication [30].

The QFT can be performed efficiently on a quantum computer with a decomposition into the product of simpler unitary matrices. The discrete Fourier transform on 2^n amplitudes can be implemented as a quantum circuit consisting of only $O(n^2)$ Hadamard gates and controlled phase shift gates, where n is the number of qubits. This can be compared with the classical discrete Fourier transform, which takes $O(n2^n)$ gates (where n is the number of bits), which is exponentially more than $O(n^2)$.

The QFT acts on a quantum state vector (a quantum register), and the classical discrete Fourier transform acts on a vector. Both types of vectors can be written as lists of complex numbers. In the classical case, the vector can be represented with, for example, an array of floating-point numbers, and in the quantum case, it is a sequence of probability amplitudes for all the possible outcomes upon measurement (the outcomes are the basis states, or eigenstates). Because measurement collapses the quantum state to a single basis state, not every task that uses the classical Fourier transform can take advantage of the QFT's exponential speedup.

The best QFT algorithms known (as of late 2000) require only $O(n \log n)$ gates to achieve an efficient approximation, provided that a controlled phase gate is implemented as a native operation.

DEFINITION

The QFT is the classical discrete Fourier transform applied to the vector of amplitudes of a quantum state, which has length $N = 2^n$ if it is applied to a register of n qubits.

The classical Fourier transform acts on a vector $(x_0, x_1, \ldots, x_{N-1}) \in \mathbb{C}^N$ and maps it to the vector $(y_0, y_1, \ldots, y_{N-1}) \in \mathbb{C}^N$ according to the formula:

$$y_k = \frac{1}{\sqrt{N}} \sum_{j=0}^{N-1} x_j \omega_N^{-jk}, \quad k = 0, 1, 2, \ldots, N-1,$$

where $\omega_N = e^{\frac{2\pi i}{N}}$ is an Nth root of unity.

Similarly, the QFT acts on a quantum state $|x\rangle = \sum_{j=0}^{N-1} x_j |j\rangle$ and maps it to a quantum state $\sum_{j=0}^{N-1} y_j |j\rangle$ according to the formula:

$$y_k = \frac{1}{\sqrt{N}} \sum_{j=0}^{N-1} x_j \omega_N^{jk}, \quad k = 0, 1, 2, \ldots, N-1.$$

(Conventions for the sign of the phase factor exponent vary; here the quantum Fourier transform has the same effect as the inverse discrete Fourier transform, and conversely.)

The inverse QFT is given by

$$x_j = \frac{1}{\sqrt{N}} \sum_{k=0}^{N-1} y_k \omega_N^{-jk}, \quad j = 0,1,2,\ldots,N-1.$$

In case that $|x\rangle$ is a basis state, the QFT can also be expressed as the map:

$$\text{QFT} : |x\rangle \mapsto \frac{1}{\sqrt{N}} \sum_{k=0}^{N-1} \omega_N^{xk} |k\rangle.$$

Equivalently, the QFT can be viewed as a unitary matrix (or quantum gate) acting on quantum state vectors, where the unitary matrix F_N is the DFT matrix:

$$F_N = \frac{1}{\sqrt{N}} \begin{bmatrix} 1 & 1 & 1 & 1 & \cdots & 1 \\ 1 & \omega & \omega^2 & \omega^3 & \cdots & \omega^{N-1} \\ 1 & \omega^2 & \omega^4 & \omega^6 & \cdots & \omega^{2(N-1)} \\ 1 & \omega^3 & \omega^6 & \omega^9 & \cdots & \omega^{3(N-1)} \\ \vdots & \vdots & \vdots & \vdots & \ddots & \vdots \\ 1 & \omega^{N-1} & \omega^{2(N-1)} & \omega^{3(N-1)} & \cdots & \omega^{(N-1)(N-1)} \end{bmatrix},$$

where $\omega = \omega_N$. For example, in the case of $N = 4 = 2^2$ and phase $\omega = i$, the transformation matrix is:

$$F_4 = \frac{1}{2} \begin{bmatrix} 1 & 1 & 1 & 1 \\ 1 & i & -1 & -i \\ 1 & -1 & 1 & -1 \\ 1 & -i & -1 & i \end{bmatrix}.$$

EXAMPLE: COMPUTATION OF QFT FOR 2-QUBITS USING MATRIX METHOD

For a 2-qubit system, the QFT matrix is a unitary matrix of size 4×4. The general form of the QFT_n matrix for n-qubits is given by:

$$(QFT_n)_{jk} = \frac{1}{\sqrt{2^n}} e^{2\pi i \cdot jk/2^n}$$

Where:

j and k range from 0 to $2^n - 1$, corresponding to all possible states for the n-qubit system.
The factor $\frac{1}{\sqrt{2^n}}$ normalizes the matrix to ensure that the QFT matrix is unitary (its conjugate transpose equals its inverse).

For a 2-qubit system (where $n = 2$):

The matrix size is 4×4 (because $2^2 = 4$).

Both j and k range from 0 to 3.

To calculate the 2-qubit QFT matrix, we use the general formula:

$$(QFT_2)_{jk} = \frac{1}{\sqrt{4}} e^{2\pi i \cdot \frac{jk}{4}} = \frac{1}{2} e^{2\pi i \cdot \frac{jk}{4}}$$

For each value of j and k, we calculate the corresponding complex exponential:
When $j = 0$:

$$(QFT_2)_{0k} = \frac{1}{2} e^0 = \frac{1}{2}, \quad k = 0,1,2,3$$

So the first row is: $\left[\frac{1}{2}, \frac{1}{2}, \frac{1}{2}, \frac{1}{2}\right]$.
When $j = 1$:

$$(QFT_2)_{1k} = \frac{1}{2} e^{2\pi i \cdot \frac{1k}{4}} = \frac{1}{2}[1, i, -1, -i]$$

So the second row is: $\left[\frac{1}{2}, \frac{i}{2}, \frac{-1}{2}, \frac{-i}{2}\right]$.
When $j = 2$:

$$(QFT_2)_{2k} = \frac{1}{2} e^{2\pi i \cdot \frac{2k}{4}} = \frac{1}{2}[1, -1, 1, -1]$$

So the third row is: $\left[\frac{1}{2}, \frac{-1}{2}, \frac{1}{2}, \frac{-1}{2}\right]$.
When $j = 3$:

$$(QFT_2)_{3k} = \frac{1}{2} e^{2\pi i \cdot \frac{3k}{4}} = \frac{1}{2}[1, -i, -1, i]$$

So the fourth row is: $\left[\frac{1}{2}, \frac{-i}{2}, \frac{-1}{2}, \frac{i}{2}\right]$.

Thus, the 2-qubit QFT matrix is:

$$QFT_2 = \frac{1}{2}\begin{bmatrix} 1 & 1 & 1 & 1 \\ 1 & i & -1 & -i \\ 1 & -1 & 1 & -1 \\ 1 & -i & -1 & i \end{bmatrix}$$

We can now apply this to the computational basis states.

1. QFT on $|00\rangle$:

$$QFT_2|00\rangle = \frac{1}{2}\begin{bmatrix} 1 & 1 & 1 & 1 \\ 1 & i & -1 & -i \\ 1 & -1 & 1 & -1 \\ 1 & -i & -1 & i \end{bmatrix}\begin{bmatrix} 1 \\ 0 \\ 0 \\ 0 \end{bmatrix} = \frac{1}{2}\begin{bmatrix} 1 \\ 1 \\ 1 \\ 1 \end{bmatrix}$$

So the result is:

$$QFT_2|00\rangle = \frac{1}{2}(|00\rangle + |01\rangle + |10\rangle + |11\rangle)$$

2. QFT on $|01\rangle$:

$$QFT_2|01\rangle = \frac{1}{2}\begin{bmatrix} 1 & 1 & 1 & 1 \\ 1 & i & -1 & -i \\ 1 & -1 & 1 & -1 \\ 1 & -i & -1 & i \end{bmatrix}\begin{bmatrix} 0 \\ 1 \\ 0 \\ 0 \end{bmatrix} = \frac{1}{2}\begin{bmatrix} 1 \\ i \\ -1 \\ -i \end{bmatrix}$$

So the result is:

$$QFT_2|01\rangle = \frac{1}{2}(|00\rangle + i|01\rangle - |10\rangle - i|11\rangle)$$

3. QFT on $|10\rangle$:

$$QFT_2|10\rangle = \frac{1}{2}\begin{bmatrix} 1 & 1 & 1 & 1 \\ 1 & i & -1 & -i \\ 1 & -1 & 1 & -1 \\ 1 & -i & -1 & i \end{bmatrix}\begin{bmatrix} 0 \\ 0 \\ 1 \\ 0 \end{bmatrix} = \frac{1}{2}\begin{bmatrix} 1 \\ -1 \\ 1 \\ -1 \end{bmatrix}$$

So the result is:

$$QFT_2|10\rangle = \frac{1}{2}(|00\rangle - |01\rangle + |10\rangle - |11\rangle)$$

4. QFT on $|11\rangle$:

$$QFT_2|11\rangle = \frac{1}{2}\begin{bmatrix} 1 & 1 & 1 & 1 \\ 1 & i & -1 & -i \\ 1 & -1 & 1 & -1 \\ 1 & -i & -1 & i \end{bmatrix}\begin{bmatrix} 0 \\ 0 \\ 0 \\ 1 \end{bmatrix} = \frac{1}{2}\begin{bmatrix} 1 \\ -i \\ -1 \\ i \end{bmatrix}$$

So the result is:

$$QFT_2|11\rangle = \frac{1}{2}(|00\rangle - i|01\rangle - |10\rangle + i|11\rangle)$$

Thus, the QFT results on the computational basis states are:

$QFT_2|00\rangle = \frac{1}{2}(|00\rangle + |01\rangle + |10\rangle + |11\rangle)$: The QFT on the state $|00\rangle$ transforms it into an equal superposition of all 4 computational basis states ($|00\rangle$, $|01\rangle$, $|10\rangle$, and $|11\rangle$), with equal amplitude of $\frac{1}{2}$ for each.

$QFT_2|01\rangle = \frac{1}{2}(|00\rangle + i|01\rangle - |10\rangle - i|11\rangle)$: The QFT on the state $|01\rangle$ results in a linear combination of the computational basis states, where the phases of the amplitudes alternate between positive and negative (with imaginary units i and $-i$) for certain basis states, indicating a phase shift in the transformation.

$QFT_2|10\rangle = \frac{1}{2}(|00\rangle - |01\rangle + |10\rangle - |11\rangle)$: Similarly, applying the QFT on $|10\rangle$ results in a superposition of all computational basis states. The amplitudes involve alternating signs without any imaginary components, again showing a phase shift but without complex coefficients.

$QFT_2|11\rangle = \frac{1}{2}(|00\rangle - i|01\rangle - |10\rangle + i|11\rangle)$: The QFT on the state $|11\rangle$ leads to a similar superposition, but with alternating phases represented by $\pm i$, indicating complex phase shifts.

COMPUTATION OF 2-QUBIT QFT USING QUANTUM CIRCUIT

The QFT on a 2-qubit system can be computed step by step using quantum gates. Let's break down the procedure for calculating the QFT on a two-qubit system.

STEP 1: INITIALIZE THE QUBITS

We start with the two qubits in the state $|00\rangle$:

$$|00\rangle = |q_0, q_1\rangle$$

STEP 2: APPLY THE HADAMARD GATE TO THE FIRST QUBIT

The first step in the QFT is to apply the Hadamard gate H to the first qubit:

$$H|00\rangle = \frac{1}{\sqrt{2}}(|00\rangle + |10\rangle)$$

STEP 3: APPLY THE CONTROLLED-Z GATE (PHASE SHIFT)

The second part of the QFT is applying controlled-phase gates. The controlled-phase gate applies a phase shift to the second qubit depending on the state of the first qubit. The controlled-phase gate is a diagonal matrix that applies a phase of $e^{2\pi i/2^n}$ to the second qubit if the first qubit is in the state $|1\rangle$.

For two qubits, the controlled-phase gate is represented as a controlled-Z gate, and it applies a phase shift of $e^{2\pi i/2^2} = e^{i\pi/2} = i$ to the second qubit if the first qubit is in the state $|1\rangle$.

Let's apply this operation. Initially, the system state is:

$$\frac{1}{\sqrt{2}}(|00\rangle + |10\rangle)$$

The phase is applied to the second qubit when the first qubit is in the state $|1\rangle$. So, the second term $|10\rangle$ will acquire a phase of $e^{i\pi/2}$.

After applying the controlled-phase gate, the state of the system becomes:

$$\frac{1}{\sqrt{2}}\left(|00\rangle + e^{i\pi/2}|10\rangle\right)$$

Thus, after applying the controlled-phase gate, the state of the system is:

$$\frac{1}{\sqrt{2}}(|00\rangle + i|10\rangle)$$

STEP 4: APPLY THE HADAMARD GATE TO THE SECOND QUBIT

Next, we apply the Hadamard gate to the second qubit:

$$H\left(\frac{1}{\sqrt{2}}(|00\rangle + |10\rangle)\right) = \frac{1}{2}(|00\rangle + |01\rangle + |10\rangle + |11\rangle)$$

STEP 5: SWAP THE QUBITS

Finally, we swap the qubits to reflect the computational basis ordering:

$$QFT_2|00\rangle = \frac{1}{2}(|00\rangle + |01\rangle + |10\rangle + |11\rangle)$$

Thus, we have confirmed that:

$$QFT_2|00\rangle = \frac{1}{2}(|00\rangle + |01\rangle + |10\rangle + |11\rangle)$$

2.3.4   QUANTUM CIRCUIT FOR IMPLEMENTING QFT

The quantum circuit for implementing the QFT uses two types of gates. The first is the Hadamard gate H, which transforms the single-qubit state $|x_k\rangle$ as:

$$H|x_k\rangle = \frac{1}{\sqrt{2}}(|0\rangle + e^{\frac{2\pi i x_k}{2}}|1\rangle)$$

The second is a two-qubit controlled rotation gate CROT_k, given in block-diagonal form:

$$\text{CROT}_k = \begin{bmatrix} I & 0 \\ 0 & U_{\text{ROT}} \end{bmatrix}$$

where U_{ROT} is a single-qubit rotation matrix used in quantum computing. It represents a quantum gate that applies a phase shift to the state of a qubit.

The matrix form of U_{ROT} is:

$$U_{\text{ROT}} = \begin{bmatrix} 1 & 0 \\ 0 & e^{\frac{2\pi i}{2^k}} \end{bmatrix}$$

This matrix represents a single-qubit rotation gate that applies a phase shift to the quantum state of a qubit.

The element 1 represents the state $|0\rangle$, meaning the $|0\rangle$ state is unchanged by this operation.

The element $e^{\frac{2\pi i}{2^k}}$ is the phase factor applied to the state $|1\rangle$. It introduces a rotation in the complex plane, with the magnitude of the rotation controlled by the value of k.

The phase shift $e^{\frac{2\pi i}{2^k}}$ is a rotation in the complex plane, where the exponent k controls the amount of rotation. Larger values of k correspond to smaller phase shifts.

In quantum circuits, U_{ROT} is used to apply phase shifts to qubits. This is particularly useful in algorithms like the QFT, where control over the phase of quantum states is important.

For multi-qubit systems, the rotation angle may depend on the position of the qubit, controlled by k. This is seen in gates like the Controlled Rotation (CROT) gate, where one qubit controls the rotation of another.

The Controlled Rotation (CROT) gate acts on the two-qubit state $|x_l x_j\rangle$ as follows:

$$\text{CROT}_k |0 x_j\rangle = |0 x_j\rangle$$

This means that if the control qubit is in state $|0\rangle$, the target qubit remains unchanged, regardless of the state of x_j.

$$\text{CROT}_k |1 x_j\rangle = e^{\frac{2\pi i x_j}{2^k}} |1 x_j\rangle$$

If the control qubit is in state $|1\rangle$, the target qubit undergoes a phase shift $e^{\frac{2\pi i x_j}{2^k}}$, where x_j represents the state of the target qubit and k controls the magnitude of the phase shift.

Thus, the general action of CROT_k on the two-qubit state $|x_l x_j\rangle$ is:

$$\text{CROT}_k |0 x_j\rangle = |0 x_j\rangle$$

and

$$\text{CROT}_k |1 x_j\rangle = e^{\frac{2\pi i x_j}{2^k}} |1 x_j\rangle$$

2.3.4.1 Approximate QFT

As the QFT circuit becomes large, the time spent on increasingly slight rotations becomes significant. It is found that rotations below a certain threshold can be ignored, leading to the approximate QFT. This is particularly important for physical implementations, as reducing the number of operations minimizes decoherence and potential gate errors.

2.3.4.2 Application of QFT to Periodic Functions

When the QFT is applied to a state whose amplitudes are given by a periodic function $a(x) = a_x$ with period r, where r is a power of 2, the result is:

$$\text{QFT}\{a(x)\} = A(x) = 0 \quad \text{except when} \quad x \text{ is a multiple of } \frac{N}{r}$$

The equation reflects the periodic nature of the function $a(x)$ and QFT. The QFT is designed to extract the periodic components of a function by transforming it into the Fourier basis. When the function $a(x)$ has a periodic structure with period r, the QFT will isolate the frequencies corresponding to this periodicity. These frequencies present as non-zero Fourier coefficients at specific multiples of $\frac{N}{r}$, where N is the size of the system, and r is the period. The result is that for most values of x, the Fourier coefficients $A(x)$ will be zero, while for multiples of $\frac{N}{r}$, the coefficients will be non-zero, reflecting the periodic nature of the underlying function.

In algorithms like Shor's algorithm, this property is crucial for identifying the period r. By applying the QFT, we can extract these non-zero coefficients corresponding to the periodic structure, enabling us to determine the hidden period of the function efficiently. Thus, the QFT highlights only those components that are related to the underlying periodicity, while other components are discarded (i.e., have zero amplitude).

The QFT is a powerful tool in quantum computing that can perform calculations much faster than the classical Fast Fourier Transform (FFT). The QFT needs only $O(n^2)$ operations, while the classical FFT requires $O(nN)$ operations. This means that the QFT can solve problems much more efficiently, especially for large inputs.

2.3.5 QUANTUM PHASE ESTIMATION

QPE is a quantum algorithm that estimates the eigenvalue of a unitary operator. QPE aims to extract the phase *phi* associated with the eigenvalue of a unitary operator acting on a quantum state. This phase information is critical in algorithms such as Shor's algorithm for factoring large numbers and other quantum algorithms for solving mathematical problems. The main goal of QPE is to estimate the phase ϕ corresponding to the eigenvalue $e^{2\pi i\phi}$ of a unitary operator U, given that U acts on a quantum state $|\psi\rangle$ as $U|\psi\rangle = e^{2\pi i\phi}|\psi\rangle$ [31].

2.3.5.1 The Quantum Phase Estimation Algorithm

QPE is based on the principle of quantum interference. The algorithm utilizes two quantum registers: one for the "phase" part and another for the quantum state whose phase we are trying to estimate. Given a unitary operator U, QPE estimates the phase ϕ such that:

$$U|\psi\rangle = e^{2\pi i\phi}|\psi\rangle$$

The algorithm proceeds as follows:

1. **Initial State Preparation:** For the initial preparation, consider two quantum registers in which the first register is initialized to a state $|0\rangle^{\otimes t}$ where t is

the number of qubits used to encode the phase, and the second register is prepared in the state $|\psi\rangle$, which is the eigenstate of the unitary U.

$$|\text{initial}\rangle = |0\rangle^{\otimes t} \otimes |\psi\rangle$$

2. **Apply Hadamard Transform:** A Hadamard gate is applied to each qubit in the first register. This step creates a superposition of all possible states in the first register.

$$H^{\otimes t}|0\rangle^{\otimes t} = \frac{1}{\sqrt{2^t}} \sum_{k=0}^{2^t-1} |k\rangle$$

3. **Apply Controlled-U Operations:** For each qubit j in the first register, apply the controlled-U^{2^j} operation (U is a unitary operator, which means it preserves the norm and corresponds to a reversible transformation in quantum mechanics. The power 2^j indicates that U is applied 2^j times in succession.), which applies U^{2^j} on the second register if the jth qubit of the first register is $|1\rangle$. This step entangles the two registers.

$$C_{U^{2^j}}|k\rangle \otimes |\psi\rangle = |k\rangle \otimes U^{2^j}|\psi\rangle$$

4. **Inverse Quantum Fourier Transform (IQFT):** After applying the controlled-unitary operations, the first register is subjected to the inverse QFT. The QFT transforms the computational basis states into superposition states that encode the phase ϕ. The inverse QFT on t qubits is defined as:

$$\text{QFT}^{-1}(|k\rangle) = \frac{1}{\sqrt{2^t}} \sum_{k=0}^{2^t-1} e^{2\pi i \frac{k}{2^t} x}|x\rangle$$

where x represents the output state of the quantum register.

5. **Measurement:** Finally, the first register is measured. The outcome of the measurement gives an approximation of the phase ϕ as a binary fraction:

$$\phi \approx \frac{k}{2^t}$$

where k is the measurement result.

Error and Precision

The accuracy of the phase estimation depends on the number of qubits t used in the algorithm. A larger t results in more precise estimates of the phase. The error in the phase estimation can be quantified as:

$$\text{Error} = \frac{1}{2^t}$$

Thus, increasing t improves the precision of the estimated phase.

QPE is a powerful quantum algorithm that provides an efficient way to estimate the phase of eigenvalues of unitary operators. Its implementation is a critical component of several quantum algorithms, with broad applications in fields such as cryptography, quantum chemistry, and machine learning.

2.3.6 SHOR'S ALGORITHM FOR FACTORING

Shor's Factorization Algorithm was proposed by Peter Shor in 1994. It suggests that quantum mechanics allows the factorization of integers to be performed in polynomial time, rather than the exponential time required by classical algorithms. This could have a drastic impact on the field of data security, which is based on the prime factorization of large numbers. Many polynomial-time algorithms for integer multiplication (e.g., Euclid's Algorithm) exist, but no polynomial-time algorithm for factorization has been discovered until Shor's proposal. Shor's Factorization Algorithm is designed to factorize non-prime integers N. A factoring problem can be turned into a period-finding problem in polynomial time, and an efficient period-finding algorithm can be used to factor integers efficiently [32].

2.3.6.1 Fundamental Theorem of Arithmetic

It has been known for a very long time that every integer $n \geq 2$ can be uniquely factored into product of prime powers. This is stated in the Fundamental Theorem of Arithmetic. Mathematicians have always been interested in the problem of how to factor a random integer into its prime factors. The best currently known classical factoring algorithm is the number field sieve which, to factor an integer n, takes an asymptotic running time of:

$$O\left(\exp\left(c \cdot (\log n)^{1/3} \cdot (\log\log n)^{2/3}\right)\right)$$

for some constant c.

Shor's Quantum Algorithm: Shor's quantum algorithm takes asymptotically $O\left((\log n)^2 \cdot \log\log n \cdot \log\log\log n\right)$ steps, along with a polynomial amount of time on a classical computer to convert the output of the quantum computer to the factors of n.

Impact on Cryptography: Much of modern cryptography is based on the assumption that no fast (i.e., polynomial time) factoring algorithm or discrete logarithm algorithm exists. The most important cryptosystems based on these assumptions are the RSA (Rivest-Shamir-Adleman) and ElGamal cryptosystems. These would be broken if Shor's algorithm could be physically realized for sufficiently large integers.

Quantum Parallelism: Many quantum algorithms use quantum analogs of classical computation as at least part of their computation. Quantum algorithms often start by creating a quantum superposition and then feeding it into a quantum version U_f

of a classical circuit that computes a function f. This setup, called quantum parallelism, accomplishes nothing by itself; any algorithm that stopped at this point would have no advantage over a classical algorithm. However, this construction leaves the system in a state that quantum algorithm designers have found to be a useful starting point. Shor's algorithm begins with the quantum parallelism setup.

2.3.7 GROVER'S ALGORITHM FOR QUANTUM SEARCHING

Quantum computing has revolutionized approaches to solving computational problems. One of the most significant quantum algorithms is Grover's algorithm, proposed by Lov Grover in 1996. It is specifically designed for unstructured search problems, achieving a quadratic speedup by reducing the search time to $O(\sqrt{N})$ compared to the $O(N)$ time required by classical algorithms. Where N represents the total number of possible entries in an unstructured search space [33].
If we are searching for a specific item in an unsorted database, N is the total number of items.

For example:

If we have $N = 1,000,000$ possible solutions, a classical search takes $O(N) = 1,000,000$ steps in the worst case.
Grover's algorithm, however, only takes $O(\sqrt{N}) \approx 1000$ steps, providing a quadratic speedup.

Classical vs. Quantum Search

In a classical context, searching for a specific element in an unstructured database of N items requires $O(N)$ operations in the worst case. Grover's algorithm, influence quantum parallelism and interference, significantly reduces the complexity to $O(\sqrt{N})$. However, Grover's algorithm provides a quantum speedup by utilizing the principles of quantum superposition and amplitude amplification.

Unstructured Search Problem

The problem involves searching for an unknown element x in an unsorted database such that $f(x) = 1$ (where f is a binary-valued function indicating the solution). Classically, no better strategy than exhaustive search exists.

Grover's Algorithm: Key Concepts

Grover's algorithm exploits the following fundamental quantum principles:

1. **Superposition**: Enables the simultaneous evaluation of all possible database entries.
2. **Oracle**: A black-box function used to mark the correct solution state.
3. **Amplitude Amplification**: Enhances the probability amplitude of the solution states while diminishing the others.

4. **Quantum Interference**: Used to constructively and destructively interfere with amplitudes to achieve amplification.

The Grover's algorithm in detail

Figure 2.13 shows the block diagram of Grover's algorithm. The algorithm consists of the following steps:

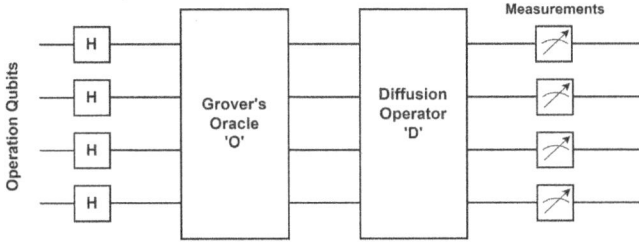

Figure 2.13 Block diagram of grover's algorithm

H is the Hadamard gate.
O is the oracle that marks the target state.
D is the diffusion operator.
Measurement is performed at the end to obtain the search result.

Initialization: Prepare the quantum system in a uniform superposition state of N basis states using the Hadamard gate. For a system with n qubits ($N = 2^n$):

$$|\psi_0\rangle = \frac{1}{\sqrt{N}} \sum_{x=0}^{N-1} |x\rangle$$

Oracle Query: Apply the oracle U_f that flips the sign of the amplitude of the solution state $|s\rangle$ such that:

$$U_f|x\rangle = \begin{cases} -|x\rangle & \text{if } x = s, \\ |x\rangle & \text{otherwise.} \end{cases}$$

Grover Diffusion Operator: Perform the Grover diffusion operator G, which inverts the amplitudes about their mean:

$$G = 2|\psi_0\rangle\langle\psi_0| - I$$

This step amplifies the solution state amplitude while reducing others.

Iterative Process

Repeat the Oracle and Diffusion operations $O(\sqrt{N})$ times to maximize the probability of measuring the correct solution.

Measurement: Finally, measure the quantum state to observe the solution with high probability.

Mathematical Analysis of Grover's Algorithm

Grover's algorithm iteratively amplifies the amplitude of the solution state by rotating the quantum state in a subspace defined by the initial uniform superposition and the marked (solution) state. The rotation angle per iteration is given by:

$$\theta = \arcsin(1/\sqrt{N})$$

where N is the total number of possible states in the search space. After approximately $O(\sqrt{N})$ iterations, the probability of measuring the solution state approaches unity.

Amplitude Evolution

Let $|\psi_t\rangle$ represent the quantum state after t iterations of Grover's algorithm. The state evolves as:

$$|\psi_t\rangle = \cos((2t+1)\theta)|\psi_{non\text{-}solution}\rangle + \sin((2t+1)\theta)|\psi_{solution}\rangle$$

where $|\psi_{non\text{-}solution}\rangle$ represents the component orthogonal to the solution state. This follows from the repeated application of the Grover oracle and diffusion operator, which together perform a rotation in this two-dimensional subspace.

Convergence Condition

The probability of measuring the solution state is maximized when:

$$(2t+1)\theta \approx \frac{\pi}{2}$$

which gives the optimal number of iterations as:

$$t \approx \frac{\pi}{4}\sqrt{N}$$

ensuring that the probability of measuring the solution state is close to unity.

This analysis highlights how Grover's algorithm efficiently increases the likelihood of finding the correct solution in $O(\sqrt{N})$ steps, providing a quadratic speedup over classical brute-force search.

Practical Considerations

1. Impact of Quantum Noise and Decoherence: The success of Grover's algorithm hinges on the precision of quantum gates. However, quantum systems are prone to interference from their surroundings, leading to decoherence and noise. These factors can degrade computational accuracy, necessitating the use of error correction and the development of quantum systems capable of withstanding these challenges.
2. Challenges in Scalability: Deploying Grover's algorithm for extensive datasets requires quantum systems with a large number of qubits and robust connectivity. Current hardware limitations, including short coherence times and imperfect gate operations, present significant obstacles to scaling the technology.

3. Flexibility in Approximation: Grover's algorithm exhibits resilience in cases with multiple valid solutions or scenarios where near-optimal solutions are sufficient. This adaptability broadens its utility, especially in domains like optimization, where exact solutions may not be strictly required.

Grover's algorithm represents the power of quantum computing, providing a compelling quadratic speedup for unstructured search problems. As quantum technologies advance, Grover's algorithm has potential for solving real-world problems in optimization, cryptography, and beyond [34].

2.3.8 SIMON'S ALGORITHM FOR COLLISION FINDING

Simon's algorithm is one of the foundational quantum algorithms that highlights the potential speedup achievable through quantum computing. Initially developed by Daniel Simon in 1994, the algorithm solves the ***collision finding problem*** exponentially faster than any known classical algorithm [35].

Problem statement
The collision finding problem addressed by Simon's algorithm can be defined as follows:
Given a black-box function $f : \{0,1\}^n \to \{0,1\}^n$ satisfying the promise:

$$f(x) = f(y) \iff x \oplus y = s,$$

for some unknown binary string $s \in \{0,1\}^n$, the task is to find the string s.

Quantum notation
- Qubits: $|0\rangle$ and $|1\rangle$.
- Superposition: $|\psi\rangle = \frac{1}{\sqrt{2^n}} \sum_{x \in \{0,1\}^n} |x\rangle$. - Measurement outcomes collapse to classical values.

Hadamard Transformation
The Hadamard gate (H) plays a key role in creating superpositions. Applying $H^{\otimes n}$ on an n-qubit input:

$$|x\rangle \xrightarrow{H^{\otimes n}} \frac{1}{\sqrt{2^n}} \sum_{y \in \{0,1\}^n} (-1)^{x \cdot y} |y\rangle.$$

2.3.8.1 Simon's Algorithm

Simon's algorithm, introduced by Daniel Simon in 1994, was one of the first quantum algorithms to demonstrate an exponential speedup over classical methods. It determines a hidden bit string s for a function $f : \{0,1\}^n \to \{0,1\}^n$ with a guaranteed periodicity property [36].

The algorithm proceeds through three main steps: initialization, superposition and oracle query, and measurement.

Step 1: Initialization Prepare a quantum register with $2n$ qubits initialized to the $|0\rangle$ state:

$$|0\rangle^{\otimes n} \otimes |0\rangle^{\otimes n}.$$

Step 2: Superposition and Oracle Query

Step 2.1: Applying Hadamard Gates to the first register

$$H^{\otimes n}|0\rangle^{\otimes n} = \frac{1}{\sqrt{2^n}} \sum_{x \in \{0,1\}^n} |x\rangle.$$

The resulting quantum state is:

$$\frac{1}{\sqrt{2^n}} \sum_{x \in \{0,1\}^n} |x\rangle|0\rangle.$$

Step 2.2: Querying the Oracle U_f

$$U_f|x\rangle|y\rangle = |x\rangle|y \oplus f(x)\rangle.$$

This results in:

$$\frac{1}{\sqrt{2^n}} \sum_{x \in \{0,1\}^n} |x\rangle|f(x)\rangle.$$

Since $f(x)$ is two-to-one, we have $f(x) = f(x')$ if and only if $x' = x \oplus s$, introducing a hidden structure.

Step 3: Uncomputing and Measurement

Step 3.1: Measuring the Second Register collapses the first register to:

$$\frac{1}{\sqrt{2}} \left(|x\rangle + |x \oplus s\rangle\right).$$

Step 3.2: Applying Hadamard Transform Again to the first register:

$$H^{\otimes n} \frac{1}{\sqrt{2}} \left(|x\rangle + |x \oplus s\rangle\right)$$

produces the interference pattern:

$$\frac{1}{\sqrt{2^{n+1}}} \sum_{y \in \{0,1\}^n} \left((-1)^{x \cdot y} + (-1)^{(x \oplus s) \cdot y}\right) |y\rangle.$$

Using the dot product property:

$$(-1)^{(x \oplus s) \cdot y} = (-1)^{x \cdot y}(-1)^{s \cdot y},$$

leading to the condition:

$$s \cdot y = 0 \quad \text{mod } 2.$$

Step 3.3: Measuring the First Register gives equations of the form:

$$y_1 s_1 \oplus y_2 s_2 \oplus \cdots \oplus y_n s_n = 0.$$

Repeating $O(n)$ times yields n independent equations, solving for s using Gaussian elimination.

Analysis and Complexity

Classical approach: Requires $O(2^{n/2})$ queries to determine s.
Quantum approach: Requires only $O(n)$ oracle queries.

Resource Requirements

Quantum Gates: $O(n^2)$ operations.
Oracle Calls: $O(n)$ queries.
Qubit Count: $2n$ qubits.

Simon's algorithm demonstrates the exponential advantage of quantum algorithms under the quantum query model, serving as a precursor to the more famous Shor's algorithm.

REFERENCES

1. Kasirajan, V. (2021). *Fundamentals of quantum computing*. Springer International Publishing.
2. Bhat, H. A., Khanday, F. A., Kaushik, B. K., Bashir, F., & Shah, K. A. (2022). Quantum computing: fundamentals, implementations and applications. *IEEE Open Journal of Nanotechnology, 3*, 61–77.
3. Khang, A., Rath, K. C., Panda, N., & Kumar, A. (2024). Quantum mechanics primer: fundamentals and quantum computing. In *Applications and principles of quantum computing* (pp. 1–24). IGI Global Scientific Publishing.
4. Rønnow, T. F., Wang, Z., Job, J., Boixo, S., Isakov, S. V., Wecker, D., . . . & Troyer, M. (2014). Defining and detecting quantum speedup. *Science, 345*(6195), 420–424.
5. Grover, L. K. (2001). From Schrödinger's equation to the quantum search algorithm. *American Journal of Physics, 69*(7), 769–777.
6. Schlosshauer, M. (2019). Quantum decoherence. *Physics Reports, 831*, 1–57.
7. Shnirman, A., Makhlin, Y., & Schön, G. (2002). Noise and decoherence in quantum two-level systems. *Physica Scripta, 2002*(T102), 147.
8. Devitt, S. J., Munro, W. J., & Nemoto, K. (2013). Quantum error correction for beginners. *Reports on Progress in Physics, 76*(7), 076001.
9. Kitaev, A. Y. (1997). Quantum computations: algorithms and error correction. *Russian Mathematical Surveys, 52*(6), 1191.
10. Niu, S., Suau, A., Staffelbach, G., & Todri-Sanial, A. (2020). A hardware-aware heuristic for the qubit mapping problem in the NISQ era. *IEEE Transactions on Quantum Engineering, 1*, 1–14.
11. Bravyi, S., Dial, O., Gambetta, J. M., Gil, D., & Nazario, Z. (2022). The future of quantum computing with superconducting qubits. *Journal of Applied Physics, 132*(16), 160902.

12. Jaeger, G. (2007). Classical and quantum computing. *Quantum Information: An Overview*, 203–217. Springer New York.
13. Acín, A., Bruß, D., Lewenstein, M., & Sanpera, A. (2001). Classification of mixed three-qubit states. *Physical Review Letters, 87*(4), 040401.
14. Bragyinsky, V. B., & Khalili, F. Y. (1995). *Quantum measurement*. Cambridge University Press.
15. Akhtarshenas, S. J. (2011). Concurrence of superpositions of many states. *Physical Review A—Atomic, Molecular, and Optical Physics, 83*(4), 042306.
16. James, D. F., Kwiat, P. G., Munro, W. J., & White, A. G. (2001). Measurement of qubits. *Physical Review A, 64*(5), 052312.
17. Ficek, Z., & Swain, S. (2005). *Quantum interference and coherence: theory and experiments* (Vol. 100). Springer Science & Business Media.
18. Katz, N., Ansmann, M., Bialczak, R. C., Lucero, E., McDermott, R., Neeley, M., . . . & Korotkov, A. N. (2006). Coherent state evolution in a superconducting qubit from partial-collapse measurement. *Science, 312*(5779), 1498–1500.
19. Horodecki, R., Horodecki, P., Horodecki, M., & Horodecki, K. (2009). Quantum entanglement. *Reviews of Modern Physics, 81*(2), 865–942.
20. Merzbacher, E. (2002). The early history of quantum tunneling. *Physics Today, 55*(8), 44–49.
21. Mosseri, R., & Dandoloff, R. (2001). Geometry of entangled states, Bloch spheres and Hopf fibrations. *Journal of Physics A: Mathematical and General, 34*(47), 10243.
22. Hu, P., Li, Y., Mong, R. S., & Singh, C. (2024). Student understanding of the Bloch sphere. *European Journal of Physics, 45*(2), 025705.
23. Bacon, D. (2006). *Dirac notation and basic linear algebra for quantum computing*. CSE 599d-Quantum Computing.
24. Yilmaz, Y. I. L. M. A. Z., Bozkurt, H., & Cakan, S. (2016). On orthonormal sets in inner product quasilinear spaces. *Creative Mathematics and Informatics, 25*(2), 237–247.
25. Patera, J., & Zassenhaus, H. (1988). The Pauli matrices in n dimensions and finest gradings of simple Lie algebras of type A_{n-1}. *Journal of Mathematical Physics, 29*(3), 665–673.
26. Longe, P. (1966). The properties of the Pauli matrices A, B, C and the conjugation of charge. *Physica, 32*(3), 603–610.
27. Helsen, J., Wallman, J. J., & Wehner, S. (2018). Representations of the multi-qubit Clifford group. *Journal of Mathematical Physics, 59*(7): 072201.
28. DiVincenzo, D. P. (1998). Quantum gates and circuits. *Proceedings of the Royal Society of London. Series A: Mathematical, Physical and Engineering Sciences, 454*(1969), 261–276.
29. Möttönen, M., & Vartiainen, J. J. (2006). Decompositions of general quantum gates. In *Trends in Quantum Computing Research*, 149. Nova Science Publishers.
30. Weinstein, Y. S., Pravia, M. A., Fortunato, E. M., Lloyd, S., & Cory, D. G. (2001). Implementation of the quantum Fourier transform. *Physical Review Letters, 86*(9), 1889.
31. D'Ariano, G. M., Macchiavello, C., & Sacchi, M. F. (1998). On the general problem of quantum phase estimation. *Physics Letters A, 248*(2–4), 103–108.
32. Thamaraimanalan, T., Singh, B., Mohankumar, M., & Korada, S. K. (2024, March). Performance analysis of Shor's algorithm for integer factorization using quantum and classical approaches. In *2024 10th International Conference on Advanced Computing and Communication Systems (ICACCS)* (Vol. 1, pp. 2591–2595). IEEE.

33. Galindo, A., & Martin-Delgado, M. A. (2000). Family of Grover's quantum-searching algorithms. *Physical Review A, 62*(6), 062303.
34. Morales, M. E., Tlyachev, T., & Biamonte, J. (2018). Variational learning of Grover's quantum search algorithm. *Physical Review A, 98*(6), 062333.
35. Brassard, G., & Hoyer, P. (1997, June). An exact quantum polynomial-time algorithm for Simon's problem. In *Proceedings of the Fifth Israeli Symposium on Theory of Computing and Systems* (pp. 12–23). IEEE.
36. Bonnetain, X. (2021). Tight bounds for Simon's algorithm. In *Progress in Cryptology–LATINCRYPT 2021: 7th International Conference on Cryptology and Information Security in Latin America, Bogotá, Colombia, October 6–8, 2021, Proceedings 7* (pp. 3–23). Springer International Publishing.

Section III

Shor's Algorithm: Factoring and Cryptanalysis

3 Shor's Algorithm: Factoring and Cryptanalysis

"Shor's algorithm shows that quantum computers could solve certain problems much more efficiently than classical computers, potentially breaking widely used cryptographic systems."

— Peter Shor

SUMMARY

This chapter focuses on Shor's algorithm, particularly its application to factoring and cryptanalysis. It begins with an overview of Shor's algorithm, detailing the classical extraction of periods from measured values and the quantum gates required for the Quantum Fourier Transform (QFT). Further, this chapter explores the applications and limitations of Shor's algorithm, including its impact on RSA (Rivest-Shamir-Adleman) encryption. A literature review follows, discussing Shor's algorithm in the context of quantum computation, its effectiveness on RSA, and the effects of imperfections on its factorization process. The section also includes an experimental study of Shor's algorithm using IBM Q, followed by a practical implementation of factoring numbers $N = 21$ and $N = 35$. Further, it covers resource estimation, quantum simulations, and different types of simulators in IBM Qiskit, including state vector, QASM, Matrix Product State (MPS), and stabilizer simulators, providing insights into their use cases and the limits of classical simulation.

3.1 INTRODUCTION

Shor's Factorization Algorithm, proposed by Peter Shor in 1994 [1], suggests that quantum mechanics can factorize numbers in polynomial time (the time required to factor large numbers increases more slowly compared to classical algorithms), as opposed to the exponential time (the time required to factor large numbers increases very quickly as the numbers grow) required by classical algorithms. This discovery could significantly impact data security, which relies on the difficulty of factoring large composite numbers. While there are polynomial-time algorithms for tasks like integer multiplication (e.g., Euclid's Algorithm: It is a classical method used to find the greatest common divisor (GCD) of two integers. The GCD of two numbers is the largest integer that divides both of them without leaving a remainder.), no polynomial-time algorithm for factorization had been found before Shor's work.

DOI: 10.1201/9781003606338-3

Shor developed a method to turn a factoring problem into a ***period-finding*** problem, which can be solved efficiently using quantum mechanics.

The fundamental theorem of arithmetic states that every integer $n \geq 2$ can be uniquely factored into a product of powers of primes. For centuries, mathematicians have worked on finding ways to factor random integers into their prime factors. The best-known classical algorithm for factoring is the number field sieve, which has an asymptotic running time of

$$O\left(\exp\left(c\left(\log n\right)^{1/3}\left(\log\log n\right)^{2/3}\right)\right)$$

for some constant c. In contrast, Shor's quantum algorithm takes

$$O\left((\log n)^2 (\log\log n)(\log\log\log n)\right)$$

steps, along with some polynomial-time work on a classical computer to convert the quantum computer's output into factors [2].

Modern cryptography often depends on the assumption that no fast (polynomial-time) factoring algorithm or discrete logarithm algorithm exists. Key cryptosystems, such as RSA and ElGamal, are based on this assumption. If Shor's algorithm could be implemented for sufficiently large integers, these cryptosystems could be easily broken. Many quantum algorithms use quantum versions of classical computations. Quantum algorithms often start by creating a quantum superposition, which is then processed by a quantum version U_f of a classical function f. This setup, known as quantum parallelism, doesn't provide an advantage by itself; however, it sets up the system in a way that is useful for further steps. Shor's algorithm begins with this quantum parallelism step to efficiently solve the factorization problem.

3.2   OVERVIEW OF SHOR'S ALGORITHM

Shor's algorithm consists of the following two parts:

Conversion of the problem of factorizing to the problem of finding the period. This part can be implemented with classical method [2].

Finding the period using the QFT.

In Shor's algorithm, the input is a non-prime number N and the output is a non-trivial factor of N.

Algorithm: It contains a few steps; only in step 2 is the use of a quantum computer required.

1. Choose any random number, let's say a, such that $1 < a < N$ so that they are co-primes of each other (i.e., a is a number less than N and has no factors in common with N).

2. A quantum computer is used to determine the unknown period r of the function [$f_{a,N}(r) = a^r \mod N$. If r is an odd integer, then go back to Step 1. Else, move to Step 3.
3. Since r is an even integer, calculate $(a^{\frac{r}{2}} - 1)(a^{\frac{r}{2}} + 1) \equiv 0 \pmod{N}$. Now, if the value of $(a^{\frac{r}{2}} - 1) \equiv 0 \pmod{N}$, go back to Step 1 and choose a different value for a. If the value of $(a^{\frac{r}{2}} \pm 1) \not\equiv 0 \pmod{N}$ (non-trivial), then move to Step 4.
4. Compute $p = \gcd\left(a^{\frac{r}{2}} - 1, N\right)$ and $q = \gcd\left(a^{\frac{r}{2}} + 1, N\right)$. The answer required is p, which is one of the prime factors of the given number N.
5. Compute the other prime factor q using $q = N/p$. Finally, the prime factors for the given N are found. So, $N = p \times q$. (where $\times$ indicates multiplication symbol)

3.2.1 CLASSICAL EXTRACTION OF THE PERIOD FROM THE MEASURED VALUE

This section sketches a purely classical algorithm for extracting the period from the measured value v obtained from the quantum core of Shor's algorithm. When the period r happens to be a power of 2, the QFT gives exact multiples of $N/r = 2^n/r$, which makes the period easy to extract. In this case, the measured value v is equal to $j \cdot 2^n/r$ for some j. Most of the time j and r will be relatively prime, in which case reducing the fraction $v/2^n$ to its lowest terms will yield a fraction j/r whose denominator is the period r.

Let us see how to obtain a good guess for r when it is not a power of 2. In general, the QFT gives only approximate multiples of the scaled frequency, which complicates the extraction of the period from the measurement. When the period is not a power of 2, a good guess for the period can be obtained from the continued fraction expansion of $v/2^n$. Shor shows that with high probability v is within $1/2$ of some multiple of $2^n/r$, say $j \cdot 2^n/r$.

The reason why n was chosen to satisfy $N^2 \leq 2^n < 2N^2$ becomes apparent when we try to extract the period r from the measured value v. In the high-probability case that

$$\left| v - j \cdot \frac{2^n}{r} \right| < \frac{1}{2}$$

for some j, the left inequality $N^2 \leq 2^n$ implies that

$$\left| \frac{v}{2^n} - \frac{j}{r} \right| < \frac{1}{2 \cdot 2^n} \leq \frac{1}{2N^2}.$$

In general, the difference between two distinct fractions p/q and p'/q' with denominators less than M (where M defines the maximum size for the denominator that can be considered in the continued fraction expansion) is bounded:

$$\left| \frac{p}{q} - \frac{p'}{q'} \right| = \left| \frac{pq' - p'q}{qq'} \right| > \frac{1}{M^2}.$$

Thus, there is at most one fraction p/q with denominator $q < M$ such that $\left|\frac{v}{2^n} - \frac{p}{q}\right| < \frac{1}{M^2}$. In the high-probability case that v is within $1/2$ of $j \cdot 2^n/r$, this fraction will be j/r.

The fraction p/q can be computed using a continued fraction expansion as shown below. We take the denominator q of the obtained fraction as our guess for the period. This guess will be correct whenever j and r are relatively prime [3].

3.2.2 CLASSICAL EXTRACTION OF THE PERIOD FROM THE MEASURED VALUE

This section gives us a purely classical algorithm for extracting the period from the measured value v obtained from the quantum core of Shor's algorithm. When the period r happens to be a power of 2, the QFT gives exact multiples of $N/r = 2^n/r$, which makes the period easy to extract. In this case, the measured value v is equal to $j \cdot 2^n/r$ for some j. Most of the time j and r will be relatively prime, in which case reducing the fraction $v/2^n$ to its lowest terms will yield a fraction j/r whose denominator is the period r.

Let us see how to obtain a good guess for r when it is not a power of 2. In general, the QFT gives only approximate multiples of the scaled frequency, which complicates the extraction of the period from the measurement. When the period is not a power of 2, a good guess for the period can be obtained from the continued fraction expansion of $v/2^n$. Shor shows that with high probability v is within $1/2$ of some multiple of $2^n/r$, say $j \cdot 2^n/r$.

The reason why n was chosen to satisfy $N^2 \leq 2^n < 2N^2$ becomes apparent when we try to extract the period r from the measured value v. In the high-probability case that

$$\left|v - j \cdot \frac{2^n}{r}\right| < \frac{1}{2}$$

for some j, the left inequality $N^2 \leq 2^n$ implies that

$$\left|\frac{v}{2^n} - \frac{j}{r}\right| < \frac{1}{2 \cdot 2^n} \leq \frac{1}{2N^2}.$$

In general, the difference between two distinct fractions p/q and p'/q' with denominators less than M is bounded:

$$\left|\frac{p}{q} - \frac{p'}{q'}\right| = \left|\frac{pq' - p'q}{qq'}\right| > \frac{1}{M^2}.$$

Thus, there is at most one fraction p/q with denominator $q < M$ such that $\left|\frac{v}{2^n} - \frac{p}{q}\right| < \frac{1}{M^2}$. In the high-probability case that v is within $1/2$ of $j \cdot 2^n/r$, this fraction will be j/r.

The fraction p/q can be computed using a continued fraction expansion as shown below. We take the denominator q of the obtained fraction as our guess for the period. This guess will be correct whenever j and r are relatively prime.

3.2.3   CONTINUED FRACTION EXPANSION

The unique fraction with a denominator less than M that is within $1/M^2$ of $v/2^n$ can be obtained efficiently from the continued fraction expansion of $v/2^n$ as follows [4]. Using the sequences:

$$a_0 = \left\lfloor \frac{v}{2^n} \right\rfloor, \quad \varepsilon_0 = \frac{v}{2^n} - a_0,$$

$$a_i = \left\lfloor \frac{1}{\varepsilon_{i-1}} \right\rfloor, \quad \varepsilon_i = \frac{1}{\varepsilon_{i-1}} - a_i,$$

$$p_0 = a_0, \quad p_1 = a_1 a_0 + 1, \quad p_i = a_i p_{i-1} + p_{i-2},$$

$$q_0 = 1, \quad q_1 = a_1, \quad q_i = a_i q_{i-1} + q_{i-2}.$$

Compute the first fraction $\frac{p_i}{q_i}$ such that $q_i < M \leq q_{i+1}$.

EXAMPLE OF CONTINUED FRACTION EXPANSION

Let's work through a simple example to understand how continued fraction expansion is used to extract the period in Shor's algorithm.

Let $v = 15$ and $2^n = 32$, so the value to expand is $\frac{v}{2^n} = \frac{15}{32} = 0.46875$.

STEP 1: INITIAL SETUP

We begin by computing the first term in the continued fraction expansion:

$$a_0 = \left\lfloor \frac{v}{2^n} \right\rfloor = \lfloor 0.46875 \rfloor = 0$$

Since 0.46875 is greater than 0 but less than 1, the floor of 0.46875 is: 0
   Next, calculate the fractional part:

$$\varepsilon_0 = \frac{v}{2^n} - a_0 = 0.46875 - 0 = 0.46875$$

STEP 2: RECURSION FOR FURTHER TERMS

Now, we compute the next terms:

$$a_1 = \left\lfloor \frac{1}{\varepsilon_0} \right\rfloor = \left\lfloor \frac{1}{0.46875} \right\rfloor = \lfloor 2.131 \rfloor = 2$$

The new fractional part is:

$$\varepsilon_1 = \frac{1}{\varepsilon_0} - a_1 = 2.131 - 2 = 0.131$$

Next, compute:

$$a_2 = \left\lfloor \frac{1}{\varepsilon_1} \right\rfloor = \left\lfloor \frac{1}{0.131} \right\rfloor = \lfloor 7.63 \rfloor = 7$$

The new fractional part is:

$$\varepsilon_2 = \frac{1}{\varepsilon_1} - a_2 = 7.63 - 7 = 0.63$$

STEP 3: CONTINUED FRACTION EXPANSION

Now, we compute the numerators and denominators using the recurrence relations:

$$p_0 = a_0 = 0, \quad p_1 = a_1 a_0 + 1 = 1, \quad p_2 = a_2 p_1 + p_0 = 7$$

$$q_0 = 1, \quad q_1 = a_1 = 2, \quad q_2 = a_2 q_1 + q_0 = 15$$

STEP 4: BEST FRACTION

We find the best fraction $\frac{p_2}{q_2} = \frac{7}{15}$, which is the best approximation of $\frac{15}{32}$.
Thus, the period r is 15.

3.3   NUMBER OF QUANTUM GATES REQUIRED TO PERFORM QFT

To compute QFT (refer section 2.3.3) for two qubits, Qubit 1 requires a Hadamard
(H) gate and $(n-1)$ controlled rotation (R) gates, resulting in a total of n gates.
Qubit 2 requires a Hadamard gate and $(n-2)$ controlled R gates, resulting in a total
of $(n-1)$ gates.

The QFT on n qubits requires n Hadamard gates and $\frac{n(n+1)}{2}$ controlled rotation
gates. Each controlled rotation gate requires two CNOT gates and a few (approximately 4) single-qubit rotation gates.

Thus, the overall scaling of the QFT is $O(n^2)$, which represents a polynomial scaling of the number of gates with respect to the number of input qubits. This polynomial scaling is a key reason why Shor's algorithm is considered an efficient quantum
algorithm [5].

3.4   APPLICATIONS OF SHOR'S ALGORITHM

The main application of Shor's algorithm is in the field of cryptography, where it
poses a potential threat to widely used encryption and digital signature schemes
based on the difficulty of factoring large numbers. Here are some detailed applications:

BREAKING RSA ENCRYPTION

RSA (Rivest-Shamir-Adleman) is a widely used public-key cryptosystem that relies on the difficulty of factoring the product of two large prime numbers. Shor's algorithm, when implemented on a sufficiently powerful quantum computer, can efficiently factorize the RSA modulus, thus breaking the encryption. This poses a significant threat to the security of data encrypted using RSA [2].

IMPACT ON PUBLIC KEY INFRASTRUCTURE (PKI)

Many secure communication protocols, including HTTPS for secure web browsing, rely on PKI for key exchange and digital signatures. If Shor's algorithm becomes practical, it could compromise the security of PKI-based systems, leading to potential vulnerabilities in online communication and e-commerce [6].

CRYPTOGRAPHIC HASH FUNCTIONS

Shor's algorithm doesn't directly attack cryptographic hash functions, but the security of many hash-based algorithms relies on the difficulty of factoring large numbers. If the underlying encryption in a hash-based scheme is broken, it can have cascading effects on the security of the entire system [7].

POST-QUANTUM CRYPTOGRAPHY

Shor's algorithm motivates the search for new cryptographic algorithms that are secure against quantum attacks. Post-quantum cryptography aims to develop encryption schemes that would remain secure even in the presence of quantum computers. Research in this area includes lattice-based cryptography, hash-based cryptography, code-based cryptography, and more [8].

OPTIMIZATION PROBLEMS

Shor's algorithm is not only applicable to factoring but can also be adapted for solving certain mathematical optimization problems. This aspect of the algorithm has applications in fields such as chemistry, physics, and materials science for simulating quantum systems.

3.5 LIMITATIONS OF SHOR'S ALGORITHM

The implementation of Shor's algorithm has several limitations and challenges:

QUANTUM COMPUTER REQUIREMENTS

Shor's algorithm requires a sufficiently large and fault-tolerant quantum computer to be practical. Building and maintaining a large quantum computer with a sufficient number of stable qubits and low error rates remains a significant technical challenge [9].

QUANTUM ERROR CORRECTION

Quantum computers are susceptible to errors due to various factors, such as deco-herence and environmental interactions. Implementing quantum error correction to maintain the stability of qubits over the course of a computation is crucial for the success of Shor's algorithm [10].

PHYSICAL QUBIT COUNT

Shor's algorithm's efficiency depends on the number of physical qubits in the quantum computer. The number of logical qubits needed for factoring an n-bit number is proportional to $O((\log n)^2)$. A circuit developed by Beauregard uses $2n + 3$ qubits and $O(n^3 \log n)$ elementary quantum gates. Achieving the required number of qubits for practical applications poses a considerable technological barrier [11].

QUANTUM GATE OPERATIONS

The algorithm involves a large number of quantum gate operations, and maintaining the coherence of these operations is challenging. Implementing these gates accurately and coherently is essential for the algorithm's success [3].

POST-QUANTUM CRYPTOGRAPHY SOLUTIONS

While Shor's algorithm poses a potential threat to classical cryptographic systems, it has also motivated research in post-quantum cryptography. New cryptographic algorithms and protocols are being developed to resist quantum attacks, ensuring secure communication in a post-quantum era. Key approaches include lattice-based cryptography (e.g., NTRUEncrypt, NTRUSign), hash-based schemes (e.g., XMSS), code-based systems (e.g., McEliece), multivariate polynomial methods (e.g., Rainbow, UOV), and isogeny-based techniques (e.g., SIDH). The U.S. National Institute of Standards and Technology (NIST) has initiated a standardization process for post-quantum cryptography, evaluating candidate algorithms to select and standardize quantum-resistant cryptographic algorithms for various applications [12, 13].

QUANTUM KEY DISTRIBUTION (QKD)

Quantum key distribution uses the principles of quantum mechanics to secure communication channels. While not a post-quantum replacement for traditional cryptographic primitives, QKD provides secure key distribution that is theoretically immune to quantum attacks [14].

3.6   LITERATURE REVIEW OF SHOR'S ALGORITHM

3.6.1   SHOR'S ALGORITHM AND QUANTUM COMPUTATION

Quantum information theory constitutes the foundation of quantum computation. Initially, the model mimics classical probabilistic systems, where a physical device

X embodies finite states—like a bit represented by –0,1″. This state information is described through probability vectors, offering insights into the possible outcomes. Upon observation, the state changes, transitioning the knowledge vector. Operations on X, typically limited to deterministic or random actions, are represented by matrices. These operations mirror real-world physical processes and are conveyed through stochastic matrices, encapsulating meaningful transformations [15].

This model generalizes seamlessly for sets beyond –0, 1″, adapting to the dimensionality of the underlying states. In quantum information, the classical state representation pivots to quantum bits or qubits. Similar to classical bits, qubits assume states –0, 1″, but the key distinction lies in their representation. The emergence of quantum computation stems from the understanding that traditional computing, based on classical physics, faces limitations when dealing with complex problems. Information and computation are fundamentally linked to physical theories. When quantum effects, such as quantum interference and entanglement, become significant at the atomic and subatomic levels, a new model for computation arises. Quantum computers operate by manipulating quantum bits or qubits, which can exist in multiple states simultaneously, enabling parallel processing on an unprecedented scale.

Shor's algorithm for factoring large numbers, a problem considered computationally intractable for classical computers, showcases the potential of quantum computation. The algorithm utilizes quantum properties to efficiently factorize numbers by employing the quantum discrete Fourier transform and quantum logic gates. This breakthrough demonstrates the superior computational capability of quantum systems in solving certain complex problems. Theoretical models for quantum computation include the Turing-machine model adapted to quantum mechanics and the implementation of quantum networks using quantum logic gates.

Quantum computing, a revolutionary field, gained prominence with Peter Shor's 1994 presentation of an algorithm that exponentially reduce the computational complexity of integer factorization. This breakthrough directly challenged the RSA algorithm, a cornerstone of digital security, as Shor's quantum algorithm threatened the traditional difficulty of factoring large integers on classical computers. Shor's algorithm depends crucially on the principles of quantum mechanics and operates on quantum states, ushering in a new era of computational possibilities [16].

3.6.2 RSA WITH SHOR'S ALGORITHM

The RSA cryptosystem, introduced by Rivest, Shamir, and Adleman in 1977, is the foundation of modern public-key cryptography, widely used in secure communications, digital signatures, and encryption protocols. Its security relies on the computational hardness of factoring large integers -a problem believed to be intractable for classical computers when sufficiently large key sizes (e.g., 2048 or 4096 bits) are used. However, the beginning of quantum computing and Shor's algorithm threaten to weaken RSA's security by efficiently solving the integer factorization problem [17].

The RSA cryptosystem is fundamentally based on modular arithmetic and number theory, with its core security relying on the computational difficulty of certain mathematical problems. At the heart of RSA lies the large integer factorization problem: given a composite number $N = p \times q$ where p and q are large prime numbers, recovering the prime factors p and q from N is computationally infeasible for sufficiently large N. This difficulty is complemented by Euler's Theorem, which states that for any integer m coprime with N (i.e., $\gcd(m,N) = 1$), the congruence $m^{\phi(N)} \equiv 1$ mod N holds, where $\phi(N) = (p-1)(q-1)$ is Euler's totient function. The key generation process in RSA involves selecting a public key (e,N) where e is chosen such that $\gcd(e,\phi(N)) = 1$, and computing the private key d as the modular inverse of e modulo $\phi(N)$, expressed as $d \equiv e^{-1} \mod \phi(N)$.

The security of RSA against classical computers primarily depends on two computational assumptions: the hardness of integer factorization and the related difficulty of solving the discrete logarithm problem. The best-known classical algorithm for factorization, the General Number Field Sieve (GNFS), has sub-exponential complexity of $O\left(e^{(\log N)^{1/3}(\log \log N)^{2/3}}\right)$, which makes RSA secure when sufficiently large key sizes are used. In practical implementations, RSA faces various vulnerabilities beyond mathematical attacks, including side-channel attacks such as timing attacks, power analysis, and fault injection attacks that can compromise the security of RSA implementations. To address these concerns and ensure long-term security against advancing computational capabilities, the National Institute of Standards and Technology (NIST) recommends using RSA keys of at least 2048 bits for classical security, with 3072 or 4096 bits recommended for more long-term security requirements [18].

3.6.3 EFFECTS OF IMPERFECTIONS FOR SHOR'S FACTORIZATION ALGORITHM

The implementation of Shor's algorithm in real quantum computing systems faces significant challenges due to various types of imperfections and errors. The most advanced experimental demonstration of Shor's algorithm to date was performed on a seven-qubit nuclear magnetic resonance (NMR) based quantum computer, which successfully factorized the number $N = 15$ [19]. While this achievement represented a major milestone in quantum computation, several simplifications to the original algorithm were necessary to accomplish this result, including the use of prior knowledge about the factors to reduce the computational complexity [20].

Several important effects of errors on the algorithm's performance have been observed in these early experiments. For instance, in the factorization of $N = 15$, researchers found that:

Decoherence errors caused by interactions with the environment led to a gradual loss of quantum information.

Imperfect gate operations introduced computational errors that accumulated throughout the algorithm's execution.

Measurement errors affected the final probability distribution of results.

However, since these experiments were limited to very small numbers (specifically $N = 15$), they could not provide meaningful insights into how these error effects scale with larger input sizes. More recent numerical simulations have attempted to address this limitation by investigating larger values of N:

1. Fowler and Hollenberg [21] examined the impact of finite precision in quantum phase rotations within the QFT component of Shor's algorithm, considering values up to $N = 33$.
2. Wang et al. [22] studied dynamical phase errors in the algorithm's implementation, demonstrating how these errors grow with increasing circuit depth.
3. Chen and Wang [16] analyzed discrete qubit flip errors for factorizations up to $N = 247$, showing that the error rate scales approximately linearly with the number of logical qubits required.

A concrete example of these error effects can be seen in the case of factoring $N = 21$. Numerical simulations show that:

With perfect gates, the success probability is approximately 50%.
Introducing just 1% gate error reduces the success probability to about 30%.
At 5% gate error, the success probability drops below 10%.

These studies collectively demonstrate that while Shor's algorithm theoretically offers exponential speedup for integer factorization, practical implementations face significant challenges from various error sources. The error correction requirements grow rapidly with the input size N, suggesting that fault-tolerant quantum computers with thousands of physical qubits will be necessary to factor cryptographically relevant numbers (e.g., $N \geq 2048$ bits) [18].

3.6.4   NUMBER OF QUBITS REQUIRED FOR SHOR'S ALGORITHM

The number of qubits needed to factor an integer of n bits using Shor's algorithm on a quantum computer is minimized. A circuit which uses $2n + 3$ qubits and $O(n^3 \log(n))$ elementary quantum gates in a depth of $O(n^3)$ to implement the factorization algorithm. The circuit is computable in polynomial time on a classical computer and is completely general as it does not rely on any property of the number to be factored. To reduce the number of qubits, a variant of a quantum addition algorithm described by Draper is used. Other techniques used to reduce the number of qubits are the hardwiring of classical values and the sequential computation of the Fourier transform [23].

3.6.5   EXPERIMENTAL STUDY OF SHOR'S FACTORING ALGORITHM USING THE IBM Q

Implementation of Shor's factoring algorithm on the IBM Q quantum processor, specifically focusing on the ibmqx5 superconducting chip, is proposed. The experimental challenges arise from the error-prone nature of physical qubits and gates. While previous works have attempted Shor's algorithm on various setups, such as

NMR, trapped ions, photons, and superconducting qubits, many implementations involve oversimplified versions equivalent to coin flipping, lacking the true quantum hardware. This work stands out by providing a proof-of-principle demonstration with compiled Shor's algorithm for factoring $N = 15, 21$, and 35, utilizing only five, six, and seven superconducting qubits, respectively [24].

Classical processing is strategically employed alongside quantum computation to compensate for device limitations, and efforts are made to minimize noise effects by reducing the number of physical qubits and circuit depth. The experimental results are analyzed quantitatively using the square of statistical overlap (SSO) and qualitatively using probability plots. The success of the algorithm is evaluated through a comparison of the measured probability distribution and the theoretically predicted distribution for the period, utilizing SSO for the analysis.

3.7 IMPLEMENTATION OF SHOR'S ALGORITHM

Shor's factoring algorithm utilizes the power of quantum computation to efficiently determine the period of the function $f(x) = a^x \mod N$, where a is a randomly chosen small number that shares no common factors with N. From this period, classical number-theoretic techniques can be applied to factor N with high probability.

The algorithm primarily relies on two key quantum computational components: modular exponentiation (computation of $a^x \mod N$) and the IQFT. Both operations take about $O(l^3)$ steps to complete, where l is the number of bits needed to represent the number being factored. This is much faster compared to classical prime factorization methods, which need around $O(2^{l^{1/3}})$ steps and become extremely slow as l increases [25, 26].

The implementation of Shor's algorithm can be divided into four distinct steps, as depicted in Figure 3.1. In Shor's algorithm, one of the most computationally intensive steps is implementing a quantum circuit to evaluate the function $f(x) = a^x \mod N$ on a superposition of 2^n inputs. Here, n is the number of qubits in the input register, allowing the quantum computer to evaluate $f(x)$ for all $x \in \{0, 1, \dots, 2^n - 1\}$ simultaneously via quantum parallelism.

The complete source code for the experimental implementation of Shor's algorithm is available on GitHub at: `https://github.com/mohanyaso/Shor.git`.

Let $f : \{0, 1, 2, \dots, N - 1\} \to \{0, 1, 2, \dots, N - 1\}$ be a periodic function of period r, meaning that

$$f(x) = f(x + r) \quad \forall x \in \{0, 1, 2, \dots, N - 1\},$$

and the values $f(x), f(x+1), f(x+2), \dots, f(x+r-1)$ are all distinct.

From the properties of modular arithmetic and period finding, the periodic function can be written as:

$$f(x) = a^x \mod N.$$

Example: Evaluating $5^{117} \mod 19$

To illustrate, let us calculate $5^{117} \mod 19$. The binary representation of 117 is:

$$117 = 1110101_2 = 2^6 + 2^5 + 2^4 + 2^2 + 2^0 = 64 + 32 + 16 + 4 + 1.$$

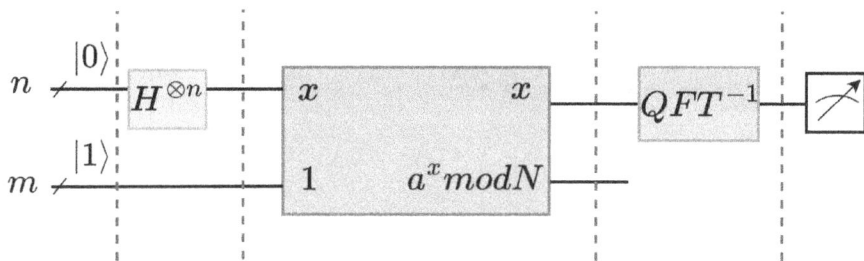

Figure 3.1 Period finding function of Shor's algorithm

Thus, we can express 5^{117} mod 19 as:

$$5^{117} \quad \text{mod } 19 = 5^{64+32+16+4+1} \quad \text{mod } 19 = (5^{64} \times 5^{32} \times 5^{16} \times 5^4 \times 5^1) \quad \text{mod } 19.$$

Using modular arithmetic:

$$5^1 \quad \text{mod } 19 = 5,$$
$$5^4 \quad \text{mod } 19 = 17,$$
$$5^{16} \quad \text{mod } 19 = 16,$$
$$5^{32} \quad \text{mod } 19 = 9,$$
$$5^{64} \quad \text{mod } 19 = 5.$$

Substituting these values:

$$5^{117} \quad \text{mod } 19 = (5 \times 9 \times 16 \times 17 \times 5) \quad \text{mod } 19 = 61200 \quad \text{mod } 19 = 1.$$

Unitary Operator for Modular Exponentiation

From the above discussion on modular exponentiation, it is evident that a unitary operator can be used to perform step-by-step   mod N operations, leading to the condition:

$$a^x \quad \text{mod } N = 1.$$

This can be achieved using the phase estimation algorithm, as x appears as the power of a. This requires a controlled unitary operation of the form $U^1, U^2, U^4, U^8, \ldots$, where the powers are $2^0, 2^1, 2^2, 2^3, \ldots$.

Quantum Phase Estimation (QPE) is a quantum algorithm used to estimate the phase corresponding to an eigenvalue of a given unitary operator. The eigenvalues of a unitary operator always have unit modulus, meaning their absolute value is 1. These eigenvalues are characterized by their phase, and therefore, QPE can be described as retrieving either the phase or the eigenvalue itself [27].

If $|y\rangle = |0\rangle$, then $|y \otimes f(x)\rangle$ becomes $|f(x)\rangle$, which provides an easy way to evaluate $f(x)$. This means that when the first register $|y\rangle$ is in the state $|0\rangle$, the second

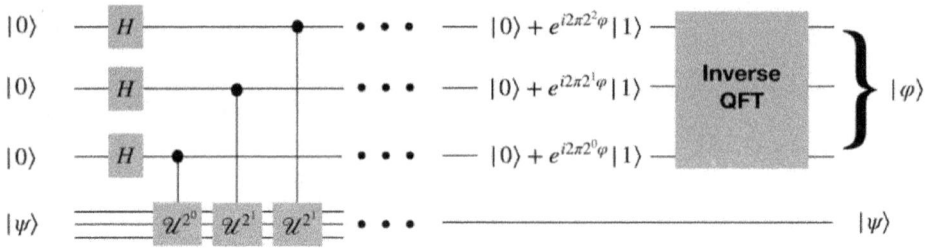

Figure 3.2   Outline of phase estimation algorithm

register's state simplifies to $|f(x)\rangle$, which directly gives us the result of evaluating the function $f(x)$ (Figure 3.2).

Thus, the input to the second register will be $|0\rangle$ for n qubits, without applying superposition. This means the second register is initially in the state $|0\rangle^{\otimes n}$, and superposition is not applied immediately, which simplifies the function evaluation process. [28].

Note: The reverse order of the output state relative to the desired QFT. Therefore, we must reverse the order of the qubits.

3.7.1   FACTORING $N = 21$ USING SHOR'S ALGORITHM

The following steps have to be followed:

Step 1: Choose a random integer a, where $1 < a < N$.
Let $a = 6$. Find the $\gcd(a,N)$ and check whether it is coprime with N or not.

$$\gcd(6,21) = 3,$$

so, 6 is not coprime with N.
Now, let $a = 11$. Find the $\gcd(a,N)$:

$$\gcd(11,21) = 1,$$

so, 11 is coprime with N.

From Table 3.1 it is clear that the possible values of "a" are 2, 4, 5, 8, 10, 11, 13, 16, 17, 19, 20.

Table 3.2 shows the result of raising 11 to the power of x and then taking the remainder when divided by 21 (modulo 21).

When $x = 0$, 11^{0} mod $21 = 1$ because any number raised to the power of 0 is 1, and the remainder when dividing 1 by 21 is 1.
When $x = 1$, 11^{1} mod $21 = 11$ because any number raised to the power of 1 is the number itself, and the remainder when dividing 11 by 21 is 11.
When $x = 2$, 11^{2} mod $21 = 16$ because the remainder of 121 divided by 21 is 16.

Table 3.1

Possible values of \a" for $N = 21$

gcd(2,21) = 1	gcd(12,21) = 3
gcd(3,21) = 3	gcd(13,21) = 1
gcd(4,21) = 1	gcd(14,21) = 7
gcd(5,21) = 1	gcd(15,21) = 3
gcd(6,21) = 3	gcd(16,21) = 1
gcd(7,21) = 7	gcd(17,21) = 1
gcd(8,21) = 1	gcd(18,21) = 3
gcd(9,21) = 3	gcd(19,21) = 1
gcd(10,21) = 1	gcd(20,21) = 1
gcd(11,21) = 1	

Table 3.2

Representation of $11^x \mod 21$ **for various values of** x

x	0	1	2	3	4	5	6	7	8	9	10	11	12
$11^x \mod 21$	1	11	16	8	4	2	1	11	16	8	4	2	1

The pattern continues, and it is clear that after reaching $11^6 \mod 21 = 1$, the sequence starts repeating. This is because of the concept of periodicity in modular arithmetic (Figures 3.3 and 3.4).

Step 3: Check if x is even. Here, the obtained period is 6, which is an even number. Now, calculate:

$$(a^{x/2} - 1)(a^{x/2} + 1) = 0 \mod N.$$

We have:

$$(a^{x/2} - 1) \neq 0 \mod N \quad \text{(non-trivial)}.$$

For $a = 11$, with $x = 6$, we get:

$$11^{6/2} - 1 \mod 21 \neq 0.$$

This simplifies to:

$$11^3 - 1 \mod 21 \neq 0.$$

Now compute:

$$11^3 = 1331, \quad 1331 - 1 = 1330.$$

Finally:

$$1330 \mod 21 \neq 0.$$

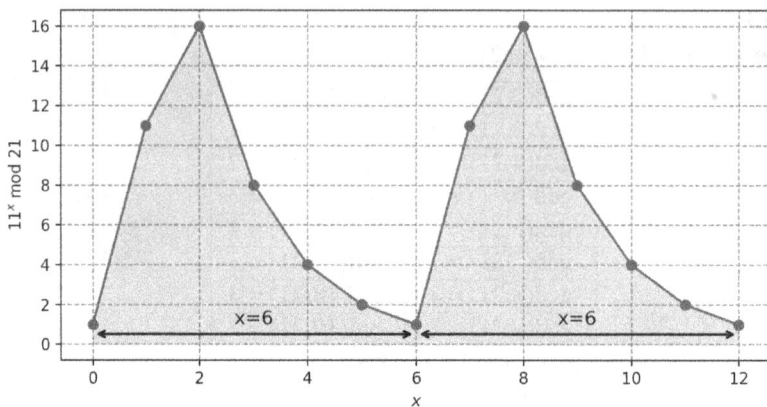

Figure 3.3   Representation of the periodic function 11^x mod 21

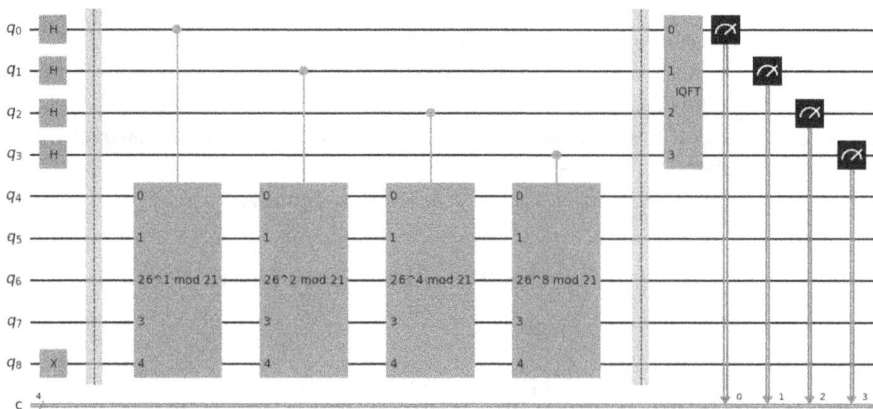

Figure 3.4   Quantum circuit to find factor for $N = 21$ for $a = 11$

We compute:

$$1330 \mod 21 = 7 \neq 0.$$

Step 4: Compute $p = \gcd(a^{x/2} - 1, N)$.
We calculate:

$$p = \gcd(11^3 - 1, 21).$$

Since:

$$11^3 - 1 = 1330,$$

we get:

$$p = \gcd(1330, 21) = 7.$$

Step 5: Compute the other prime factor q using $q = \frac{N}{p}$.
Finally, the prime factors for the given N are found:

$$q = \frac{N}{p} = \frac{21}{7} = 3.$$

Thus, the factors for $N = 21$ are $p = 7$ and $q = 3$, so:

$$N = p \times q = 7 \times 3.$$

Computation of Period for $2^x \mod 21$

Let us check the Modulus Computation for $a = 2$ with $\gcd(2, 21) = 1$. Since $\gcd(2, 21) = 1$, we know that 2 is coprime with 21. The task is to find the period of the function $2^x \mod 21$ by examining its values for different values of x.

Step 1: Choose a random integer a, where $1 < a < N$.
Let us try with $a = 2$ now.

Step 2: The first register is initialized with a superposition of all states. We now calculate $2^x \mod 21$ for various values of x to observe the periodicity.

Table 3.3

Representation of $2^x \mod 21$ for various values of x

x	0	1	2	3	4	5	6	7	8	9	10	11	12
$2^x \mod 21$	1	2	4	8	16	11	1	2	4	8	16	11	1

From Table 3.3, we can observe that the sequence $2^x \mod 21$ repeats itself after reaching $2^6 \mod 21 = 1$. Therefore, the period of the sequence is 6.

Step 3: Check if the Period r is Even.
We have already determined the period $r = 6$ for $2^x \mod 21$, and since 6 is an even number, we proceed to the next step.

Next, let us compute the prime factors using the following expression:

$$(a^{x/2} - 1)(a^{x/2} + 1) = 0 \mod N$$

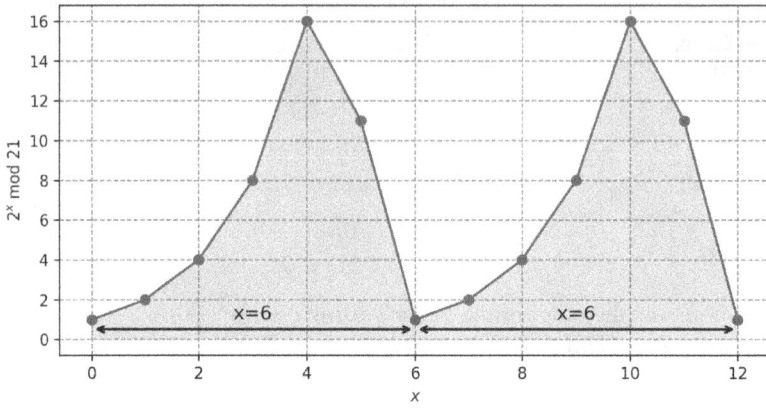

Figure 3.5   Representation of the periodic function $2^x \bmod 21$

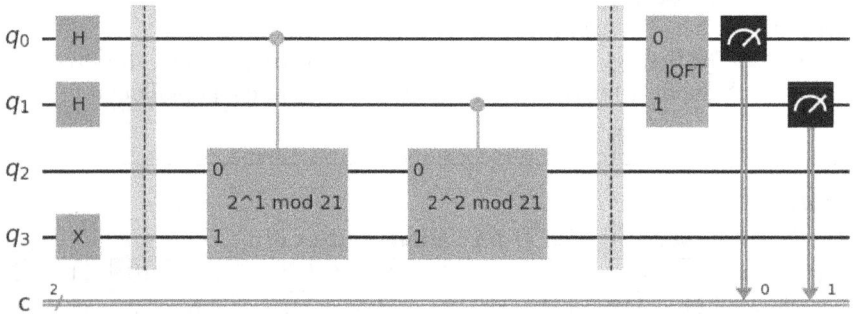

Figure 3.6   Quantum circuit to find factor for $N = 21$ for $a = 2$

For $a = 2$ and $x = 6$, we calculate (Figures 3.5 and 3.6):

$$(2^{6/2} - 1)(2^{6/2} + 1) = (2^3 - 1)(2^3 + 1) = (8 - 1)(8 + 1) = 7 \times 9$$

Now, let us check modulo 21:

$$(2^3 - 1) \mod 21 = 7 \mod 21 \neq 0$$

This confirms that $2^{x/2} - 1 \neq 0 \mod 21$, and thus it is a non-trivial factor. Now, let's proceed to the next step.

Step 4: Compute $p = \gcd(2^{x/2} - 1, 21)$
The greatest common divisor (gcd) of $2^{x/2} - 1$ and $N = 21$:

$$p = \gcd(2^3 - 1, 21) = \gcd(7, 21)$$

Since $\gcd(7, 21) = 7$, we find that $p = 7$.

Step 5: Compute the Other Prime Factor q
Now, we compute the other prime factor q using the formula:

$$q = \frac{N}{p} = \frac{21}{7} = 3$$

Thus, the prime factors of $N = 21$ are $p = 7$ and $q = 3$, and we can write:

$$N = p \times q = 7 \times 3 = 21$$

The prime factorization of $N = 21$ is $21 = 7 \times 3$, which is found using the periodicity of $2^x \mod 21$.

Table 3.4 compares various values of a for $N = 21$, displaying the period, prime factors, number of qubits required for IQFT, number of Hadamard gates, and the number of controlled rotation (CROT) gates required.

For optimal quantum circuit design, it is essential to select a value for a such that the period is non-trivial and reasonable. A periodicity of 1, as observed with $a = 7$, does not provide useful information for factorization. The goal is to select the smallest a that yields the maximum period.

The numbers a that are co-prime with $N = 21$ (i.e., $\gcd(a, 21) = 1$) are:

$$a \in \{2, 4, 5, 8, 10, 11, 13, 16, 17, 19, 20\}$$

The periodicities for the values of a are as follows:

For $a = 2$, the period $x = 6$
For $a = 4$, the period $x = 3$
For $a = 5$, the period $x = 6$
For $a = 8$, the period $x = 2$
For $a = 10$, the period $x = 6$
For $a = 11$, the period $x = 6$
For $a = 13$, the period $x = 2$

Table 3.4

Quantum computation parameters

S.No.	Random number a	Period x	Prime Factors	Number of qubits required for IQFT	Number of H gates	Number of CROT gates
1.	2	6	7, 3	2	2	3
2.	4	3	7, 3	3	3	6
3.	5	6	7, 3	3	3	6
4.	8	2	7, 3	4	4	10
5.	10	6	7, 3	4	4	10
6.	11	6	7, 3	4	4	10
7.	13	2	7, 3	4	4	10
8.	16	2	7, 3	5	5	15
9.	17	6	7, 3	5	5	15
10.	19	6	7, 3	5	5	15
11.	20	2	7, 3	5	5	15

For $a = 16$, the period $x = 3$
For $a = 17$, the period $x = 6$
For $a = 19$, the period $x = 6$
For $a = 20$, the period $x = 2$

The optimal choice is $a = 2$, $a = 5$, $a = 10$, $a = 11$, $a = 17$, or $a = 19$, as these values yield a period of 6. Among these, $a = 2$ is the smallest value that provides the maximum period.

For efficient factorization using Shor's algorithm, $a = 2$ is the optimal choice as it provides a period of 6, which ensures a reasonable period and optimal quantum circuit design.

3.7.2   FACTORING $N = 35$ USING SHOR'S ALGORITHM

The following steps are involved in factoring $N = 35$ using Shor's algorithm.
Step 1: Choose a Random Integer a, $1 < a < N$
Select a random integer a such that $1 < a < N$. Here, let $a = 3$.
Compute the $\gcd(a, N)$:
$$\gcd(3, 35) = 1$$

Since $\gcd(3, 35) = 1$, 3 is co-prime with 35, and Shor's algorithm can proceed to the next step.
Step 2: Initialize the First Register with Superposition of All States. Find the Period x.

The next step in Shor's algorithm is to initialize the quantum register in a superposition of all possible states. The goal is to find the period x, such that $a^x \mod N = 1$.

To find the period x, we compute powers of a modulo N for successive values of x:

$$a^1 \mod 35 = 3^1 \mod 35 = 3$$
$$a^2 \mod 35 = 3^2 \mod 35 = 9$$
$$a^3 \mod 35 = 3^3 \mod 35 = 27$$
$$a^4 \mod 35 = 3^4 \mod 35 = 16$$
$$a^5 \mod 35 = 3^5 \mod 35 = 13$$
$$a^6 \mod 35 = 3^6 \mod 35 = 4$$
$$a^7 \mod 35 = 3^7 \mod 35 = 12$$
$$a^8 \mod 35 = 3^8 \mod 35 = 6$$
$$a^9 \mod 35 = 3^9 \mod 35 = 18$$
$$a^{10} \mod 35 = 3^{10} \mod 35 = 14$$
$$a^{11} \mod 35 = 3^{11} \mod 35 = 2$$
$$a^{12} \mod 35 = 3^{12} \mod 35 = 1$$

The period x is the smallest integer such that $a^x \mod 35 = 1$. From the computations above, it is evident that:

$$x = 12$$

Thus, the period x is 12.

Table 3.5 shows the calculation of 3^x and $3^x \mod 35$ for various values of x and the corresponding divisor (35).

Table 3.5: Powers of 3 modulo 35 for increasing values of x

a	x	3^x	Divisor (N)	$3^x \mod 35$
3	0	1	35	1
3	1	3	35	3
3	2	9	35	9
3	3	27	35	27
3	4	81	35	11
3	5	243	35	33
3	6	729	35	29
3	7	2,187	35	17
3	8	6,561	35	16
3	9	19,683	35	13
3	10	59,049	35	4
3	11	177,147	35	12

a	x	3^x	Divisor (N)	3^x mod 35
3	12	531,441	35	1
3	13	15,943,023	35	3
3	14	47,829,069	35	9
3	15	143,489,073	35	27
3	16	430,467,213	35	11
3	17	1,291,404,163	35	33
3	18	3,874,204,689	35	29
3	19	11,622,261,467	35	17
3	20	34,867,784,401	35	16
3	21	104,603,532,203	35	13
3	22	313,810,595,609	35	4
3	23	941,431,781,827	35	12
3	24	2,824,295,536,481	35	1
3	25	84,728,886,609,443	35	3

The pattern continues and it is clear that after reaching 3^{12} mod $35 = 1$, the sequence starts repeating. This is because of the concept of periodicity in modular arithmetic. In modular arithmetic, numbers repeat after a certain interval, known as the period.

In this case, the smallest period x for which 3^x mod $35 = 1$ is 12. This means that for any x greater than 12, the sequence will repeat the same values as for earlier powers of 3. For example, we observe:

$$3^{12} \quad \text{mod } 35 = 1, \quad 3^{13} \quad \text{mod } 35 = 3, \quad 3^{14} \quad \text{mod } 35 = 9, \quad \dots$$

This repeating behavior is a key feature in Shor's algorithm, as the period x is used to help find the prime factors of N.

Step 3: Check If x is Even

The period $x = 12$ is even, so we can proceed to the next step.

Now, calculate:

$$(a^{x/2} - 1)(a^{x/2} + 1) \equiv 0 \quad \text{mod } N$$

First, calculate $a^{x/2} - 1$ mod N and $a^{x/2} + 1$ mod N. Here, $x = 12$, so we compute $a^{12/2} = a^6$.

$$3^6 \quad \text{mod } 35 = 729 \quad \text{mod } 35 = 29$$

Now, check:

$$(3^6 - 1) \quad \text{mod } 35 = (729 - 1) \quad \text{mod } 35 = 728 \quad \text{mod } 35 = 7 \neq 0$$

Since $(3^6 - 1)$ mod $35 \neq 0$, we proceed to compute the next part (Figures 3.7 and 3.8).

$$(3^6 + 1) \quad \text{mod } 35 = (729 + 1) \quad \text{mod } 35 = 730 \quad \text{mod } 35 = 30 \neq 0$$

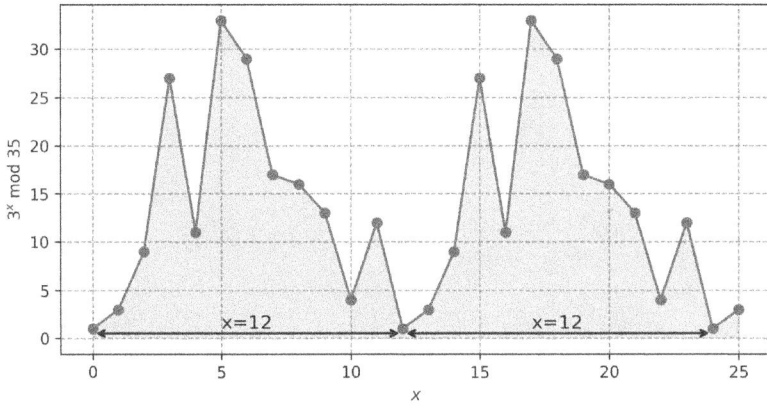

Figure 3.7 Representation of the periodic function $3^x \mod 35$

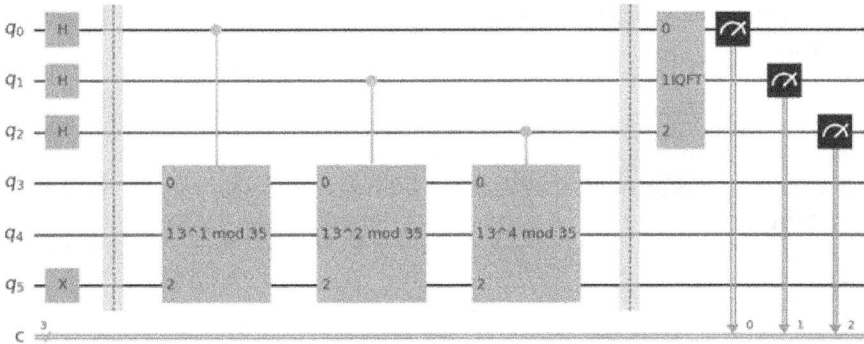

Figure 3.8 Quantum circuit to find factor for $N = 35$ for $a = 3$

Thus, neither $3^6 - 1 \mod 35$ nor $3^6 + 1 \mod 35$ equals 0 modulo 35. This is a non-trivial result.

Step 4: Compute $p = \gcd(a^{x/2} - 1, N)$

Now, compute:

$$p = \gcd(3^6 - 1, 35) = \gcd(728, 35)$$

$$\gcd(728, 35) = 7$$

Thus, $p = 7$.

Step 5: Compute the Other Prime Factor q

Using the formula $q = \frac{N}{p}$, we compute:

$$q = \frac{35}{7} = 5$$

The prime factors of $N = 35$ are $p = 7$ and $q = 5$, obtained using Shor's algorithm.

3.8   DISCUSSION AND RESOURCE ESTIMATION

Table 3.6 provides the resource estimation to factor a number using Shor's algorithm using various optimization methods. The number of logical qubits required, the circuit depth, which is a measure of how many time steps or layers of gates are required to implement the quantum circuit and the number of Toffoli gates needed in the quantum circuit. Toffoli gates are commonly used in quantum computing and act as reversible classical AND gates. These metrics are important in quantum computing for evaluating the efficiency and resource requirements of quantum circuits. Lower depths and gate counts are generally desirable for better quantum circuit performance.

Table 3.6

Comparison between the different optimizations studied of the resource estimations

References	Logical qubits	Depth	Toffoli count
[23]	$2n+3$	$144n^3 \lg(n) \;+\; O(n^2 \lg(n))$	$576n^3 \lg^2(n) \;+\; O(n^3 \lg(n))$
[29]	$2n+2$	$52n^3 + O(n^2)$	$64n^3 \lg(n) \;+\; O(n^3)$
[30]	$3n \;+\; 0.002n \lg(n)$	$500n^2 + n^2 \lg(n)$	$0.3n^3 \;+\; 0.0005n^3 \lg(n)$

3.9   QUANTUM SIMULATIONS

Quantum Simulation (or just, Simulation) will refer to the process of performing operations corresponding to a quantum computational algorithm or circuit on a classical computer. The algorithms or circuits are represented by gate operations (or transformations) that are applied on one or more quantum bits (qubits) which are the fundamental unit of information. The operations themselves are represented by unitary matrices. Therefore, quantum simulations are classical programs that perform matrix multiplications. It should also be pointed out that, in general, these matrices have complex entries [31].

3.9.1   SCALING OF QUANTUM SIMULATIONS

The size of the matrices present in a simulation program is determined by the number of qubits present in a given quantum circuit. If a circuit contains n qubits, then the operations defined on it will be unitary matrices of size $2^n \times 2^n = 2^{2n}$. This implies the memory (space) and consequently, the time complexity of matrix multiplications performed in a simulation of this circuit will in general scale exponentially with the number of qubits present in the circuit. Increasing the number of qubits in a circuit by one will double the memory required for storing the matrices [32].

3.9.2   THE EXTENT OF SIMULATION

It should be noted that classical simulations only involve the simulation of the operations performed by a quantum computer on a given initial state (input) leading to a final state (output). The internal degrees of freedom (internal state) of the quantum computer are not considered in this simulation. Due to this reason, these kinds of simulations are incapable of considering the actual physical transformations being applied to the qubits. As a result, these simulations do not account for the impact of noise or the practical challenges involved in applying quantum gate operations.

3.9.3   WHAT INFORMATION CAN A SIMULATION GIVE?

Quantum simulations, provide an explicit connection between the input and output of a given quantum circuit. Details such as the circuit depth and volume, the actual number of quantum gates, and the number of ancillary qubits required cannot be obtained by only performing simulations of this kind. Aspects pertaining to the quantum circuit implemented on a real quantum machine depend on the qubit topology of the quantum processor and the optimal sequence of gate operation is typically determined using a compiler or a transpiler. This problem is exacerbated further in the case of Shor's algorithm due to the fact that the gate operations involved in the quantum circuit change based on the number being factorized (N) and the number selected as the base of exponentiation (a). However, an approximate number of gates required for a possible implementation may still be estimated.

3.9.4   BOUNDS ON THE CLASSICAL SIMULATION

Classical simulation of Shor's algorithm will not be possible if the size of the modular exponentiation (ME) matrix exceeds the available memory (RAM) on the system. The size of the ME matrix can be approximately estimated by observing that the ME matrix is represented as a sequence of $n+1$ qubit operations, where one qubit acts as a controlling qubit. The number of such operations required to perform the ME operation is $O(n^3)$ [33].

It is therefore reasonable to assume that $O(n^3)$ nonzero entries are present in each row/column of the ME matrix. This means the number of nonzero entries of the ME matrix can be approximately stated to be:

$$2^{(n+1)} \times n^3.$$

Python uses 64-bit double variables to represent floats. Therefore, the approximate memory required to store the ME matrix is given by:

$$2 \times 64 \times 2^{(n+1)} \times n^3 \text{ bits.}$$

where,

64: Each float takes 64 bits (Python's `float` is usually a C `double`).
2: Accounts for real and imaginary parts, assuming complex numbers.
2^{n+1}: Likely represents the number of rows or columns, based on the quantum state space size.
n^3: Common in modular exponentiation circuits or matrix operations for n-bit integers (e.g., gate count or matrix size).

3.10   TYPES OF SIMULATORS IN IBM QISKIT

IBM Qiskit provides various simulators for quantum computing. These simulators allow users to simulate quantum circuits and algorithms without needing access to actual quantum hardware [34]. Here are some of the main types of simulators available in Qiskit:

1. State Vector Simulator
2. QASM Simulator
3. Matrix Product State (MPS) Simulator
4. Unitary Simulator
5. Stabilizer Simulator

3.10.1   STATE VECTOR SIMULATOR

The State Vector Simulator in IBM Qiskit is a tool for simulating ideal quantum circuits. It allows users to compute and visualize the quantum state vector at each step of the circuit's evolution. This simulator is particularly useful for small-scale quantum circuits where the number of qubits is manageable, typically up to 32 qubits. It supports general noise modeling [35].

Supported gates:

["u1","u2", "u3", "u", "p", "r", "rx", "ry", "rz", "id", "x", "y", "z", "h", "s", "sdg", "sx", "t", "tdg", "swap", "cx", "cy", "cz", "csx", "cp", "cu1", "cu2", "cu3", "rxx", "ryy", "rzz", "rzx", "ccx", "cswap", "mcx", "mcy", "mcz", "mcsx", "mcp", "mcu1", "mcu2", "mcu3", "mcrx", "mcry", "mcrz", "mcr", "mcswap", "unitary", "diagonal", "multiplexer", "initialize", "kraus", "roerror", "delay']

FUNCTIONALITY

Quantum State Representation:

The State Vector Simulator calculates and stores the quantum state vector, which represents the complete state of the quantum system. The state vector is a complex vector containing information about the probability amplitudes of all possible combinations of qubit states.

Step-by-Step Evolution:

As the quantum circuit is executed, the State Vector Simulator tracks the evolution of the quantum state vector at each step. It applies the quantum gates in the circuit to the current state vector to compute the resulting state after each gate.

Visualization:

The simulator provides tools to visualize the quantum state vector at any point during the simulation. Users can inspect the probability amplitudes of individual quantum states and analyze the behavior of the quantum system.

3.10.1.1 Use Cases

Education and Learning:

The State Vector Simulator is an invaluable tool for teaching and learning quantum computing concepts. Students can experiment with quantum circuits and observe how different gates and operations affect the quantum state. Visualizing the state vector helps in understanding quantum superposition, entanglement, and other fundamental principles.

Small-Scale Simulations:

For small-scale quantum computations where the number of qubits is limited, the State Vector Simulator provides an accurate and efficient way to simulate the quantum system. It is particularly useful for exploring quantum algorithms on systems with a manageable number of qubits.

LIMITATIONS

Exponential Resource Requirements

The amount of memory required to store the state vector grows exponentially with the number of qubits in the system. As a result, the State Vector Simulator becomes impractical for simulating circuits with a large number of qubits, typically beyond a few dozen qubits.

In quantum mechanics, the state of a quantum system consisting of n qubits can be represented by a complex vector of size 2^n, where each element of the vector corresponds to the probability amplitude of a particular quantum state.

Mathematically, the size of the state space S for n qubits is given by $S = 2^n$. This shows that the state space grows exponentially with the number of qubits. For example, with just 20 qubits, the state space already has $2^{20} = 1,048,576$ dimensions, and with 50 qubits, the state space has $2^{50} \approx 1.125 \times 10^{15}$ dimensions.

When simulating a quantum circuit using the state vector approach, the simulator needs to store and manipulate this entire state vector at each step of the computation. Therefore, the amount of memory required for simulation also grows exponentially with the number of qubits.

To calculate the amount of memory required to store the state vector for a quantum system with n qubits, we need to consider the size of the state space, which is 2^n, and the size of each complex number representing the probability amplitude. The size of each complex number depends on the precision used to represent it. Typically, each complex number requires 16 bytes for the real part and 16 bytes for the imaginary part, resulting in a total of 32 bytes per complex number.

Therefore, the amount of memory M required to store the state vector in bytes is given by:

$$M = 2^n \times 32$$

In terms of gigabytes (GB), this can be expressed as:

$$M_{\text{GB}} = \frac{2^n \times 32}{2^{30}}$$

Let's consider an example: Suppose we want to simulate a quantum system with 20 qubits. Then, the amount of memory required in bytes is:

$$M = 2^{20} \times 32 = 33,554,432 \text{ bytes}$$

And in gigabytes:

$$M_{\text{GB}} = \frac{33,554,432}{2^{30}} \approx 0.031 \text{ GB}$$

This calculation shows that even for a relatively small number of qubits, such as 20, the amount of memory required for storing the state vector is significant, around 0.031 GB. As the number of qubits increases, the memory requirement grows exponentially. For example, with 50 qubits, the memory requirement would be on the order of terabytes [36].

Idealized Simulation:

The State Vector Simulator assumes ideal conditions without any noise or errors in the quantum computation. In reality, quantum systems are susceptible to noise, decoherence, and other sources of errors, which are not captured by this simulator.

Computational Complexity:

While the State Vector Simulator provides accurate results for small-scale quantum circuits, the computational complexity increases rapidly with the size of the circuit. As a result, simulating large circuits can become computationally intensive and time-consuming.

3.10.2 QASM SIMULATOR

The QASM (Quantum Assembly Language) Simulator in IBM Qiskit is a tool for simulating quantum circuits by generating classical instructions that mimic the behavior of the quantum gates in the circuit. Unlike the State Vector Simulator, which directly computes and stores the quantum state vector, the QASM Simulator simulates the execution of a quantum circuit by generating a sequence of classical instructions that emulate the behavior of the quantum gates. This approach allows for the simulation of larger circuits and is particularly useful for simulating noisy quantum circuits and for performance analysis.

Supported Gates:

["u1", "u2", "u3", "u", "p", "r", "rx", "ry", "rz", "id", "x", "y", "z", "h", "s", "sdg", "sx", "t", "tdg", "swap", "cx", "cy", "cz", "csx", "cp", "cu1", "cu2", "cu3", "rxx", "ryy", "rzz", "rzx", "ccx", "cswap", "mcx", "mcy", "mcz", "mcsx", "mcp", "mcu1", "mcu2", "mcu3", "mcrx", "mcry", "mcrz", "mcr", "mcswap", "unitary", "diagonal", "multiplexer", "initialize", "kraus", "roerror", "delay"]

FUNCTIONALITY

Classical Emulation:

The QASM Simulator emulates the behavior of quantum gates using classical instructions. It maintains a classical state vector that represents the state of the quantum system and applies classical operations to simulate the effects of quantum gates.

Stochastic Simulation:

In addition to deterministic simulation, the QASM Simulator supports stochastic simulation, where noise and errors can be introduced to mimic the behavior of real quantum hardware. This feature allows users to study the effects of noise and decoherence on quantum algorithms and error mitigation techniques.

Measurement and Sampling:

The simulator supports measurement operations, which collapse the quantum state and produce classical outcomes. Users can perform measurements and sample from the resulting classical probability distribution to observe the outcomes of quantum computations.

Gate Decomposition:

Quantum gates that are not directly supported by classical computers, such as controlled gates and multi-qubit gates, are decomposed into sequences of elementary gates that can be simulated classically. This decomposition allows the QASM Simulator to handle a wide range of quantum circuits efficiently.

Use Cases:

Noisy Circuit Simulation:

The QASM Simulator is used to simulate noisy quantum circuits by introducing random errors and noise into the simulation. This allows users to study the effects of noise on quantum algorithms and to develop error mitigation strategies.

Performance Analysis:

Researchers and developers use the QASM Simulator to analyze the performance of quantum algorithms and circuits. By simulating large-scale circuits and measuring their execution times, users can identify bottlenecks and optimize their implementations.

Algorithm Development:

Quantum algorithm developers use the QASM Simulator to prototype and debug quantum algorithms before running them on actual quantum hardware. The simulator provides a flexible and efficient environment for testing and refining quantum algorithms.

LIMITATIONS

Classical Resource Limits

Despite its ability to simulate larger quantum circuits compared to the State Vector Simulator, the QASM Simulator still faces significant limitations when it comes to classical computational resources. Although the QASM Simulator does not require the storage of the full quantum state vector, the resources needed to simulate quantum circuits with increasing numbers of qubits and gates can become prohibitively expensive.

Simulating very large circuits requires significant computational resources in terms of both time and memory. The complexity of simulating a quantum circuit depends on several factors, including the number of qubits, the types of gates, and the structure of the quantum algorithm. For circuits with many qubits or highly complex gate operations, the classical resources required for simulation may exceed the capabilities of typical classical computing systems.

Suppose we want to simulate a quantum circuit with n qubits using the QASM Simulator. The computational complexity of simulating this circuit depends on its specific properties:

Polynomial Complexity: If the quantum circuit exhibits polynomial complexity, the memory and processing power required for simulation will grow polynomially with n. For example, a circuit with a complexity of $O(n^2)$ means that as the number of qubits increases, the memory and processing power requirements will grow quadratically with n. Such circuits are generally easier to simulate on classical hardware compared to exponentially complex circuits, but they still impose significant resource demands for larger systems.

Exponential Complexity: If the quantum circuit has exponential complexity, the memory and processing power required to simulate it will grow exponentially with n. A circuit with complexity $O(2^n)$ will require exponentially more resources as the number of qubits increases. For large values of n, simulating such circuits becomes infeasible due to the exponential growth of resource requirements. This means that even for relatively small quantum circuits with, for example, 50 or more qubits, classical simulation using the QASM Simulator becomes unmanageable due to the sheer amount of computational power and memory required.

In practice, classical resource limits often constrain the size and complexity of quantum circuits that can be effectively simulated. As the number of qubits increases, the simulator's performance degrades, and simulations may become prohibitively slow or even infeasible on standard classical hardware.

Approximate Simulation

While the QASM Simulator can simulate quantum circuits with a variety of gates and quantum operations, it does so through classical emulation of quantum gates. This process can introduce approximation errors, which can become noticeable, especially in circuits involving large numbers of qubits or when noise is introduced into the system.

Approximation Errors: Classical emulation of quantum gates cannot capture the full fidelity of a real quantum system. Although the QASM Simulator provides accurate results for many quantum circuits, especially those with a relatively small number of qubits, the approximation errors can become significant when simulating larger and more complex systems. The simulator relies on classical methods for representing quantum states and applying quantum operations, which can lead to discrepancies between the simulated results and what would occur on a true quantum computer.

Noise and Errors: The QASM Simulator is capable of simulating quantum circuits with noise models to some extent, but it may not fully replicate the quantum noise present in actual quantum hardware. In real quantum devices, noise such as decoherence and gate errors plays a crucial role in the system's behavior. The QASM Simulator might not perfectly capture the impact of such noise, potentially leading to inaccurate predictions in noisy quantum systems. For circuits involving quantum error correction or complex noise models, the QASM Simulator may be limited in its ability to provide realistic simulations.

Lack of Realistic Quantum Interactions: Some aspects of quantum behavior, such as quantum entanglement and superposition, can be difficult to model accurately in a classical simulator. While the QASM Simulator can perform accurate calculations for circuits without noise and with ideal gates, its ability to simulate real-world quantum interactions that involve imperfections and noise is inherently limited by the classical nature of the underlying simulation.

Limitations in Quantum Gate Modeling

Another limitation of the QASM Simulator arises in how it models certain quantum gates. While it supports a wide range of quantum gates, some advanced quantum operations may be difficult to simulate with high accuracy or require additional approximations. The modeling of quantum gates such as multi-qubit operations, entangling gates, or non-trivial quantum circuits could become computationally expensive. Simulating these gates accurately requires sophisticated methods that may not always be feasible with classical resources.

The QASM Simulator is a powerful tool for simulating quantum circuits on classical hardware, but it is subject to limitations in terms of computational resources, approximation errors, and noise modeling. These limitations are particularly important when simulating large-scale quantum circuits with many qubits or circuits that involve complex interactions between qubits. As quantum computing hardware continues to advance, the QASM Simulator serves as an important tool for testing and validating quantum algorithms, but it cannot fully replicate the behavior of a real quantum computer. Users must be mindful of these limitations when using the simulator for research or educational purposes.

3.10.3 MATRIX PRODUCT STATE (MPS) SIMULATOR:

The MPS Simulator is a specialized tool for simulating one-dimensional quantum systems using MPS representations. It is particularly efficient for simulating one-dimensional quantum circuits or chains of interacting qubits. MPS are a tensor network representation that can capture the entanglement structure of quantum states in a compact form, making them suitable for simulating large quantum systems with limited computational resources.

Supported Gates:

["unitary", "t", "tdg", "id", "cp", "u1", "u2", "u3", "u", "cx", "cz", "x", "y", "z", "h", "s", "sdg", "sx", "swap", "p", "ccx", "delay", "roerror"]

Efficient Operations and Representations

The MPS Simulator can efficiently perform operations such as applying quantum gates, computing expectation values, and simulating time evolution. These operations can be implemented using algorithms tailored for MPS, which exploit the locality of interactions in one-dimensional quantum systems.

Consider a one-dimensional chain of N qubits, where each qubit can be in a superposition of states $|0\rangle$ and $|1\rangle$. We aim to simulate the quantum state of this system using the MPS representation. In this representation, the quantum state of the entire system is expressed as a tensor network of matrices, where each matrix represents the state of one qubit conditioned on the states of its neighboring qubits. The number of parameters required to represent the state grows polynomially with the size of the system, as opposed to exponentially, as seen in the full state vector representation.

MPS Representation

In the MPS representation, the quantum state of N qubits is represented as a tensor network composed of N matrices. Each matrix corresponds to the state of one qubit conditioned on the states of its neighboring qubits. Specifically, each matrix in the MPS tensor has dimensions $D_{\text{in}} \times D \times D_{\text{out}}$, where:

D_{in} is the input dimension, representing the number of incoming connections (from the previous qubit),

D_{out} is the output dimension, representing the number of outgoing connections (to the next qubit),

D is the bond dimension, which characterizes the entanglement between neighboring qubits.

In the case of a one-dimensional chain of qubits with nearest-neighbor interactions, as in the provided example, each qubit is connected to its two neighboring qubits. Therefore, for each qubit in the chain (except the first and last qubits), we have $D_{in} = D_{out} = 2$. Additionally, the bond dimension D determines the entanglement capacity of the MPS representation and is typically chosen to be small to ensure efficiency.

Thus, for a chain of N qubits, the dimensions of the MPS tensor representation would be $2 \times 2 \times N$, where 2 corresponds to the input and output dimensions for each qubit. N corresponds to the number of qubits in the chain. The MPS tensor is then contracted along the chain to compute expectation values, simulate time evolution, or perform other operations on the quantum state.

Example: 10 Qubit System

For a 10-qubit system ($N = 10$) using a tensor network with only $2 \times 2 \times N = 40$ parameters, this is significantly smaller than the $2^N = 1024$ parameters required for the full state vector representation. This demonstrates the advantage of using the MPS representation for simulating large quantum systems, offering both computational efficiency and a reduced memory footprint.

ENTANGLEMENT HANDLING:

While MPS inherently limit the entanglement between neighboring qubits, the simulator can handle entanglement across longer distances by employing techniques such as matrix product operators or higher-order tensor networks. Entanglement handling in MPS simulations involves techniques to efficiently represent and manipulate entanglement across qubits in a quantum system. One common approach is to use Matrix Product Operators (MPOs) or higher-order tensor networks. Here, is an equation to illustrate how MPOs can be used for entanglement handling in MPS simulations. Let's consider a one-dimensional chain of N qubits with nearest-neighbor interactions. The quantum state of this system can be represented using an MPS tensor network. We can express the quantum state $|\psi\rangle$ of the system as:

The quantum state $|\psi\rangle$ of a one-dimensional system of N qubits can be expressed in the MPS form as:

$$|\psi\rangle = \sum_{S_1, S_2, \ldots, S_N} A_{S_1}^{[1]} A_{S_2}^{[2]} \ldots A_{S_N}^{[N]} |S_1 S_2 \ldots S_N\rangle$$

Where:

$A^{[i]}$ is the matrix associated with the ith qubit, with dimensions $D \times D$, where D is the bond dimension. (The **bond dimension**, denoted by D, is a parameter that determines the size of the matrices $A_{S_i}^{[i]}$ in the MPS representation. Specifically, each matrix has dimensions $D \times D$. The bond dimension controls the amount of entanglement that the MPS can capture: a larger D allows for the representation of more entangled quantum states, while a smaller D restricts the expressiveness to states with limited entanglement.)

S_i represents the state of the ith qubit, which can be either $|0\rangle$ or $|1\rangle$.

In this representation, each matrix $A^{[i]}$ encodes the information about the state of the ith qubit, and the product over all $A^{[i]}$'s represents the full quantum state of the system. The bond dimension D controls the amount of entanglement between neighboring qubits.

To handle entanglement across longer distances in quantum systems, we introduce Matrix Product Operators (MPOs). MPOs are higher-dimensional analogs of MPS tensors and represent operators instead of quantum states.

Consider an MPO W that describes a two-qubit interaction between qubits i and $i+1$. The MPO W can be expressed as:

$$W = \sum_{\alpha,\beta,\gamma,\delta} W_{\alpha\beta\gamma\delta} |\alpha\beta\rangle\langle\gamma\delta|$$

Where:

$W_{\alpha\beta\gamma\delta}$ are the elements of the MPO tensor.
α and γ represent the states of qubit i.
β and δ represent the states of qubit $i+1$.

To apply the MPO W to the MPS tensor network representing the quantum state, we contract the MPO tensor W with the MPS tensors associated with qubits i and $i+1$. This results in a new MPS tensor network that represents the entangled state of qubits i and $i+1$.

Mathematically, the contraction of the MPO W with the MPS tensors can be expressed as:

$$A^{[i]}_{S_i}A^{[i+1]}_{S_{i+1}} = \sum_{\alpha,\beta,\gamma,\delta} W_{\alpha\beta\gamma\delta}A^{[i]}_{S_i\alpha}A^{[i+1]}_{\beta S_{i+1}}$$

Where:

$A^{[i]}_{S_i}$ and $A^{[i+1]}_{S_{i+1}}$ are the updated MPS tensors after applying the MPO W.

By introducing MPOs and performing contractions with MPS tensors, the MPS simulator can efficiently handle entanglement across longer distances in the quantum system. This enables the simulation of more complex quantum states and dynamics, where entanglement is distributed over a broader range of qubits.

LIMITATIONS:

Limited to 1D Systems:

The MPS Simulator is designed specifically for simulating one-dimensional quantum systems. It may not be suitable for simulating higher-dimensional systems or systems with complex spatial structures.

Limited Entanglement:

MPS inherently limit the entanglement between neighboring qubits. While this makes them efficient for simulating certain types of quantum systems, it also restricts their applicability to systems with strong entanglement.

3.10.4   UNITARY SIMULATOR

A unitary simulator is a type of quantum simulator designed to simulate the unitary evolution of quantum systems. In quantum mechanics, unitary evolution refers to the evolution of quantum states under the action of unitary operators, which preserve the norm and inner product of quantum states. These unitary operators are foundational in quantum computing, as they represent reversible transformations on quantum states, such as quantum gates.

Advantages of Unitary Simulators

Exact Simulation

Unitary simulators provide an exact simulation of quantum systems by directly applying unitary operators to quantum states. This ensures accurate results without any approximation errors.

A unitary operator U is defined by the property that its adjoint (or conjugate transpose) $U^\dagger$ is equal to its inverse:

$$U^\dagger U = UU^\dagger = I$$

where I is the identity operator. This property guarantees that the norm and inner product of quantum states are preserved under the action of the unitary operator, which is crucial for maintaining the consistency and integrity of quantum information.

Schrodinger Equation and Time Evolution

In quantum mechanics, the time evolution of a quantum state $|\psi(t)\rangle$ is governed by the Schrödinger equation:

$$i\hbar \frac{d}{dt}|\psi(t)\rangle = H|\psi(t)\rangle$$

where H is the Hamiltonian operator that represents the total energy of the quantum system. The solution to this equation is given by the unitary time evolution operator $U(t)$:

$$|\psi(t)\rangle = U(t)|\psi(0)\rangle$$

where $U(t) = e^{-\frac{iHt}{\hbar}}$ is the unitary time evolution operator generated by the Hamiltonian H. In a unitary simulator, the time evolution of a quantum system is simulated by discretizing time and applying small time steps of the unitary operator $U(\delta t)$ repeatedly. This process is mathematically represented as:

$$|\psi(t + \delta t)\rangle = U(\delta t)|\psi(t)\rangle$$

where δt represents a small time step. The accuracy of the simulation depends on the fidelity of the unitary operators used during the simulation. Since unitary operators are exact representations of quantum transformations, applying them to quantum states ensures accurate simulation results without introducing any approximation errors.

Reversibility

A key property of unitary operations is that they are reversible. This feature enables unitary simulators to allow for backward simulation, providing the ability to reverse quantum operations and compare states at different times. Reversibility in unitary simulations is important for various tasks, including debugging, state verification, and backward time evolution in quantum systems.

In a unitary simulator, backward simulation refers to the ability to simulate the evolution of a quantum state in reverse time, effectively "undoing" the quantum operations that were previously applied. This is achieved by applying the inverses of the unitary operations in reverse order.

For example, let's consider a quantum state $|\psi\rangle$ at some initial time t_0, and let $U(t)$ represent the unitary time evolution operator from time t_0 to time t. The state $|\psi(t)\rangle$ is given by:

$$|\psi(t)\rangle = U(t)|\psi(t_0)\rangle$$

Now, suppose we want to simulate the evolution of the state backward from time t to t_0. We can achieve this by applying the inverse of each unitary operator in reverse order. Mathematically, this is represented as:

$$|\psi(t_0)\rangle = U(t_0 - t)U(t_0 - t_1)\ldots U(t_0 - t_{n-1})|\psi(t)\rangle$$

where $U(t_0 - t)$, $U(t_0 - t_1)$, etc., represent the inverse of the unitary evolution operators corresponding to each time step, applied in reverse order. This process "reverses" the effect of the unitary evolution, allowing us to recover the quantum state at the earlier time t_0.

Applications of Unitary Simulators

Unitary simulators are essential for simulating quantum systems that undergo reversible transformations, such as quantum circuits where quantum gates represent unitary operations. Their ability to accurately simulate the evolution of quantum states over time makes them invaluable tools in the study of quantum dynamics, quantum chemistry, and quantum algorithms.

Furthermore, the reversibility property of unitary simulators has significant applications in areas like quantum error correction, where simulating the effects of noise and corrections requires both forward and backward simulations. Similarly, unitary simulators are used in quantum tomography, where one needs to reverse quantum evolution to compare the simulated and actual quantum states for error analysis.

Unitary simulators provide an exact and efficient way to simulate the evolution of quantum systems by applying unitary operators. Their key advantages include the preservation of quantum state properties through exact simulation, reversibility that enables backward simulation, and the ability to simulate complex quantum dynamics with high accuracy. These characteristics make unitary simulators powerful tools for quantum computing and the study of quantum systems.

Efficiency for Circuit Simulation:

Unitary simulators are efficient for simulating quantum circuits composed of a small to moderate number of qubits. They can handle various types of quantum gates and circuit structures. Unitary simulators operate by directly applying sequences of unitary operators to the initial quantum state. This direct application allows for efficient simulation without the need for explicit state vector representations. Instead of storing the entire state vector, the simulator only needs to keep track of the current quantum state and apply unitary operations as needed.

LIMITATIONS OF UNITARY SIMULATORS:

Memory Requirements:

Unitary simulators require memory resources proportional to the size of the quantum state space, which grows exponentially with the number of qubits. This limits their scalability for simulating large quantum systems.

The memory requirements of a unitary simulator grow exponentially with the number of qubits N, as each qubit requires two complex amplitudes (real and imaginary parts) to represent its quantum state. Therefore, the total memory requirement M can be expressed as:

$M = 2^N$ Where: M is the total memory requirement. N is the number of qubits.

Computational Complexity

The computational complexity of a unitary simulator is primarily determined by the number of operations required to simulate the quantum circuit. The complexity of simulating a quantum system depends on several factors, including the number of qubits, the type of gates used, and the overall structure of the quantum circuit.

For a quantum circuit with N qubits, the number of quantum gates G typically scales with N or a polynomial function of N. The quantum gates are the fundamental building blocks of quantum circuits, and the number of gates G required to simulate a circuit depends on the complexity of the circuit itself. Thus, the computational complexity C can be approximated as:

$$C = O(G)$$

Where:

C is the computational complexity of the simulation.
G is the number of gates in the quantum circuit.

In a unitary simulator, each quantum gate is applied to the quantum state, and the simulation must compute the resulting quantum state after each operation. The time required for each gate application depends on the type of gate and its matrix representation. For example, single-qubit gates require applying a 2x2 matrix to the quantum state vector, while two-qubit gates require applying a 4x4 matrix. The total number of operations increases as the number of gates in the quantum circuit increases.

3.10.4.1   Efficient Simulation for Small to Moderate Numbers of Qubits

Unitary simulators are generally considered efficient for simulating quantum circuits with a small to moderate number of qubits, where both memory requirements and computational complexity are manageable on classical computers. This means that the total memory requirement and computational complexity should be polynomial or quasi-polynomial functions of N, allowing for efficient simulation.

For example, the state vector representation of a quantum system with N qubits requires storing 2^N complex amplitudes, which grows exponentially with N. However, by using efficient simulation methods, such as the MPS representation or other tensor network-based methods, unitary simulators can reduce the memory complexity and enable the simulation of larger quantum systems with fewer resources.

In practice, unitary simulators are most effective for quantum systems where the number of qubits N is not too large (typically $N \leq 30$ to 40, depending on the specific simulation method). For larger systems, alternative approaches, such as quantum-inspired classical simulations or approximate methods, may be necessary to overcome the exponential growth of computational complexity.

Computational Complexity of Different Quantum Gates

The computational cost for simulating a quantum circuit also depends on the types of quantum gates used in the circuit. The basic gates, such as single-qubit gates (e.g., X, Y, Z, H) and two-qubit gates (e.g., $CNOT, CZ, SWAP$), typically have polynomial complexity. For each gate, a matrix operation is performed, and the size of the matrix depends on the number of qubits involved in the operation.

Single-qubit gates typically require $O(1)$ operations.
Two-qubit gates, such as CNOT, require $O(N^2)$ operations to simulate a circuit of N qubits.

This means that while single-qubit gates can be simulated efficiently, two-qubit gates (which are essential for quantum entanglement) require more resources. As a result, simulating circuits with a large number of two-qubit gates can lead to significant increases in computational complexity.

The computational complexity of unitary simulators is primarily determined by the number of gates in the quantum circuit, which typically scales polynomially with the number of qubits. Unitary simulators are efficient for simulating quantum circuits with a small to moderate number of qubits, where both memory and computational complexity are manageable on classical computers. However, as the number of qubits increases, the exponential growth of computational resources required becomes a significant challenge, particularly for circuits with a large number of two-qubit gates. For larger quantum systems, alternative methods or approximations may be necessary to handle the computational complexity efficiently.

3.10.5   STABILIZER SIMULATOR

The stabilizer simulator is a quantum simulator designed specifically for simulating stabilizer circuits, which are a special class of quantum circuits that can be efficiently simulated classically. These circuits are especially useful for studying quantum error correction codes and fault-tolerant quantum computing schemes. The stabilizer simulator is an efficient simulator of Clifford circuits and can simulate noisy evolution if the noise operators are also Clifford gates.

Supported Gates

The stabilizer simulator supports the following gates that are part of the Clifford group and other stabilizer operations:

$$\text{Gates} = \{\text{cx, cy, cz, id, x, y, z, h, s, sdg, sx, swap, delay, roerror}\}$$

Where:
- cx, cy, cz are controlled gates (such as CNOT, CY, CZ).
- id is the identity gate.
- x, y, z are Pauli gates.
- h is the Hadamard gate.
- s, sdg are phase gates (S and S†).
- sx is the square root of X gate (i.e., $\sqrt{X}$).
- swap is the SWAP gate.
- delay represents a time delay in the quantum circuit.
- roerror simulates readout errors.

These gates are sufficient to simulate quantum circuits that use stabilizer operations, which include most quantum error correction protocols and fault-tolerant quantum computing schemes.

Stabilizer Operations

Stabilizer operations are operations that belong to the Clifford group, a subgroup of unitary operations that can be efficiently simulated classically. These operations include Pauli gates (X, Y, Z), Hadamard gates (H), and controlled-NOT (CNOT) gates, all of which are crucial for error correction and fault-tolerant quantum computation.

The key feature of stabilizer circuits is that their state evolution can be efficiently tracked using classical computational resources. This property makes stabilizer circuits particularly useful for classical simulations of quantum error correction and fault tolerance.

Stabilizer Simulator Features

Error Correction

Stabilizer simulators are often used to simulate quantum error correction protocols, such as the surface code, which rely on stabilizer operations for error detection and correction. By simulating the behavior of stabilizer-based error correction codes, these simulators enable researchers to study and optimize error correction strategies.

The surface code is a two-dimensional array of qubits arranged in a grid, with stabilizer measurements performed on plaquettes and vertices of the grid. These measurements are used to detect and correct errors that occur on the qubits.

The stabilizer generators for the surface code consist of products of Pauli operators (X and Z) associated with the qubits on each plaquette and vertex of the grid. For example, for a single vertex, the stabilizer generator might be represented as:

$$S = \prod_{\text{qubits}} Z_i$$

Where Z_i represents the Z operator acting on the ith qubit in the stabilizer.

Errors in the quantum circuit can be represented as Pauli operators (X, Y, Z) acting on the qubits. These errors occur randomly during the execution of quantum gates due to noise and imperfections in the quantum hardware. After applying the stabilizer measurements, researchers extract syndrome information from the measurement outcomes. The syndrome information indicates the presence of errors and their locations on the grid.

Based on the syndrome information obtained, error correction procedures are applied to deduce and correct the errors that occurred during the quantum computation. This typically involves determining the most likely error configuration consistent with the observed syndrome and applying corrective operations to rectify the errors.

Memory Requirement

The memory requirement of a stabilizer simulator depends on the size of the quantum system being simulated, which is determined by the number of qubits and the size of the stabilizer grid. For the surface code, the memory requirement can be approximated by the number of qubits N in the system:

$$M = O(N)$$

Where:
- M is the memory requirement.
- N is the number of qubits in the system.

This linear scaling with N makes stabilizer simulators highly efficient in terms of memory usage, particularly for error correction protocols that involve a large number of qubits.

Computational Complexity

The computational complexity of a stabilizer simulator primarily arises from two factors: performing stabilizer measurements and executing error correction procedures.

Stabilizer Measurements

Stabilizer measurements involve performing Pauli measurements on the qubits in the stabilizer grid. The computational complexity of stabilizer measurements scales with the size of the stabilizer grid, which is typically proportional to the number of qubits N:

$$C_{\text{measurement}} = O(N)$$

This linear scaling with N ensures that stabilizer measurements can be performed efficiently, even for large numbers of qubits.

Error Correction Procedures

Error correction procedures involve decoding the syndrome information obtained from stabilizer measurements to determine the error locations and types. The complexity of error correction algorithms depends on the specific decoding method used and can vary. However, it typically scales polynomially or logarithmically with the number of qubits N. A general representation of the computational complexity for error correction is:

$$C_{\text{correction}} = O(f(N))$$

Where $f(N)$ represents the complexity function for error correction algorithms.

Total Computational Complexity

The overall computational complexity of a stabilizer simulator is determined by the sum of the complexities of stabilizer measurements and error correction procedures. Therefore, the total computational complexity is:

$$C_{total} = C_{measurement} + C_{correction}$$

$$C_{total} = O(N) + O(f(N))$$

The exact computational complexity may vary depending on the specific implementation of the stabilizer simulator and the error correction algorithm used. However, the linear scaling of stabilizer measurements and the typically polynomial or logarithmic scaling of error correction make stabilizer simulators much more efficient than general-purpose simulators for circuits using stabilizer operations.

The stabilizer simulator is a powerful and efficient tool for simulating quantum circuits that use stabilizer operations, particularly those involved in quantum error correction and fault-tolerant quantum computing. By efficiently simulating circuits made up of Clifford gates, the stabilizer simulator offers a classical alternative for studying complex quantum error correction schemes like the surface code. With linear memory requirements and computational complexity that scales efficiently with the number of qubits, stabilizer simulators provide an effective means of simulating and optimizing quantum error correction protocols. Table 3.7 shows the comparison of various quantum simulators advantages and limitations.

Table 3.7: Comparison of various simulators

Criterion	State vector simulator	QASM simulator	Density matrix simulator	Matrix Product State Simulator	Stabilizer simulator	Unitary simulator
Simulation Model	Tracks state vector evolution	Tracks gate operations	Tracks density matrix	Tracks MPS parameters	Tracks stabilizer states	Tracks the overall unitary matrix of the circuit

Criterion	State vector simulator	QASM simulator	Density matrix simulator	Matrix Product State Simulator	Stabilizer simulator	Unitary simulator
Qubits	32	32	–	100	5000	14–20 (limited by matrix size)
Supported Operations	Unitary gates	Quantum gates	Unitary gates	Unitary gates	Stabilizer operations	All unitary gates
Error Modelling	No	Yes	No	No	Yes	No
Noise Model	No	Yes	No	No	Yes	No
Memory Requirement	2^N complex amplitudes	Depends on circuit size	2^{2N} complex numbers	2^{2N} parameters	2^{2N} stabilizer states	$2^N \times 2^N$ complex matrix
Computational Complexity	$O(2^N)$ operations	Depends on circuit size	$O(2^{2N})$ operations	$O(2^{2N})$ operations	$O(2^{2N})$ operations	$O(2^{3N})$ operations
Scalability	Limited to small/-moderate N	Limited to small/-moderate N	Limited to small/-moderate N	Limited to small/-moderate N	Limited to small/-moderate N	Limited to small N due to matrix size
Suitable Applications	Quantum state evolution, small circuits	Circuit execution, algorithm testing	Small system dynamics	Quantum state representation	Error correction, stabilizer codes	Analyzing overall circuit behavior

Criterion	State vector simulator	QASM simulator	Density matrix simulator	Matrix Product State Simulator	Stabilizer simulator	Unitary simulator
Examples	IBM Qiskit's Aer simulator	IBM Qiskit's QASM simulator	IBM Qiskit's density matrix simulator	QuTiP, ITensor	Qiskit's stabilizer simulator	Cirq's unitary simulator, custom matrix simulators

3.10.6 DENSITY MATRIX REPRESENTATION

In quantum mechanics, the state of a quantum system can be described by a density matrix, denoted by ρ. For a pure state $|\psi\rangle$, the density matrix is given by the outer product of the state vector with itself:

$$\rho = |\psi\rangle\langle\psi|$$

For a mixed state, which is a statistical ensemble of pure states, the density matrix is a weighted sum of the outer products of the constituent pure states.

Supported Gates

["cx", "cy", "cz", "id", "x", "y", "z", "h", "s", "sdg", "sx", "swap", "delay", "roerror"]

Functionality:

Density matrix simulators provide functionality for simulating various quantum operations and measurements on quantum systems represented by density matrices. This includes:

Unitary Evolution: Simulating the time evolution of quantum systems under unitary operations, such as quantum gates and Hamiltonian evolution.

Measurement: Calculating probabilities and expectation values of measurement outcomes for different measurement bases.

Noise and Decoherence: When simulating quantum systems, it's often essential to account for the effects of noise and decoherence, which can arise from various sources such as imperfect control operations, environmental interactions, and hardware imperfections. Lindblad operators offer a framework for modeling such noise and decoherence effects in quantum simulations.

Lindblad operators, named after the physicist Goran Lindblad, are a set of operators used to describe the effects of noise and decoherence in open quantum systems. These operators represent the interactions between the quantum system of interest and its surrounding environment, leading to irreversible processes that cause the system to lose coherence and deviate from its ideal evolution.

In density matrix simulations, Lindblad operators are added to the Hamiltonian evolution of the quantum system to simulate the effects of noise and decoherence. The Lindblad master equation, also known as the Lindblad equation, describes the time evolution of the density matrix ρ of an open quantum system under the influence of Lindblad operators.

Use Cases

Density matrix simulators are used in various applications in quantum computing and quantum information science. Simulating the behavior and performance of quantum algorithms, including those designed for quantum computation, quantum cryptography, and quantum error correction. The DM simulator can be effectively used for analyzing the properties of quantum states, such as entanglement, coherence, and purity. It is used for studying the effects of noise and errors on quantum systems and developing error mitigation strategies.

Limitations

While density matrix simulators provide a powerful tool for studying a wide range of quantum phenomena, they have limitations:

Computational Complexity: Simulating quantum systems using density matrices can be computationally intensive, especially for large systems, due to the exponential growth of the matrix size with the number of qubits.

In quantum mechanics, the density matrix ρ representing the state of an N-qubit quantum system is a $2^N \times 2^N$ matrix. Each element of the density matrix is a complex number, leading to a total of 2^{2N} complex numbers to store and manipulate. Storing a $2^N \times 2^N$ density matrix requires $O(2^{2N})$ memory space. For example, simulating a 10-qubit system requires storing a $2^{10} \times 2^{10} = 1024 \times 1024$ matrix, which contains $2^{20} = 1,048,576$ complex numbers.

Performing operations on density matrices involves matrix multiplication, addition, and other linear algebra operations. Multiplying two $2^N \times 2^N$ density matrices has a computational complexity of $O(2^{3N})$. As the number of qubits increases, the computational complexity grows exponentially, making simulations impractical for large systems.

Density matrix simulators are inherently classical algorithms and are limited by classical computational resources, making them inefficient for simulating large quantum systems beyond the capabilities of classical computers (Table 3.8).

Table 3.8

Memory requirement for various number of qubits

Number of qubits (N)	Memory requirement $2^N \times 2^N$	Computational complexity $O(2^{3N})$
1	4	8
2	16	64
3	64	512
4	256	4096
5	1,024	32,768
6	4,096	262,144
7	16,384	2,097,152
8	65,536	16,777,216
9	262,144	134,217,728
10	1.05×10^6	1,073,741,824
20	1.10×10^{12}	1.15292×10^{18}
30	1.15×10^{18}	1.23794×10^{27}
40	1.21×10^{24}	1.32923×10^{36}
50	1.27×10^{30}	1.42725×10^{45}

3.10.7 QUANTUM GATES SUPPORTED BY THE SIMULATORS

Single-Qubit Gates:

Pauli-X Gate (X): Represents a rotation of the qubit state around the X-axis of the Bloch sphere by π radians.

Pauli-Y Gate (Y): Represents a rotation of the qubit state around the Y-axis of the Bloch sphere by π radians.

Pauli-Z Gate (Z): Represents a rotation of the qubit state around the Z-axis of the Bloch sphere by π radians.

Hadamard Gate (H): Creates superposition by rotating the qubit state by $\frac{\pi}{2}$ radians about the axis that is the sum of the X and Z axes.

Phase Gate (S): Introduces a phase shift of $\frac{\pi}{2}$ radians to the $|1\rangle$ state.

$\pi/8$ **Gate (T):** Introduces a phase shift of $\frac{\pi}{4}$ radians to the $|1\rangle$ state.

Multi-Qubit Gates:

Controlled-NOT Gate (CNOT or CX): Flips the target qubit if and only if the control qubit is in the $|1\rangle$ state.

Controlled Phase Gate (CP): Applies a phase shift to the target qubit depending on the state of the control qubit.

Swap Gate (SWAP): Exchanges the states of two qubits.

Toffoli Gate (CCNOT or CCX): Flips the target qubit if and only if both control qubits are in the $|1\rangle$ state.

Arbitrary Rotation Gates:

Arbitrary Single-Qubit Rotation Gate $(R_x(\theta), R_y(\theta), R_z(\theta))$: Performs rotations about the X, Y, or Z axis of the Bloch sphere by an angle θ.
Arbitrary Two-Qubit Rotation Gate $(U(\theta, \phi, \lambda))$: Represents a general two-qubit unitary transformation.

Measurement and Initialization Gates:

Measurement Gate (M): Measures the state of a qubit in the computational basis.
Initialization Gate: Initializes a qubit to a specified state ($|0\rangle$ or $|1\rangle$).

Identity Gate:

Identity Gate (I): Performs no operation and leaves the qubit state unchanged.

These gates provide the necessary operations to manipulate and transform quantum states, allowing for the implementation of various quantum algorithms and protocols (Tables 3.9 and 3.10).

Table 3.9: Performance metrics of Shor's algorithm (number factoring)

S.No.	Given number (N)	Number of binary bits	Random number (a)	Period (r)	P	Q
1	10	4	2	4	5	2
2	15	4	2	4	5	3
3	21	8	2	4	7	3
4	221	8	3	8	13	17
5	247	8	3	8	13	19
6	289	12	4	8	17	17
7	301	12	2	8	43	7
8	437	12	7	8	23	7
9	581	12	2	8	83	7
10	667	12	6	8	23	7
11	1147	12	4	8	31	37
12	2773	12	3	8	47	59
13	8633	16	6	8	89	97
14	11573	16	12	8	71	163
15	14351	16	4	8	127	113

S.No.	Given number (N)	Number of binary bits	Random number (a)	Period (r)	P	Q
16	25777	16	17	8	149	173
17	40991	16	66	8	179	229
18	62059	16	28	8	271	229
19	64807	16	44	8	283	229
20	65473	16	13	8	233	281
21	96503	20	2	9	11,31	283
22	96983	20	2	32	331	293
23	144377	20	7	32	409	353
24	214369	20	15	32	463	463
25	77087	20	12	4	157	491
26	268951	20	5	30	449	599
27	350239	20	9	24	577	607
28	477157	20	2	34	673	709
29	667397	20	39	16	761	877
30	1980179	24	4	24	1321	1499
31	2377933	24	15	16	1489	1597
32	2652931	24	26	30	1567	1693
33	2755321	24	2	34	1721	1601
34	3138463	24	10	32	1811	1733
35	3571571	24	119	16	1913	1867
36	4024913	24	76	32	1951	2063
37	4694593	24	43	36	2131	2203
38	97713221	28	118	42	9883	9887
39	98089207	28	10	16	9901	9907
40	98525467	28	462	16	9929	9923
41	98724071	28	33	16	9941	9931
42	99161683	28	351	16	9949	9967
43	99799811	28	240	16	10007	9973
44	100460333	28	3	90	10037	10009
45	101002379	28	79	88	10061	10039
46	101364623	28	356	32	10067	10069
47	101707189	28	6	80	10091	10079
48	101969579	28	23	92	10103	10093
49	102454763	28	37	32	10133	10111

Table 3.10: Quantum resource utilization in Shor's algorithm simulation

S.No.	Given number (N)	No. of qubits	Clifford gates	T gates	T-depth	Full depth
1	10	5	225	160	108	290
2	15	5	225	160	108	290
3	21	5	225	160	108	290
4	221	7	682	492	336	882
5	247	7	682	492	336	882
6	289	7	682	492	336	882
7	301	7	682	492	336	882
8	437	7	682	492	336	882
9	581	7	682	492	336	882
10	667	7	682	492	336	882
11	1147	7	682	492	336	882
12	2773	7	682	492	336	882
13	8633	7	682	492	336	882
14	11573	7	682	492	336	882
15	14351	7	682	492	336	882
16	25777	7	682	492	336	882
17	40991	7	682	492	336	882
18	62059	7	682	492	336	882
19	64807	7	682	492	336	882
20	65473	7	682	492	336	882
21	96503	7	682	492	336	882
22	96983	11	4423	3228	2232	5764
23	144377	11	4423	3228	2232	5764
24	214369	11	4423	3228	2232	5764
25	77087	9	2997	2172	1488	3904
26	268951	11	7525	5484	3780	9825
27	350239	10	3710	2700	1860	4834
28	477157	10	6076	4412	3024	7935
29	667397	10	2145	1564	1080	2789
30	1980179	10	3710	2700	1860	4834
31	2377933	10	2145	1564	1080	2789
32	2652931	11	7525	5484	3780	9825
33	2755321	10	6076	4412	3024	7935
34	3138463	11	4423	3228	2232	5764
35	3571571	10	2145	1564	1080	2789
36	4024913	11	4423	3228	2232	5764
37	4694593	10	6076	4412	3024	7935
38	97713221	15	42120	30860	21420	55075
39	98089207	10	2145	1564	1080	2789

S.No.	Given number (N)	No. of qubits	Clifford gates	T gates	T-depth	Full depth
40	98525467	10	2145	1564	1080	2789
41	98724071	10	2145	1564	1080	2789
42	99161683	10	2145	1564	1080	2789
43	99799811	10	2145	1564	1080	2789
44	100460333	13	18070	13212	9144	23618
45	101002379	13	18070	13212	9144	23618
46	101364623	11	4423	3228	2232	5764
47	101707189	13	18070	13212	9144	23618
48	101969579	13	18070	13212	9144	23618
49	102454763	11	4423	3228	2232	5764
50	300673199	10	**Overflow error**			

The test cases used to validate Shor's algorithm on a MPS simulator are tabulated here. Each entry includes the composite number N, its binary representation length, a co-prime a, the computed period r, the prime factors P and Q, along with circuit resource metrics including the number of qubits, Clifford gates, T gates, T-depth, and full depth. For smaller values of N (such as 10, 15, and 21), the algorithm requires relatively few resources, with qubit counts ranging between 4 and 8, and minimal gate and depth requirements. This demonstrates that the algorithm is efficient and manageable on classical simulators for small composite numbers.

As N increases, particularly beyond 1000, the number of required qubits stabilizes around 12 to 16 in most cases. This group shows a consistent pattern in quantum resource usage, suggesting a predictable scaling behavior of the algorithm for mid-range input sizes. Despite the increase in number size, the T gate count and circuit depths remain largely constant across many entries, indicating the MPS simulator can handle these inputs effectively. When N enters the range of large integers (greater than 10^6), there is a marked increase in quantum circuit complexity. For example, numbers around the 28-bit size, such as 97713221 or 101969579, show a dramatic rise in resource requirements, with T gate counts exceeding 13,000 and full depths reaching above 55,000 in some cases. This highlights the computational limitations and increasing overhead involved in simulating large quantum circuits classically.

The final test case involving $N = 300673199$ results in an overflow error. This likely arises due to limitations in the simulation environment's memory or processing capability, signifying a boundary beyond which classical simulation using MPS becomes infeasible. Overall, the data demonstrates that Shor's algorithm, when executed on an MPS simulator, is efficient for small and medium-sized inputs but encounters scalability challenges for very large integers. The test cases provide valuable benchmarks for understanding the resource demands of Shor's algorithm and the performance of classical quantum circuit simulators.

REFERENCES

1. P. W. Shor, "Algorithms for quantum computation: Discrete logarithms and factoring," in Proceedings of the 35th Annual Symposium on Foundations of Computer Science, 1994, pp. 124–134, doi:10.1109/SFCS.1994.365700.

2. P. W. Shor, "Polynomial-time algorithms for prime factorization and discrete logarithms on a quantum computer," SIAM Journal on Computing, vol. 26, no. 5, pp. 1484–1509, Oct. 1997. arXiv:quant-ph/9508027, doi:10.1137/S0097539795293172, S2CID 2337707.

3. M. A. Nielsen and I. L. Chuang, "Quantum Computation and Quantum Information", 7th ed., Cambridge University Press, Dec. 2010. ISBN 978-1-107-00217-3.

4. H. Cohn, "A short proof of the simple continued fraction expansion of e," The American Mathematical Monthly, vol. 113, no. 1, pp. 57–62, 2006.

5. P. Dizdarevic and M. Ahlström, "Mathematical Analysis and Simulation of Shor's Algorithm and the Quantum Fourier Transform," 2012. pp. 1–25

6. A. Menezes, P. van Oorschot, and S. Vanstone, "Handbook of Applied Cryptography", CRC Press, 1996.

7. D. J. Bernstein, "Cryptographic hashing and its relation to factoring," Mathematics of Computation, vol. 67, no. 223, pp. 1253–1283, 1998. doi:10.1090/S0025-5718-98-00952-1.

8. National Institute of Standards and Technology (NIST), "Post-Quantum Cryptography Standardization," 2023. Available online: https://csrc.nist.gov/projects/post-quantum-cryptography.

9. J. Preskill, "Fault-tolerant quantum computation," Proceedings of the Royal Society A: Mathematical, Physical and Engineering Sciences, vol. 454, no. 1969, pp. 385–410, 1998. doi:10.1098/rspa.1998.0167.

10. A. M. Steane, "Error correcting codes in quantum theory," Physical Review Letters, vol. 77, no. 5, pp. 793–797, 1996. doi:10.1103/PhysRevLett.77.793.

11. S. Beauregard, "Circuit for Shor's algorithm using 2n+3 qubits," Quantum Information and Computation, vol. 2, no. 2, pp. 81–92, 2002. arXiv:quant-ph/0205095.

12. D. J. Bernstein, N. Heninger, P. Lou, and L. Valenta, "Post-quantum RSA," In Post-Quantum Cryptography: 8th International Workshop, PQCrypto 2017, pp. 311–329, Springer International Publishing, 2017.

13. D. Stebila and M. Mosca, Post-quantum cryptography, Cambridge University Press, 2022.

14. A. Broadbent and C. Schaffner, "Quantum cryptography beyond quantum key distribution," Designs, Codes and Cryptography, vol. 78, pp. 351–382, 2016. doi:10.1007/s10623-015-0139-x.

15. M. Amico, Z. H. Saleem, and M. Kumph, "Experimental study of Shor's factoring algorithm using the IBM Q Experience," Physical Review A, vol. 100, no. 1, p. 012305, 2019.

16. Chen, J., and Y. Wang. "Discrete qubit errors in Shor's algorithm: From $N = 15$ to $N = 247$." Physical Review A, vol. 98, no. 2, pp. 022312, 2018.

17. M. Sharma, V. Choudhary, R. S. Bhatia, S. Malik, A. Raina, and H. Khandelwal, "Leveraging the power of quantum computing for breaking RSA encryption," Cyber-Physical Systems, vol. 7, no. 2, pp. 73–92, 2021.

18. Gidney, C., and M. Ekerå. "How to factor 2048 bit RSA integers in 8 hours using 20 million noisy qubits." Quantum, vol. 5, p. 433, 2021.

19. L. M. K. Vandersypen et al., "Experimental realization of Shor's quantum factoring algorithm using nuclear magnetic resonance," Nature, vol. 414, no. 6866, pp. 883–887, Dec. 2001. arXiv:quant-ph/0112176, doi:10.1038/414883a, PMID 11780055.

20. D. G. Cory, R. Laflamme, E. Knill, et al., "NMR based quantum information processing: Achievement and prospect," Fortschritte der Physik, vol. 48, pp. 875–907, 2000.

21. A. G. Fowler, S. J. Devitt, and L. C. Hollenberg, "Implementation of Shor's algorithm on a linear nearest neighbour qubit array," arXiv preprint quant-ph/0402196, 2004.

22. Wang, D. S., et al. "The effect of dynamical phase errors on Shor's algorithm." Quantum Information Processing, vol. 16, no. 7, pp. 1–15, 2017.

23. S. Beauregard, "Circuit for Shor's algorithm using 2n+ 3 qubits," arXiv preprint quant-ph/0205095, 2002.

24. https://docs.quantum.ibm.com/verify/cloud-based-simulators

25. D. Beckman, A. N. Chari, S. Devabhaktuni, and J. Preskill, "Efficient networks for quantum factoring," Physical Review A, vol. 54, no. 2, pp. 1034–1063, Aug. 1996. doi:10.1103/physreva.54.1034.

26. A. Ekert and R. Jozsa, "Quantum computation and Shor's factoring algorithm," Reviews of Modern Physics, vol. 68, no. 3, pp. 733, 1996.

27. "Phase-estimation and factoring," ibm.com, retrieved Feb. 25, 2025.

28. D. Bernstein, "Detecting perfect powers in essentially linear time," Mathematics of Computation, vol. 67, no. 223, pp. 1253–1283, 1998. doi:10.1090/S0025-5718-98-00952-1.

29. T. Häner, M. Roetteler, and K. M. Svore, "Factoring using 2n+ 2 qubits with Toffoli based modular multiplication," arXiv preprint arXiv:1611.07995, 2016.

30. M. Ekerå, "On completely factoring any integer efficiently in a single run of an order-finding algorithm," Quantum Information Processing, vol. 20, no. 6, p. 205, June 2021. doi:10.1007/s11128-021-03069-1.

31. I. M. Georgescu, S. Ashhab, and F. Nori, "Quantum simulation," Reviews of Modern Physics, vol. 86, no. 1, pp. 153–185, 2014. doi:10.1103/RevModPhys.86.153.

32. A. J. Daley, I. Bloch, C. Kokail, S. Flannigan, N. Pearson, M. Troyer, and P. Zoller, "Practical quantum advantage in quantum simulation," Nature, vol. 607, no. 7920, pp. 667–676, 2022. doi:10.1038/s41586-022-04802-6.

33. C. Huang, M. Newman, and M. Szegedy, "Explicit lower bounds on strong quantum simulation," IEEE Transactions on Information Theory, vol. 66, no. 9, pp. 5585–5600, 2020. doi:10.1109/TIT.2020.2998938.

34. IBM Quantum, "Simulate with Qiskit Aer," Available online: https://docs.quantum.ibm.com/guides/simulate-with-qiskit-aer.

35. A. Jamadagni, A. M. Läuchli, and C. Hempel, "Benchmarking quantum computer simulation software packages: state vector simulators," arXiv preprint, arXiv:2401.09076, 2024.

36. N. Quetschlich, M. Soeken, P. Murali, and R. Wille, "Utilizing resource estimation for the development of quantum computing applications," in 2024 IEEE International Conference on Quantum Computing and Engineering (QCE), vol. 1, pp. 232–238, Sep. 2024. IEEE.

Section IV

Grover's Algorithm: Quantum Search

4 Grover's Algorithm: Quantum Search

> "Grover's algorithm provides a quadratic speedup for unstructured search problems, reducing the number of steps from $O(N)$ to $O(\sqrt{N})$."
>
> — Lov Grover

SUMMARY

This chapter explores Grover's algorithm in the context of quantum search, beginning with an overview of its mechanics. The section includes a literature survey that covers Grover's algorithm, stream ciphers, and the Grover attack, as well as quantum resource estimation. The section then introduces a simplified 4-bit Grain cipher (with a 4-bit key and 4-bit IV), detailing its design, initialization, and key stream generation. Following this, the section dives into key recovery using Grover's algorithm, with an emphasis on quantum circuit development for the simplified Grain 4-bit cipher. It outlines key steps in the circuit, such as executing the Boolean function and XORing the NFSR's fourth bit. Further, the section details the development of a Grover attack quantum circuit, describing both single and double pair methods. Experimental results are provided across multiple cases, with a summary of test cases and classical computation times. Quantum resource estimation, including the costs associated with the simplified Grain 4-bit cipher and the Grover oracle, is analyzed. The section concludes with a discussion on the results, classical and quantum resource estimations, and the potential for future enhancements to the approach.

4.1 INTRODUCTION

Quantum computing is a revolutionary paradigm that exploits the principles of quantum mechanics to solve problems more efficiently than classical computing. Among the various algorithms that highlight the power of quantum computation, Grover's algorithm stands out as a groundbreaking approach to unstructured search problems. Classically, searching an unsorted database or solving a problem where the solution has no specific structure requires linear time. For a database containing N elements, finding a specific item requires, on average, $\frac{N}{2}$ queries, and in the worst case, N queries. Grover's algorithm significantly improves this by leveraging quantum superposition, quantum interference, and measurement to achieve a quadratic speedup.

DOI: 10.1201/9781003606338-4

Specifically, it reduces the number of queries to $O(\sqrt{N})$, demonstrating a remarkable advantage over classical methods [1].

The algorithm proposed by Lov Grover in 1996, marked a significant milestone in quantum algorithm research. Grover's algorithm addresses the problem of finding a marked item in an unsorted list, which can be generalized to various optimization and combinatorial problems. It uses an oracle-based approach, where an oracle function identifies the desired solution, and a series of quantum operations amplify the probability of measuring the correct answer. Grover's algorithm is not only a practical illustration of quantum computing's potential but also a foundational concept that provides insights into quantum mechanics' capabilities and limitations. Its applications extend beyond database search, encompassing areas like cryptography, computational chemistry, and machine learning, where unstructured search problems are prevalent. In this section, we delve into the details of Grover's algorithm, beginning with the mathematical foundation, continuing with its step-by-step implementation, and concluding with its resource estimation and future enhancements.

4.2   OVERVIEW OF GROVER'S ALGORITHM

Grover's algorithm is a quantum algorithm used to search through a space of N elements for a solution efficiently [3]. It is assumed that $N = 2^n$, and each state is represented by indices in $\{0, 1\}^n$. The algorithm aims to find a state y such that:

$$f(x) = \begin{cases} 1 & \text{if } x = y, \\ 0 & \text{otherwise.} \end{cases}$$

The function f is effectively computable and provided as a black box.

Grover's algorithm significantly reduces the number of oracle calls needed compared to classical methods. It requires only $O(2^{n/2})$ oracle queries, while classical methods would need $O(2^n)$ queries.

ALGORITHM STEPS

1. **Initialize the Superposition:** Apply a Hadamard gate to each qubit in the initial state $|00\ldots0\rangle$, creating an equal superposition of all possible states:

$$|\psi\rangle = \frac{1}{\sqrt{2^n}} \sum_{x=0}^{2^n-1} |x\rangle.$$

2. **Perform Grover's Iteration** $\lfloor \frac{\pi}{4} \cdot 2^{n/2} \rfloor$ times. Each iteration consists of two main steps:

   a. **Oracle Application (U_f):**
      The Grover oracle evaluates a Boolean function $f : \{0,1\}^n \to \{0,1\}$ that identifies the solution. If x is a solution, then $f(x) = 1$; otherwise, $f(x) = 0$.
      The oracle acts as follows:

$$U_f : |x\rangle |z\rangle \to |x\rangle |z \oplus f(x)\rangle.$$

If the auxiliary qubit $|z\rangle$ is prepared in the state $\frac{1}{\sqrt{2}}(|0\rangle - |1\rangle)$, the oracle effectively applies a phase shift to the solution states:

$$U_f : |x\rangle \frac{1}{\sqrt{2}}(|0\rangle - |1\rangle) \rightarrow (-1)^{f(x)} |x\rangle \frac{1}{\sqrt{2}}(|0\rangle - |1\rangle).$$

This means the oracle negates the amplitude of solution states while leaving the others unchanged. Each call to U_f typically involves two evaluations of f and a comparison circuit.

  b. **Amplitude Amplification (Diffusion Operator):**
    The diffusion operator, represented as $2|s\rangle \langle s| - I$, where

$$|s\rangle = \frac{1}{\sqrt{2^n}} \sum_{x=0}^{2^n-1} |x\rangle,$$

increases the probability amplitude of marked states while decreasing the amplitude of unmarked states.

This operator consists of Hadamard transformations, phase shifts, and a multi-controlled NOT gate.

3. **Repeat Grover Iterations** $O(2^{n/2})$ times to amplify the probability of measuring a correct solution.

4. **Measurement:** Measure the quantum state. With high probability, the outcome will correspond to a correct solution.

4.3 LITERATURE SURVEY

4.3.1 GROVER'S ALGORITHM

A fast quantum mechanical algorithm for database search presented by Grover, L.K. [2]. Quantum computing, initially proposed in the early 1980s, harnesses the principles of quantum mechanics to perform computations. Quantum computers were found to be at least as powerful as classical computers, given that classical computers ultimately adhere to the laws of quantum mechanics. In the late 1980s and early 1990s, formal descriptions and formalizations of quantum mechanical computers emerged, demonstrating their superiority on specialized problems compared to classical counterparts. Notably, in 1994, Shor's algorithm showcased the efficiency of quantum computing by solving integer factorization, a problem that lacked efficient classical solutions. This paper introduces a quantum algorithm designed to address a practical information processing problem: searching an unsorted database for an item satisfying a specific condition. While theoretical computer science often involves examining various possibilities to determine whether they meet specific conditions, the search problem presented here has no underlying structure, making it a challenging task. Quantum mechanical systems, exploiting quantum superposition, enable simultaneous exploration of multiple states and thus speed up the process. The paper presents an algorithm with a square root speedup for this search problem. Quantum mechanical algorithms share some similarities with probabilistic algorithms, such as simulated annealing, which work with probability distributions over different states. However, quantum algorithms incorporate complex-number amplitudes to fully describe the system. The system's evolution relies on matrix transformations, particularly the Walsh-Hadamard transformation or the Fourier transformation, which give quantum algorithms their power. Additionally, selective phase rotation of amplitudes in specific states plays a crucial role in quantum algorithms, enabling intricate operations. The Literature focuses on solving the search problem, employing techniques like phase rotation and diffusion transforms. It initializes the system to an even distribution of states, executes unitary operations iteratively, and samples the resulting state. The phase rotation step and diffusion transform significantly contribute to the algorithm's success. In practical implementations, these steps involve sensing the system's state and making phase rotation decisions while preserving the system's racelessness. This approach ensures that paths leading to the same final state remain indistinguishable and capable of interference, all without classical measurements. The algorithm achieves a square root speedup in the search problem, exemplifying the power of quantum computing in addressing complex information processing challenges.

4.3.2 STREAM CIPHERS

Grain-128 stream cipher presented by Martin Hell et al. [2]. The cipher consists of three main building blocks, namely an Linear Feedback Shift Register (LFSR), an Nonlinear Feedback Shift Register (NFSR) and an output function. Before the keystream is generated the cipher must be initialized with the key and the IV. This cipher is designed with a 128-bit key size and a 96-bit Initialization Vector (IV). The 128 elements of the NFSR are initially loaded with the key bits, while the first 96 elements of the LFSR are loaded with the IV bits. Following the initialization with key and IV bits, the cipher undergoes 256 clock cycles during which it doesn't generate any keystream. Instead, the output function is looped back and combined via XOR with the input, a process applied both to the LFSR and the NFSR. Grain-128 excels in hardware environments where specific requirements are crucial. It is optimized for low gate count, minimal power consumption, and efficient use of chip area. What's remarkable about this cipher is its adaptability—with a modest investment in additional hardware, its speed can be significantly increased. What makes Grain-128 truly stand out is the combination of its 128-bit security and its efficiency in terms of gate count when implemented in hardware. There is no other 128-bit cipher that can match Grain-128 in terms of both security and hardware efficiency. This literature survey provides an in-depth exploration of Grain-128, examining its design principles, security aspects, and exceptional efficiency in hardware implementations while maintaining strong 128-bit security.

A stream cipher, known as Grain, has been introduced by M. Hell et al. [5]. This cipher has been meticulously designed with a focus on enabling efficient hardware implementation. In-depth documentation of the algorithm, along with a thorough security analysis based on well-known attack methods, has been provided to ensure its robustness. The construction of the Grain cipher is cantered around two shift registers: one featuring linear feedback and the other incorporating nonlinear feedback. These shift registers work in tandem with a nonlinear filter function to create a secure stream cipher. Notably, Grain operates with an 80-bit key size, and no vulnerabilities have been discovered that offer a more efficient attack method than exhaustive key search. In its simplest form, Grain is a bit-oriented stream cipher, producing 1 bit of output per clock cycle. However, one of its notable features is its flexibility to increase the output rate significantly, up to 16 bits per clock cycle, by Utilizing additional hardware resources. This adaptability makes Grain an attractive choice for applications requiring varying levels of throughput while maintaining a strong security posture.

In the domain of stream ciphers, an approach has been introduced by Alexander Maximov [4] involving the use of a NFSR in conjunction with a LFSR. The NFSR's state is influenced by a Boolean function denoted as $g(x)$, and the LFSR, when exhibiting strong statistical properties, plays a role in controlling the NFSR's state transitions. This study focuses on the broader "Grain" family of stream ciphers, where the keystream bits are generated through yet another Boolean function, $h(y)$, acting on the states of both the NFSR and the LFSR. The cryptographic strength of this Grain cipher family is intricately linked to the general decoding problem, particularly when assessing its vulnerability to key-recovering attacks. By carefully selecting the functions $f(\cdot)$, $g(\cdot)$, and $h(\cdot)$, there is the potential to craft a highly secure stream cipher. Indeed, Grain emerged as a promising contender for the European project ECRYPT in May 2005. Grain operates with a secret key of 80 bits in length, and its internal state spans 160 bits. It was specifically designed to be a fast and compact primitive, well-suited for efficient hardware implementation.

A simple algorithm for fast correlation attacks on stream ciphers introduced by V. Chepyzhov et al. [5] developed a novel algorithm tailored for swift correlation attacks on stream ciphers. This fresh approach brings about a notable reduction in memory requirements compared to recent proposals. Additionally, this study has uncovered the intricate relationship between the number of observed symbols, the correlation probability, and the permissible computational complexity necessary for a successful attack. The algorithm apart is its remarkable efficiency when implemented. This efficiency translates into superior performance, characterized by the highest error probability achievable within a given computational complexity constraint. While it's worth noting that the performance may vary based on the selected computational complexity, direct comparisons between different algorithms can be challenging. Nevertheless, extensive simulations consistently demonstrate that the algorithm stands as the fastest and most effective option available.

Fast correlation attacks based on turbo code techniques presented by T. Johansson et al. [6]. This study explores the domain of stream ciphers, which are recognized for their hardware-friendly characteristics, reduced complexity, and low power consumption features that are especially important in applications like telecommunications. Specifically, they examine binary additive stream ciphers, a subtype of synchronous stream ciphers. These ciphers generate a keystream sequence that is combined, bit by bit, with the plaintext sequence to produce the ciphertext. This keystream generation relies on an initialization using a secret key, resulting in a unique keystream for each key. The primary objective in stream cipher design is to efficiently create keystream sequences that closely resemble truly random ones, ensuring they are challenging to distinguish. Additionally, from a security standpoint, a robust stream cipher should be resistant to various forms of attacks, including known-plaintext attacks. In the case of synchronous stream ciphers, known-plaintext attacks are akin to uncovering the secret key that produced a given keystream sequence, making it a central challenge. In stream cipher design, LFSRs often serve as fundamental building blocks, and the secret key frequently initializes these LFSRs. There exist several classes of cryptanalytic attacks on stream ciphers, with correlation attacks being especially significant for LFSR-based stream ciphers. These attacks rely on detecting correlations between the known output sequence and the output of individual LFSRs, which can lead to effective "divide-and-conquer" attacks. To mitigate these vulnerabilities, stream ciphers often employ nonlinear Boolean functions to combine the outputs of multiple LFSRs. The aim was to break the linearity of LFSR sequences, increasing the resulting sequence's linear complexity. However, it's important to note that some level of correlation between the output and other output symbols may still persist. This study contributes to the field by introducing new algorithms for fast correlation attacks, building upon iterative decoding techniques. The algorithm comprises two parts: a pre-processing phase and a decoding phase. In the pre-processing phase, permuted versions of the LFSR-generated code reveal multiple parallel embedded convolutional codes with shared information sequences but distinct parity checks. In the decoding phase, the keystream is used to construct received sequences for these convolutional codes, which are then employed in an iterative decoding process to ascertain the correct information sequence. This approach draws parallels with turbo codes and their decoding techniques. For a fixed memory size, the proposed algorithm outperforms previous methods. For example, in a scenario with a 40-bit LFSR and a 40,000-bit observed sequence, the new algorithm's success extends to higher correlation probabilities compared to prior methods, albeit with increased computational complexity.

Algebraic attacks on stream ciphers with linear feedback, presented by N. Courtois et al. [7]. In this research work, the author explore stream ciphers characterized by linear feedback and a nonlinear combiner in their output generation process. The primary focus of their investigation is the security of these stream ciphers and the criteria necessary to defend against established cryptographic attacks. These attacks encompass various techniques, including fast correlation attacks, conditional correlation attacks, and inversion attacks. To bolster the resistance of stream ciphers against correlation-based threats, researchers have dedicated their efforts to designing Boolean functions that resist linear approximations and exhibit immunity to correlations within specific subsets of input bits. This study has resulted in a variety of proposals within the cryptographic community. Recent developments have broadened the scope of correlation attacks, introducing novel techniques that exploit correlations related to non-linear low-degree multivariate functions, encompassing all variables. These approaches have gained prominence with the advent of efficient algorithms capable of solving systems of equations involving low-degree nonlinear multivariate components. Building on previous research, this study explores the vulnerability of stream ciphers with linear feedback to algebraic attacks. These attacks revolve around the deduction of low-degree multivariate equations in state bits from the output. Importantly, these equations maintain their low-degree nature when applied to the initial state bits. This approach can be scaled across multiple states, resulting in highly over defined equation systems. Solving such systems efficiently is made possible through techniques such as linearization and eXtended Linearization (XL) methods. In contrast to prior research, where low-degree equations were obtained through the approximation of the cipher's nonlinear component, this study introduces an innovative methodology. The propose a technique that generates low-degree equations by strategically multiplying the initial equations with carefully chosen multivariate polynomials. This novel approach empowers us to cryptanalyze a wide spectrum of stream ciphers, even those adhering to established design criteria. This includes traditional designs that rely on a limited subset of state bits, which we conclusively demonstrate to be insecure regardless of the specific Boolean functions employed.

Fault analysis of stream ciphers presented by J. Hoch and A. Shamir [8]. In the field of cryptography research, fault attacks stand out as a potent cryptanalytic technique capable of penetrating a variety of cryptosystems that resist conventional attacks. While prior research has extensively explored fault attacks in the context of public key cryptosystems and block ciphers, there has been a noticeable gap in systematically studying their applicability to stream ciphers.

Improved fast correlation attacks using parity-check equations of weight 4 and 5 presented by Canteaut and M. Trabbia (2000) [9]. Fast correlation attacks, particularly those employing the Gallager iterative decoding algorithm with parity-check equations of weight 4 or 5, outperform attacks based on convolutional codes or turbo codes. The efficiency of this algorithm is primarily constrained by the time complexity of the pre-processing step. It's important to note that this pre-processing step needs to be executed just once for all subsequent operations. While alternative techniques proposed, might influence higher-weight parity-check equations, their effectiveness is substantially limited by the memory requirements of the decoding process. Consequently, in most scenarios, the Gallager algorithm emerges as the preferred choice.

Instant Ciphertext-Only Cryptanalysis of GSM encrypted communication presented by E. Barkan et al. [10]. This research work contributes into the realm of GSM (Global System for Mobile communications) and its associated security mechanisms, shedding light on cryptographic algorithms and vulnerabilities within this widely adopted cellular technology. Notably, GSM incorporates essential security measures to authenticate users and safeguard the network's integrity, with A5 serving as the encryption algorithm, A3 handling authentication, and A8 managing key agreement. However, in this research work they exposes vulnerabilities within these algorithms, particularly in the case of A5/2, which has been subjected to cryptanalysis and found susceptible to known plaintext attacks. Furthermore, this study presents a novel ciphertext-only attack on A5/2, offering a streamlined approach to breach GSM security, potentially enabling real-time active attacks on GSM networks. The study also discusses passive ciphertext-only attacks on networks using A5/1, outlining the implications of these vulnerabilities across various attack scenarios, providing insights into the intricate world of cellular network security.

Cryptanalytic Time/Memory/Data Trade-offs presented by Biryukov, A. Shamir. [11]. In the symmetric cryptosystems, two fundamental categories exist: block ciphers and stream ciphers, each characterized by distinct design principles, attack vectors, and security evaluation criteria. While extensive literature focuses on the resilience of block ciphers to various attacks, exploring aspects such as differential and linear vulnerabilities, avalanche behavior, and structural attributes like Feistel or S-P structures, stream ciphers have received comparatively less attention. The limited cohesive concepts in stream cipher analysis revolve around the utilization of LFSRs as bit generators and the examination of linear complexity and correlation resistance. This paper shifts its focus toward a specific form of cryptanalytic attack termed a time/memory trade-off attack. This attack methodology comprises two phases: a lengthy pre-processing stage, during which the attacker explores the cryptosystem's general structure and compiled extensive tables unrelated to specific keys, followed by a real-time phase, where the attacker employs these precomputed tables to swiftly determine the unknown key when provided with actual data generated using that key.

4.3.3   GROVER ATTACK AND QUANTUM RESOURCE ESTIMATION

Resource Estimation of Grover's-kind Quantum Cryptanalysis against FSR based Symmetric Ciphers presented by Ravi Anand et al. [12]. The security analysis of stream ciphers in the context of quantum computing, a relatively unexplored area compared to block ciphers. While quantum attacks on block ciphers like AES have been extensively presented. The impact of quantum algorithms on stream ciphers remains unclear. This study aims to bridge this gap and evaluate the vulnerability of stream ciphers in the quantum framework. Simply doubling the key size in stream ciphers may not be sufficient to defend against quantum attacks because these ciphers rely on internal state structures, key scheduling, and feedback mechanisms that can introduce vulnerabilities beyond brute-force key search. While Grover's algorithm reduces brute-force complexity from 2^n to $2^{n/2}$, stream ciphers may also be susceptible to quantum-accelerated algebraic attacks, state recovery techniques, and weaknesses in their initialization processes. Unlike block ciphers, where increasing key size directly improves security, stream ciphers can have structural vulnerabilities that quantum algorithms exploit more efficiently. Moreover, quantum time-memory trade-offs and precomputed quantum states could further weaken security. Instead of just increasing key length, future quantum-resistant stream cipher designs should focus on nonlinear key expansion, post-quantum cryptographic approaches, and hybrid security models to mitigate quantum threats effectively [13].

The structure and characteristics of stream ciphers differ from block ciphers, necessitating a different approach to security analysis in the quantum realm.

Considering the early stage of quantum computing, the paper acknowledges the challenge of accurately determining the cost for each quantum gate [14]. While previous research primarily focused on reducing the number of gates and qubits, this work emphasizes the reduction of circuit depth and gate count under NIST's MAXDEPTH constraint. In this research work the author provides reversible quantum circuit designs for the Grain-128-AEAD and TinyJAMBU and estimates the cost of ciphers, Grover oracle and applying Grover's algorithm for key recovery assesses various parameters including the count of Clifford gates, T-gates, T-depth, overall depth, and qubit count. The results indicate that certain ciphers, such as Grain-128-AEAD and TinyJAMBU, could be vulnerable to attacks with specific gate count complexities [15].

Quantum Grover Attack on the Simplified-AES presented by Mishaal Almazrooie et al. [16]. In this research the author presents a detailed and explicit quantum design of the Simplified-AES (S-AES) cipher, with a focus on optimizing the use of qubits. The design involves constructing quantum circuits for the fundamental components of S-AES, followed by their integration into a quantum S-AES block cipher. A CNOT synthesis technique is utilized for circuit decomposition. The complexity analysis indicates that the quantum implementation of the S-AES block cipher exhibits a polynomial quantum cost, which suggests a similar polynomial cost for AES quantum implementation. Additionally, the paper models a quantum Grover attack aimed at exhaustively searching for the secret key. The proposed quantum S-AES is incorporated into a black-box, which is queried within Grover's algorithm. Overall, this quantum design of a classical block cipher serves as a foundation for quantum cryptanalysis. It highlights that constructing a quantum circuit for a block cipher can be achieved with a polynomial cost, emphasizing the importance of exploring potential quantum threats to symmetric cryptosystems, such as applying a quantum framework to classical Algebraic attacks to enhance security analysis against quantum adversaries [17, 18].

Applying Grover's algorithm to AES: quantum resource estimates presented by Markus Grassl. et at. [19]. In the field of quantum cryptanalysis, Shor's groundbreaking work has challenged fundamental computational assumptions in classical asymmetric cryptography, particularly the hardness of integer factorization (impacting RSA, Rivest-Shamir-Adleman) and discrete logarithm computation in finite cyclic groups (affecting DSA and ECC). These problems, once believed to be intractable, can be solved efficiently using a sufficiently large quantum computer, posing a significant threat to conventional public-key cryptosystems. In the context of symmetric encryption, the impact of quantum algorithms appears less revolutionary. While a quantum variant of related-key attacks poses a threat to block ciphers when quantum access to the encryption function is available, this attack model has limitations, particularly when only a small number of plaintext-ciphertext pairs are provided, and the objective is to deduce the encryption key [20]. It has long been recognized that Grover's search algorithm could theoretically be applied to the key search problem, offering a square root speedup over classical exhaustive key search, making it the most pertinent quantum cryptanalytic advancement for block ciphers. However, despite its apparent simplicity, implementing Grover's algorithm for well-known targets like the Advanced Encryption Standard (AES) has lacked detailed logical-level resource estimation. This is particularly significant because the circuit implementation of AES must be reversible, meaning it must be embedded into a permutation. Once a reversible implementation is established, a quantum implementation can be derived, as permutations are a subset of all unitary operations [21]. This research work contributes the reversible circuits that fully implement the AES for each standardized key size (128, 192, and 256 bits) and offers resource estimates, including the number of qubits, Toffoli gates, controlled NOT gates, and NOT gates. The decomposition of reversible circuits into a universal fault-tolerant gate set, specifically the Clifford+T gates, is considered. These gates are chosen because they can be fault-tolerant implemented on a wide range of codes, including surface code families and concatenated CSS codes. This research work contributes to minimize the T-gate count, as Clifford gates are typically more efficient than T-gates. Their findings reveal that a Grover attack on AES requires a relatively low number of logical qubits, ranging from approximately 3,000 to 7,000 logical qubits. However, the extensive circuit depth poses a challenge for implementing this algorithm on a physical quantum computer, even without error correction. Notably, a significant portion of the circuit cost arises from key expansion, and the overall depth is influenced by the sequential nature of Grover's algorithm [22].

Grover on SIMON presented by Ravi Anand et al. [23]. Quantum computing and quantum communication have made significant advancements, raising concerns about the security of current cryptographic systems. Researchers have explored quantum attacks on symmetric ciphers, including attacks aimed at recovering encryption keys and methods to distinguish between various cipher constructions. Grover's algorithm, which offers a quadratic speedup in exhaustive key searches, has been a primary focus, leading to efforts to assess its impact on different ciphers. While practical fault-tolerant quantum computers are still under development, the availability of simulation facilities and small-scale quantum processors has made it necessary to investigate the practical implementation of quantum cryptanalysis. One particular area of concern is the SIMON family of lightweight block ciphers, which has been standardized by ISO and has garnered attention due to potential vulnerabilities to quantum attacks. This study presents the costs associated with applying Grover's search algorithm to various SIMON variants and attempts to implement it on IBM's quantum processors. However, due to limitations in the number of qubits available, only a reduced version of the cipher could be implemented, revealing disparities between simulation results and actual implementation. Implementing Grover's algorithm for symmetric ciphers presents a challenging task, primarily involving the creation of a reversible version of the cipher. In this research, they have successfully designed reversible versions for all SIMON variants, enabling the implementation of Grover's oracle and Grover diffusion for key search on these variants. Additionally, they have provided complete implementation code in QISKIT, estimating the required resources in terms of NOT, CNOT, and Toffoli gates. They have also included information on the T-depth of the circuits and the number of qubits needed for the attack [24].

Implementing Grover Oracles for Quantum Key Search on AES and LowMC presented by S. Jaques et al. [25]. In this work author explores the quantum attack capabilities of Grover's search algorithm against block ciphers, particularly in the context of AES and LowMC and also author explores the phenomenon of spurious keys in the context of Grover's search algorithm applied to block ciphers. Spurious keys refer to alternative keys that also map the known plaintexts to the same ciphertexts, potentially complicating the key search process. Understanding and mitigating the impact of spurious keys is crucial for effectively leveraging Grover's algorithm in cryptographic attacks. One key observation is that the presence of spurious keys may lead to multiple candidate keys, increasing the complexity of the search space. However, advancements in quantum cryptanalysis have proposed techniques such as the M-solution version of Grover's algorithm to address this challenge. This approach assigns equal probability to each spurious key and the correct key, effectively treating them as potential solutions. Furthermore, inner parallelization techniques have been explored to divide the search space into subsets, isolating spurious keys into different groups. This partitioning facilitates the identification of unique keys within each subset, streamlining the search process. Additionally, classical post-processing techniques can be employed to discard spurious keys after measurement, provided access to a sufficient number of plaintext-ciphertext pairs. Overall, the study of spurious keys explores the nature of quantum cryptanalysis and highlights ongoing efforts to enhance the efficiency and efficacy of cryptographic attacks in the quantum era.

4.4   SIMPLIFIED GRAIN 4-BIT (4-BIT KEY STREAM & 4 BIT IV)

The cipher consists of three main building blocks, namely a LFSR, NFSR, and an output function [2]. The LFSR bits are denoted by x_1, x_2, x_3, and x_4. Similarly, NFSR bits are denoted by y_1, y_2, y_3, and y_4 [26].

4.4.1   DESIGN DETAILS OF SIMPLIFIED GRAIN 4-BIT (4-BIT KEY STREAM)

The feedback polynomial of the LFSR, denoted $f(x)$, is a primitive polynomial of degree 4. It is defined as:

$$f(x) = 1 + x + x^4$$

The nonlinear feedback polynomial of the NFSR, $g(x, y)$, is defined as:

$$g(x, y) = 1 + y_1 y_3 + y_2 y_4 + y_2 + y_4 + x_4$$

The 8 memory elements in the two shift registers represent the state of the cipher. From this state, all 8 variables are taken as input to a Boolean function, $h(x, y)$. This function is of degree 2. It is defined as:

$$h(x, y) = x_1 y_1 + x_2 y_2 + x_3 y_3 + x_4 y_4$$

4.4.2 KEY AND IV INITIALIZATION

Before the keystream is generated, the cipher must be initialized with the key and the Initialization Vector (IV). The NFSR elements are loaded with the key bits, and the LFSR elements are loaded with the IV bits. After loading the key and IV bits, the cipher is clocked 8 times without producing any keystream.

The output function is XORed with the y_4 input of the NFSR, and it is fed back to both the LFSR and the NFSR, as shown in Figure 4.1.

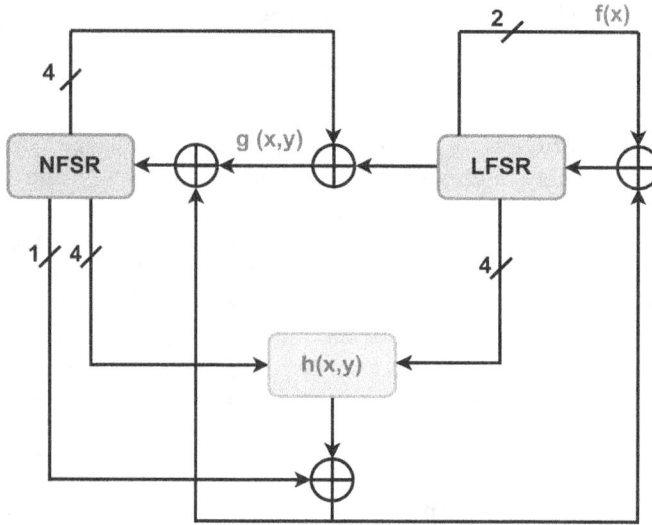

Figure 4.1   Block diagram of key initialization

4.4.3 KEY STREAM GENERATION

After the completion of 8 clocks in the key initialization process, the keystream is generated as shown in Figure 4.2. Then the keystream is XORed with the plaintext to produce the ciphertext.

4.5 KEY RECOVERY USING GROVER

Let for any key $K = \{0,1\}^4$, initialization vector $IV = \{0,1\}^4$, and plaintext $P = \{0,1\}^4$, the stream cipher $S_{K,IV,P} = C$, which generates the 4-bit ciphertext C under the key K, initialization vector IV, and plaintext P [2].

For a given ciphertext of length 4, we can apply Grover's search for key recovery as follows:

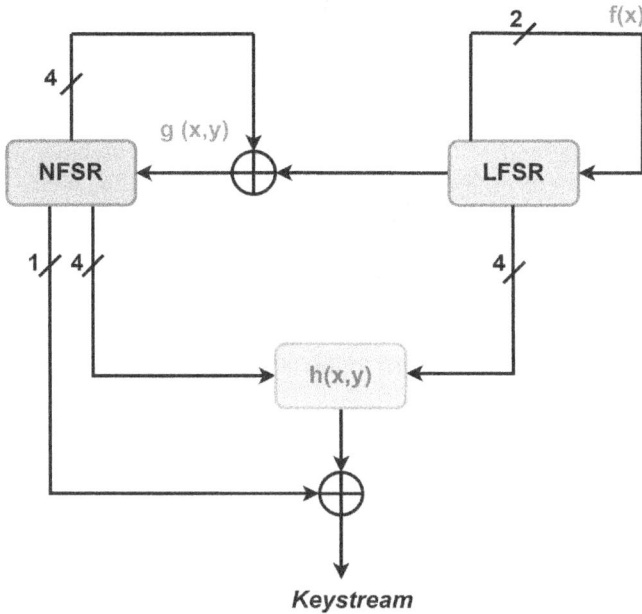

Figure 4.2 Block diagram of key stream generation

Construct a Boolean function f which takes K, IV, and P as input and satisfies:

$$f(K) = \begin{cases} 1 & \text{if } S_{K,IV,P} = C \\ 0 & \text{otherwise} \end{cases}$$

Initialize the system by making a superposition of all possible keys with the same amplitude:

$$|K\rangle = \frac{1}{2^{k/2}} \sum_{j=0}^{2^k-1} |K_j\rangle$$

For any state $|K_j\rangle$ in the superposition $|K\rangle$, rotate the phase by π radians if $f(K_j) = 1$ and leave the system unaltered otherwise.
Apply the diffusion operator.

Iterate steps 2(a) and 2(b) for $\frac{\pi}{4}\sqrt{\frac{2^k}{S}}$ times, where S is the number of solutions and k is the key size.

Measure the system and observe the state $K = K_0$ with high probability, where K_0 is the secret key.

4.6 QUANTUM CIRCUIT DEVELOPMENT OF SIMPLIFIED GRAIN 4-BIT

We need to develop a quantum version of the simplified Grain, called the simplified Grain 4-bit quantum circuit, and also the reverse version of the simplified Grain 4-bit quantum circuit. We use these quantum circuits in the Grover oracle when attacking the cipher using Grover's algorithm. There are two main building blocks in the simplified Grain 4-bit: one is key initialization, and the other is key stream generation.

4.6.1 KEY AND IV INITIALIZATION

For the quantum circuit development of key initialization, a total of 80 qubits are required. These qubits are allocated as follows:

Four qubits are designated for the LFSR, denoted as lfsr˙iv˙x.
Four qubits are allocated for the NFSR, referred to as nfsr˙key˙y.
The remaining 72 qubits are assigned as ancilla qubits or work qubits.

NOTE

In Quantum circuit implementation, qubits are indexed from 0 to $n-1$.
In LFSR feedback polynomials (e.g., $f(x) = 1 + x + x^4$), the powers start from 0 and that is why the polynomial always starts with 1.
To map polynomial powers to Qiskit qubits, we reverse the order:

$$\text{Qubit index} = n - \text{power}$$

For a 4-qubit system ($n = 4$), the mapping is as follows:

Power	Qubit Index
4	0
3	1
2	2
1	3

For the feedback polynomial $f(x) = 1 + x + x^4$:

Tap at x^1 corresponds to qubit 3.
Tap at x^4 corresponds to qubit 0.

Thus, the XOR operation is applied between qubit 3 and qubit 0.

Step 1: Executing the Feedback Polynomial $f(x)$

The first operation is to execute the feedback polynomial $f(x) = 1 + x + x^4$ for the LFSR. To achieve this, we start by using a Controlled-NOT (CNOT) gate, which functions as a classical XOR gate. This gate transfers the value of the fourth bit of the LFSR (`lfsr qubit 3`) to the ancilla qubit `ancilla qubit 0`.

Next, we apply another CNOT gate to perform an XOR operation between the LFSR's first bit (`lfsr qubit 0`) and the ancilla qubit `ancilla qubit 0`. This step effectively computes the feedback polynomial $f(x)$, and its result is stored in the ancilla qubit 0, as shown in Figure 4.3.

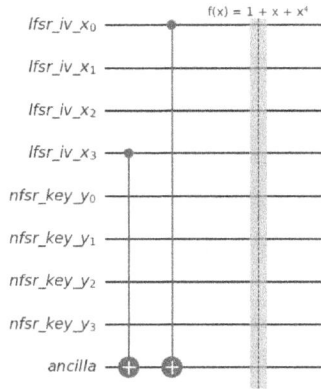

Figure 4.3   Quantum circuit development of key initialization of SGrain 4 bit—step 1

Step 2: Executing the feedback polynomial $g(x,y)$

The next operation is to execute the feedback polynomial $g(x, y) = 1 + y_1 y_3 + y_2 y_4 + y_2 + y_4 + x_4$ for the NFSR. To achieve this, we start by using a Controlled-Controlled-Not (CCNOT) gate, which acts as a classical AND gate when the target qubit is in the zero state.

The first step of $g(x, y)$ involves performing an AND operation between the fourth bit of the NFSR (`NFSR qubit 3`) and the second bit of the NFSR (`NFSR qubit 1`). This is achieved using the CCNOT gate, and the output is stored in ancilla qubit `ancilla qubit 1`.

Next, we perform another AND operation, this time between the first bit of the NFSR (`NFSR qubit 0`) and the third bit of the NFSR (`NFSR qubit 2`), using another CCNOT gate. The result of this operation is stored in ancilla qubit `ancilla qubit 2`.

By XORing the values in ancilla qubits 1 and 2, we obtain the expression $y_1 y_3 + y_2 y_4$, and this value is retained in ancilla qubit 2.

Continuing, we XOR the third bit of the NFSR (`NFSR qubit 2`) with ancilla qubit 2. This step results in $y_1 y_3 + y_2 y_4 + y_2$, and the output is saved in ancilla qubit 2.

Further, we XOR the first bit of the NFSR (`NFSR qubit 0`) with ancilla qubit 2, yielding $y_1 y_3 + y_2 y_4 + y_2 + y_4$, and ancilla qubit 2 maintains this output.

Finally, we XOR the first bit of the LFSR (LFSR `qubit` 0) with ancilla qubit 2, resulting in $y_1y_3 + y_2y_4 + y_2 + y_4 + x_4$. At this point, ancilla qubit 2 holds the value of the feedback polynomial $g(x,y)$, as shown in Figure 4.4.

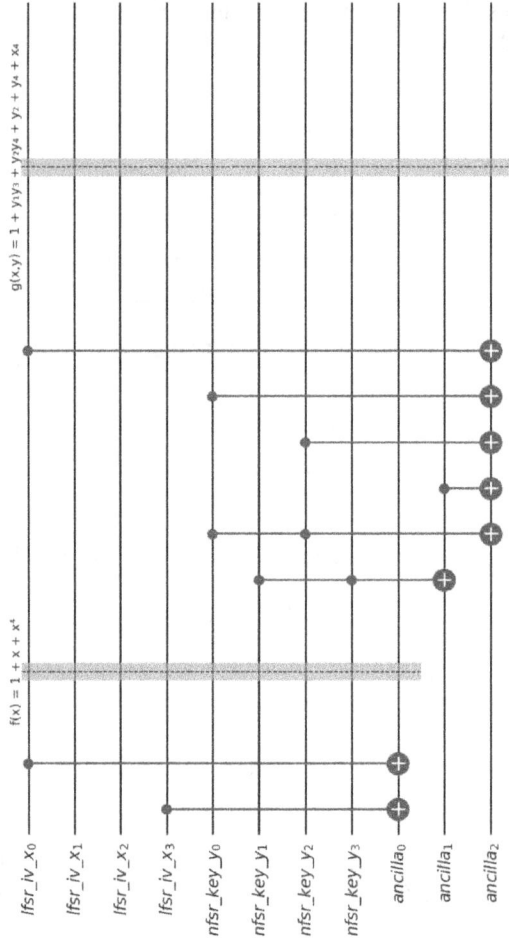

Figure 4.4 Quantum circuit development of key initialization of SGrain 4 bit—step 2

4.6.1.1   Step 3: Executing the Boolean Function $h(x,y)$

In this step, the execution of the Boolean function $h(x,y) = x_1y_1 + x_2y_2 + x_3y_3 + x_4y_4$ is performed . The process is initiated by utilizing a Controlled-Controlled-Not (CCNOT) gate. This gate operates on the fourth bit of the LFSR, specifically LFSR qubit 3, and the corresponding fourth bit of the NFSR, specifically NFSR qubit 3. The outcome of this operation is then stored in the ancilla qubit 3.

Subsequently, this process is replicated for the third bit of the LFSR (LFSR qubit 2) and the third bit of the NFSR (NFSR qubit 2), with the result being stored in ancilla qubit 4. Likewise, we repeat the procedure for the second bit of the LFSR (LFSR qubit 1) and the second bit of the NFSR (NFSR qubit 1), and the output is stored in ancilla qubit 5.

This process is also applied to the first bit of the LFSR (LFSR qubit 0) and the corresponding first bit of the NFSR (NFSR qubit 0), with the result being maintained in ancilla qubit 6.

Moving forward, we perform an XOR operation between ancilla qubit 3 and ancilla qubit 4. This results in the expression $x_1y_1 + x_2y_2$, which is preserved by ancilla qubit 4. Subsequently, we perform an XOR operation between ancilla qubit 4 and ancilla qubit 5. This yields the expression $x_1y_1 + x_2y_2 + x_3y_3$, and the result is stored in ancilla qubit 5.

Lastly, we perform an XOR operation between ancilla qubit 5 and ancilla qubit 6. This culminates in the final form of the Boolean function $h(x,y)$, specifically:

$$h(x,y) = x_1y_1 + x_2y_2 + x_3y_3 + x_4y_4,$$

and the output is maintained by ancilla qubit 6, as shown in Figure 4.5.

4.6.1.2   Step 4: XORing the Fourth Bit of NFSR with the Boolean Function $h(x,y)$

In this step, we perform an XOR operation between the first bit of the NFSR, specifically NFSR qubit 0, and the ancilla qubit 6, which holds the output of the Boolean function $h(x,y)$. This operation yields the first key bit of the key stream, which is then retained by ancilla qubit 6, as shown in Figure 4.6.

Final XOR Operations for Feedback Updates

In this step, an XOR operation is executed between ancilla qubit 6, which contains the first bit of the key stream, and ancilla qubit 0 (i.e., ancilla qubit 0 holds the feedback polynomial $f(x)$). As a result, ancilla qubit 0 now holds the conclusive feedback state for the LFSR.

In a similar manner, we conduct another XOR operation. This time, the operation takes place between ancilla qubit 6 and ancilla qubit 2 (i.e., ancilla qubit 2 holds the feedback polynomial $g(x,y)$). The outcome of this operation is once again saved in ancilla qubit 2, denoting the ultimate feedback for the NFSR, as shown in Figure 4.7.

Step 6: Shifting the Bits of LFSR and NFSR and Providing Feedback to These Shift Registers

In this step, we will perform the shift operation on both the LFSR and the NFSR using three swap gates for each shift register. However, when shifting using swap gates, the last bit ends up at the first bit position. To ensure that the first bit retains the feedback polynomial, we need to initialize it to zero.

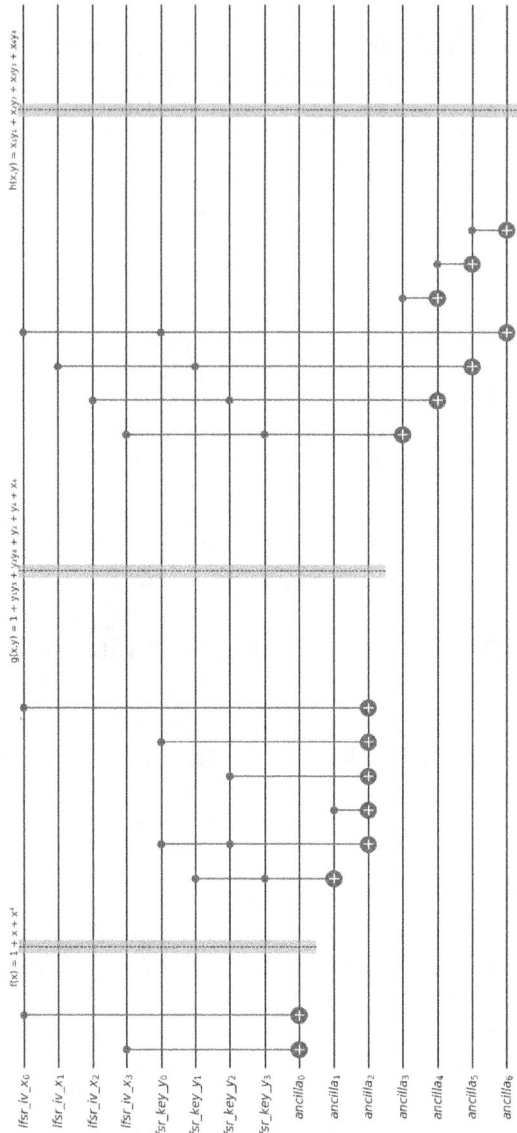

Figure 4.5 Quantum circuit development of key initialization of SGrain 4 bit—step 3

To achieve this, we utilize the extra two ancilla qubits and swap these two qubits' states to the first bit of both the LFSR and NFSR using two swap gates. This ensures that the first bit of both the LFSR and NFSR will be set to zero.

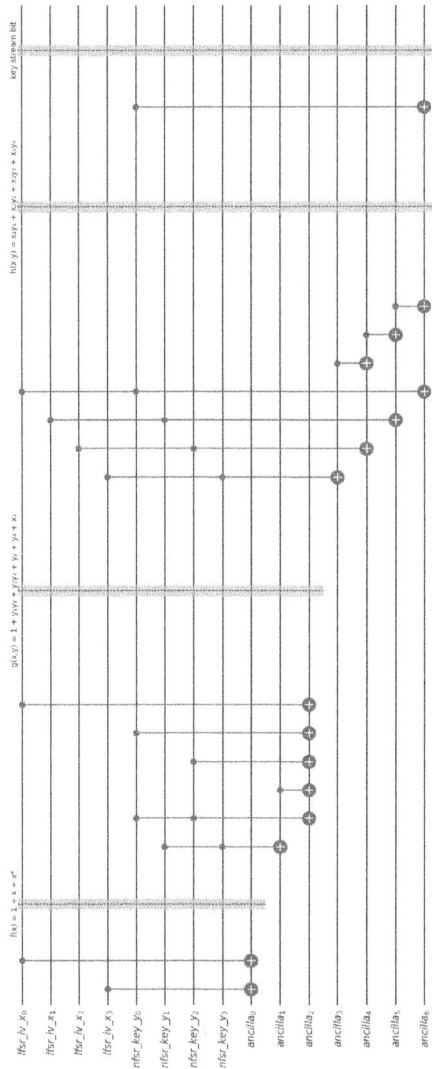

Figure 4.6 Quantum circuit development of key initialization of SGrain 4 bit—step 4

Following the initialization, we will provide feedback to both the LFSR and NFSR by using one CNOT gate for each shift register. This completes the bit shifting and feedback process for key initialization, as shown in Figure 4.8.

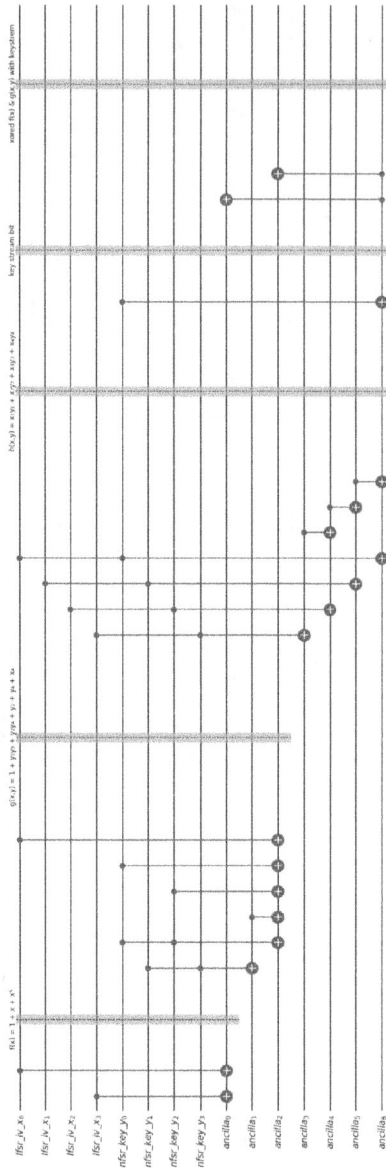

Figure 4.7 Quantum circuit development of key initialization of SGrain 4 bit—step 5

4.6.2 KEY STREAM GENERATION

In the Key Stream Generation process, the entire procedure is essentially the same as that executed in the Key Initialization process. The only difference is that we do not

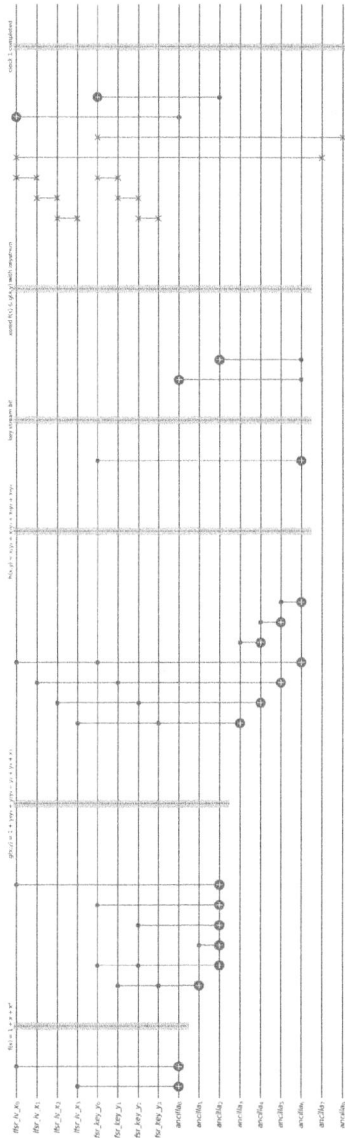

Figure 4.8 Quantum circuit of key initialization of SGrain 4 bit for one clock

perform XOR operations with the key stream bit and the functions $f(x)$ and $g(x,y)$. In total, there are 8 clock cycles in the Key Stream Generation process, resulting in an 8-bit key stream.

Ancilla qubits 6, 15, 24, 33, 42, 51, 60, and 69 hold the 8-bit key stream. The quantum circuit of key stream generation for one clock is shown in Figure 4.9.

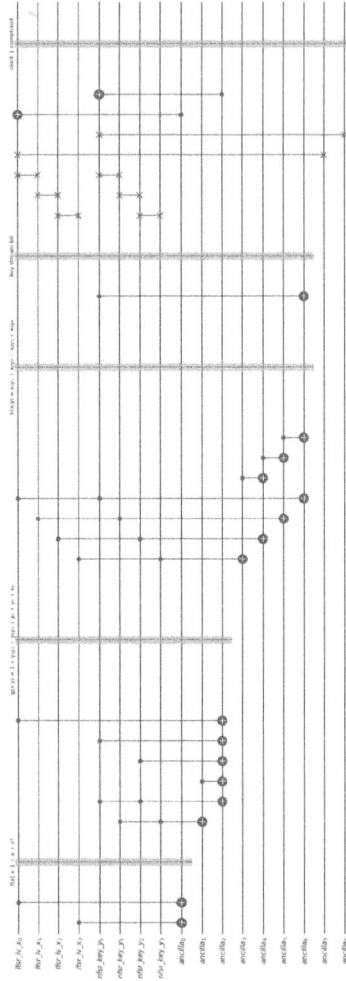

Figure 4.9 Quantum circuit of keystream generation of SGrain 4 bit for one clock

4.6.3 SIMPLIFIED GRAIN 4 BIT

We use subcircuits, such as key initialization and key stream generation, as building blocks to construct a simplified 4-bit Grain cipher. The block diagram for such a circuit is shown in Figure 4.10.

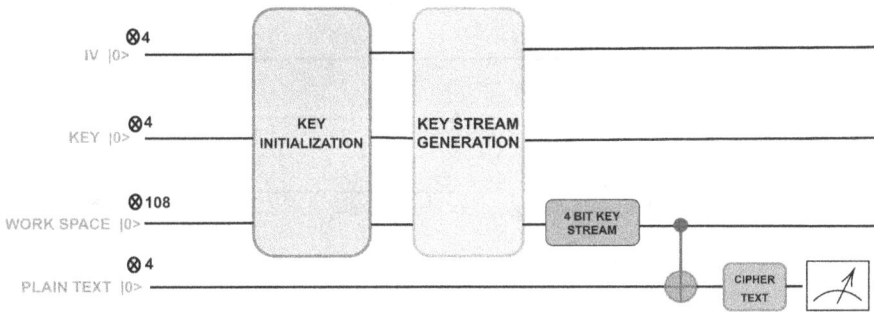

Figure 4.10   Block diagram of SGrain 4 bit quantum circuit

4.7   QUANTUM CIRCUIT DEVELOPMENT OF GROVER ATTACK

In this section, we will explore the development of quantum circuits specifically designed for implementing Grover's algorithm to perform cryptographic attacks as per [28, 29].

4.7.1   SINGLE PAIR METHOD

Consider that we are given one plaintext–ciphertext pair. The oracle is then constructed so that the given plaintext is encrypted under the same key and then computes a Boolean value which determines if the resulting ciphertext is equal to the given available ciphertext. This can be done by running one encryption circuit and then comparing the resultant ciphertext with the given ciphertext. The target qubit will be flipped if the ciphertexts match. The target qubit will be flipped if the ciphertexts match because of the phase kickback effect. In quantum circuits, when a controlled operation (like a comparison or XOR) is applied with a qubit in superposition as the control and a flag qubit as the target, any conditional phase that would have affected the target is instead "kicked back" to the control. This subtle yet powerful phenomenon enables the marking of matching states with a phase change, even without directly measuring them. This way, the target key is marked, and interference patterns formed in later steps amplify the probability of measuring this correct solution. The construction of such an oracle is shown in Figure 4.11.

4.7.2   DOUBLE PAIR METHOD

It is plausible that there may be other encryption keys capable of producing the same ciphertext from a known plaintext and IV(initialization vector). Therefore, to enhance the attack's success probability, it becomes necessary to expand the search to encompass more plaintext-ciphertext pairs. Let's consider a scenario where we have been provided with two plaintext-ciphertext pairs.

ORACLE

IV |0⟩ ⊗4

KEY |0⟩ ⊗4   H

S-GRAIN 4 BIT

S-GRAIN⁻¹ 4 BIT

Diffuser

WORK SPACE |0⟩ ⊗108

PLAIN TEXT |0⟩ ⊗4   C X • X C

CHECK QUBIT |0⟩   X H

$Repeat\ \frac{\pi}{4}\sqrt{\frac{2^k}{S}}\ times$

(Where, k − Key Size, S − No. of Sollutions)

C → Ciphertext   X → NOT Gate   H → Hadamard Gate   ∡ → Measure   → CNOT Gate

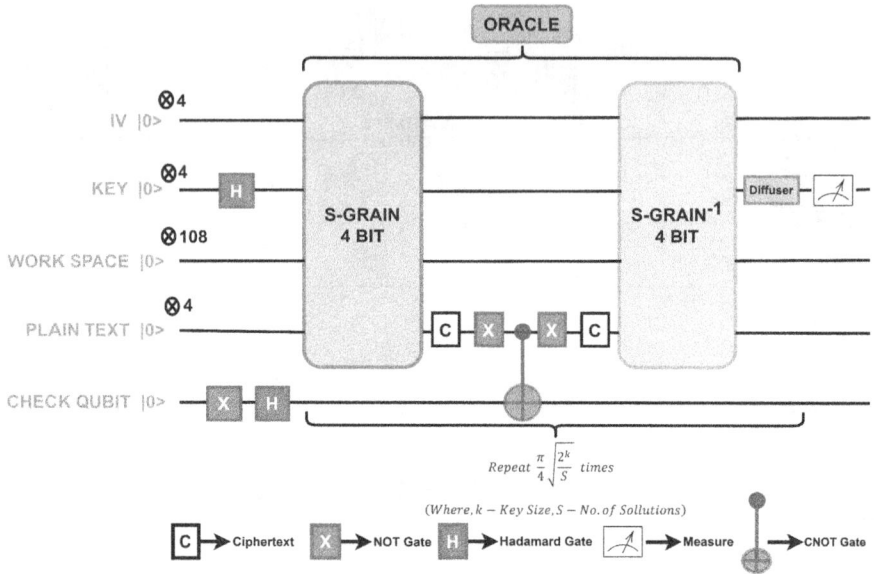

Figure 4.11   Block diagram of Grover attack single pair method

Here, we compare the first resulting ciphertext with the provided first ciphertext. To do this, we employ an ancilla qubit to verify the correspondence between the first resulting ciphertext and the given ciphertext. If the ciphertexts match, the ancilla qubit is set to 1. This is necessary because we need all control qubits to be in the —1⟩ state in order to trigger phase kickback, which is essential for marking the correct key. The ancilla qubit acts as a conditional flag only when it is 1 (indicating a match) do we allow the phase kickback to occur during the controlled operation on the target qubit.

Subsequently, by reversing all of these processes, we reset all the qubits to their initial state, which is the zero state. At this stage, we can provide another pair of plaintexts and ciphertexts and examine the second resulting ciphertext against the available given ciphertext. If both ciphertexts match, the target qubit flips. The construction of such an oracle is shown in Figure 4.12.

It is important to note that, compared to the Single Pair Method, the Double Pair Method significantly increases the depth of the process, as it involves additional checks and more qubits. However, the increase in qubits is minimal, with only one additional qubit being added per comparison, making the method more efficient while still enhancing accuracy in key recovery [27].

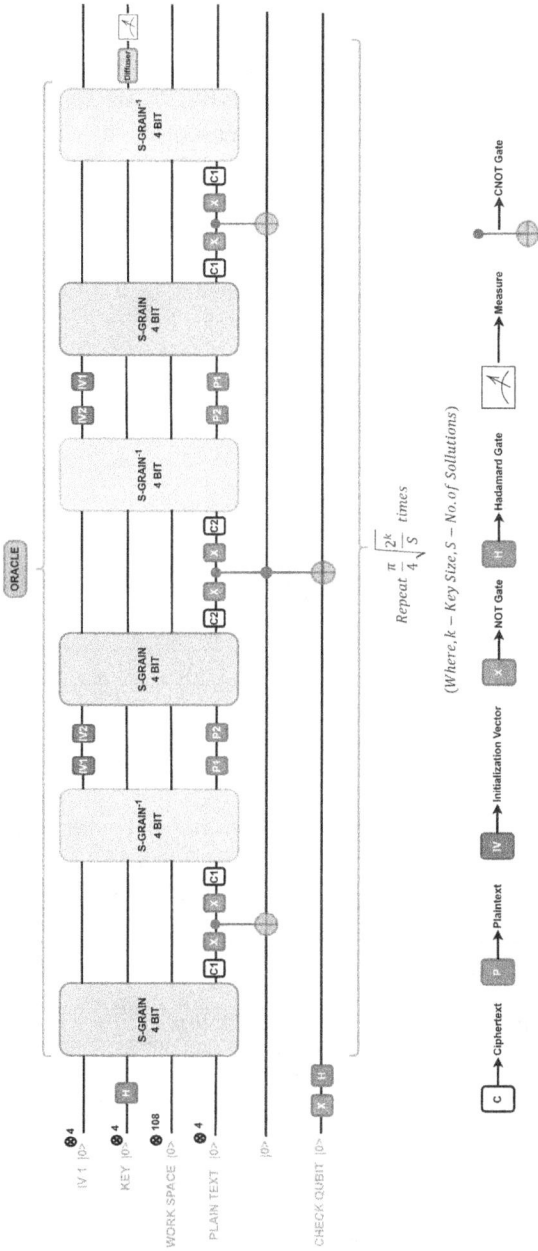

Figure 4.12 Block diagram of Grover attack double pair method

4.8 EXPERIMENTAL RESULTS

We conducted these attacks using own custom-built simulator, which is based on the Qiskit Matrix Product State (MPS) simulator. This simulator leverages a tensor-network approach using a MPS representation for quantum states, allowing efficient simulation of quantum circuits with limited entanglement. By tailoring the simulator to the specific attack framework, we were able to optimize performance and gain better control over the underlying simulation processes. The implementation code is publicly available at https://github.com/mohanyaso/Grover.git.

The following implementations are implemented on a system with the following specifications shown in Table 4.1.

Table 4.1

Hardware and software specifications

S. No.	Hardware/software	Description
1	Processor	46
2	Vendor id	Genuine Intel
3	Model Number	106
4	Model Name	Intel(R) Xeon(R) Gold 5317 CPU @ 3.00Ghz
5	CPU Speed	3400.000 MHz
6	Cache size	18432 kb
7	CPU Cores	12
8	Graphics	NVIDIA Corporation (A30) Memory Size: 24 GB GPU memory bandwidth: 933GB/s NVIDIA-SMI 525.85.12 Driver Version 525.85.12 CUDA Version 12.0
9	RAM Size	503 GB
10	Disk Capacity	4.8 TB
11	Operating System (OS)	Ubuntu 20.04.5 LTS
12	OS Type	64 bit

4.8.1 TEST CASE 1

    a. **Simplified grain 4-bit—pair 1:** Here, the given Initialization Vector (IV) is "0111", the Key is "1111", and the Plaintext is "0001". After the cipher's operation, we have obtained the ciphertext "0100".
    The obtained result from the Simplified Grain 4-bit cipher is shown in Figure 4.13.

    b. **Simplified grain 4 bit—pair 2:** Here, the given Initialization Vector (IV) is "0110", the Key is "1111", and the Plaintext is "1001". After the cipher's

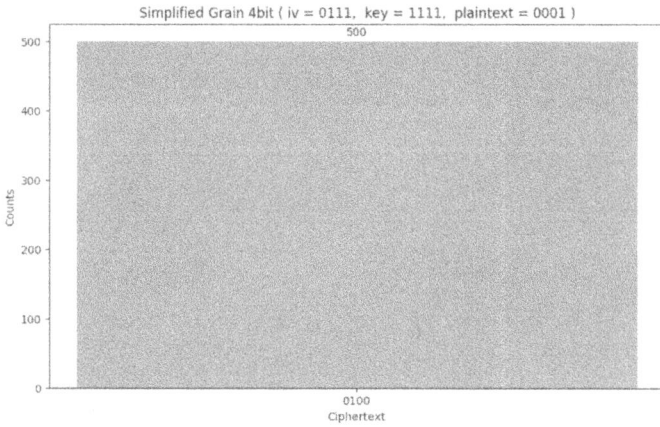

Figure 4.13 Histogram output of simplified grain 4 bit—Test case 1 (Pair 1)

operation, we have obtained the ciphertext "1010". The obtained result from the Simplified Grain 4-bit cipher is shown in Figure 4.14. In the Grover

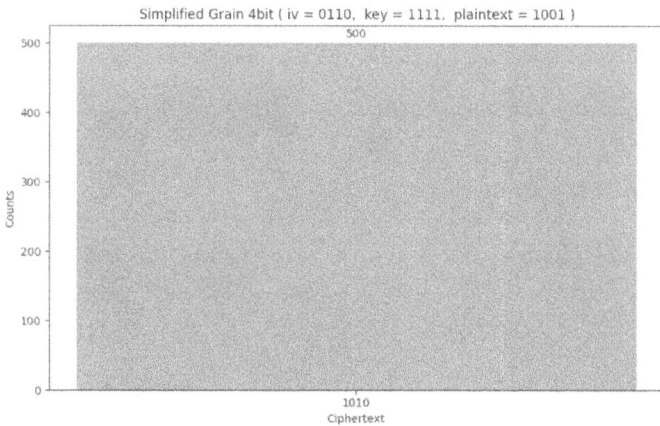

Figure 4.14 Histogram output of simplified grain 4 bit—Test case 1 (Pair 2)

attack, we collect samples from both Pair 1 and Pair 2, as listed in Table 4.2. In a single-pair attack, we exclusively utilize Pair 1. However, in a double-pair attack, we make use of data from both pairs.

c. **Grover attack for one iteration:**
   i. **Single pair method:**
      In the single-pair attack, we provided the Initialization Vector (IV) 0111, plaintext 0001, and ciphertext 0100, resulting in three keys. One key is 0111, the second one is 1101, and the last one is the expected key, 1111, as illustrated in Figure 4.15.

Table 4.2

Inputs and outputs of 4-bit case 1

Pair	IV (Initialization vector)	Key	Plaintext	Obtained ciphertext
Pair 1	0111	1111	0001	0010
Pair 2	0110	1111	1001	1010

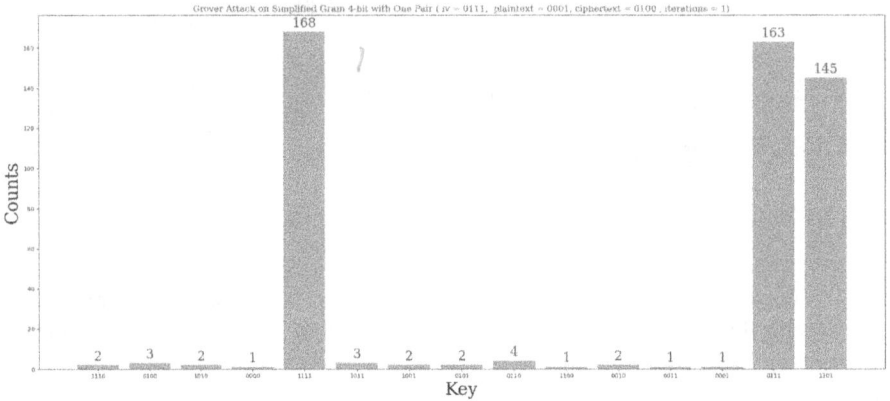

Figure 4.15   Histogram output of Grover attack single pair method—Test case 1

ii. **Double pair method:**
In the double pair method, we are given two sets of IV, plaintext, and ciphertext. Set 1 consists of IV_1 (0111), $Plaintext_1$ (0001), and $Ciphertext_1$ (0100). Set 2 includes IV_2 (0110), $Plaintext_2$ (1001), and $Ciphertext_2$ (1010). By using these two sets, we have successfully obtained a unique key, which matches the expected key 1111, as shown in Figure 4.16.

4.8.2   TEST CASE 2

a. **Simplified grain 4 bit—Pair 1:** Here, the given Initialization Vector (IV) is 1010, the Key is 1001, and the Plaintext is 0110. After the cipher's operation, we have obtained the ciphertext 0100. The obtained result from the Simplified Grain 4-bit cipher is shown in Figure 4.17.

b. **Simplified grain 4 bit—Pair 2:** Here, the given Initialization Vector (IV) is 1111, the Key is 1001, and the Plaintext is 0110. After the cipher's

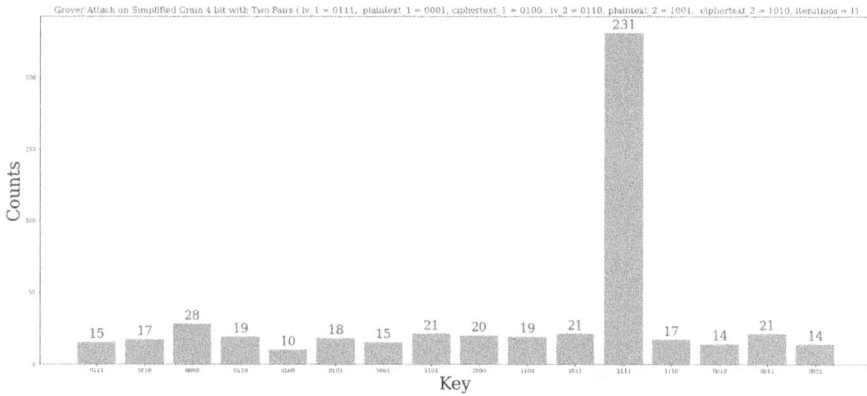

Figure 4.16 Histogram output of Grover attack double pair parallel method—Test case 1

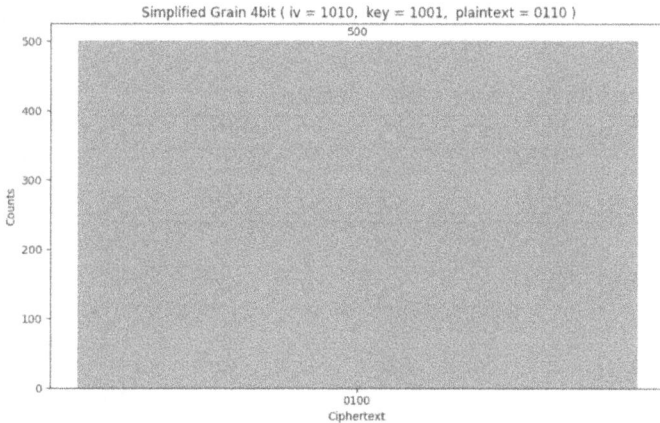

Figure 4.17 Histogram output of simplified grain 4 bit—Test case 2 (Pair 1)

operation, we have obtained the ciphertext 0101. The obtained result from the Simplified Grain 4-bit cipher is shown in Figure 4.18.

In the Grover attack, we collect samples from both Pair 1 and Pair 2 listed in Table 4.3. In a single-pair attack, we exclusively utilize Pair 1. However, in a double-pair attack, we make use of data from both pairs.

c. **Grover attack for one iteration:**
   i. **Single pair method:**
      In the single-pair attack, we provided the Initialization Vector (IV) 1010, plaintext 0110, and ciphertext 0100, resulting in two keys. One key is 1000, while the other is the expected key, 1001, as illustrated in Figure 4.19.

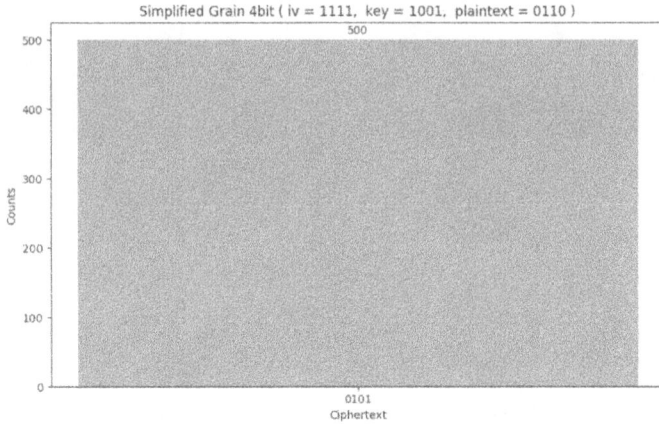

Figure 4.18   Histogram output of simplified grain 4 bit—Test case 2 (Pair 2)

Table 4.3

Inputs and outputs of Sgrain 4-bit – Test case 2

Pair	IV (Initialization vector)	Key	Plaintext	Obtained ciphertext
Pair 1	1010	1001	0110	0100
Pair 2	1111	1001	0110	0101

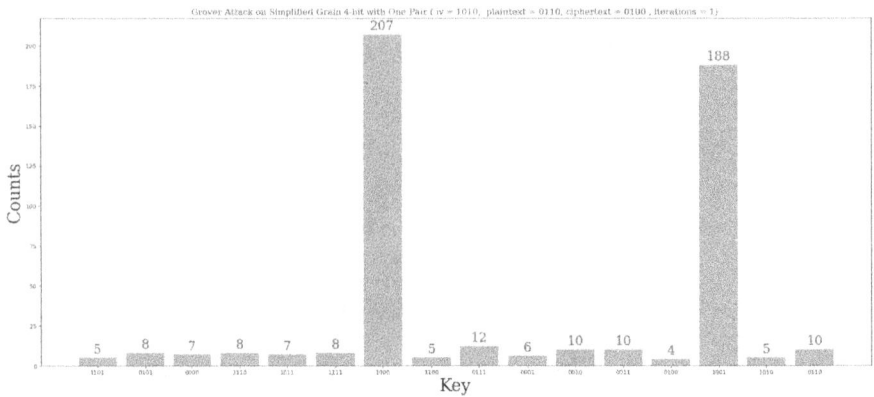

Figure 4.19   Histogram output of Grover attack single pair method—Test case 2

ii. **Double pair method:**

In the double pair method, we are given two sets of IV, plaintext, and ciphertext. Set 1 consists of IV_1 (1010), Plaintext$_1$ (0110), and

Ciphertext$_1$ (0100). Set 2 includes IV$_2$ (1111), Plaintext$_2$ (0110), and Ciphertext$_2$ (0101). By using these two sets, we have successfully obtained a unique key, which matches the expected key, 1001, as shown in Figure 4.20.

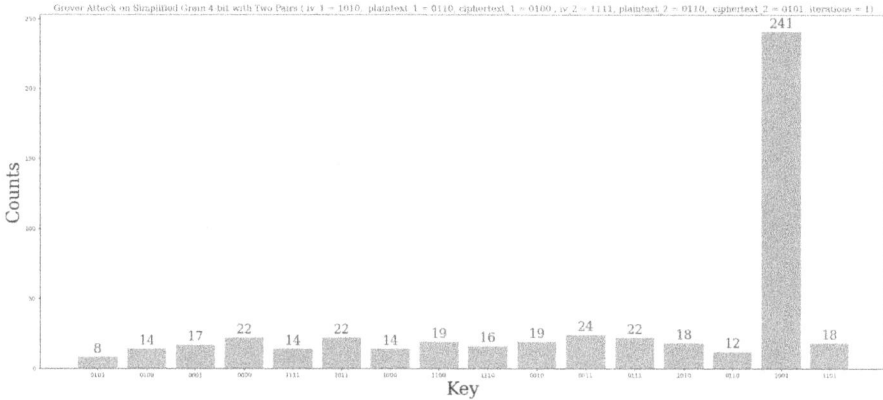

Figure 4.20   Histogram output of Grover attack double pair method—Test case 2

4.8.3   TEST CASE 3

a. **Simplified grain 4 bit—pair 1:** Here, the given Initialization Vector (IV) is 1011, the Key is 1100, and the Plaintext is 1001. After the cipher's operation, we have obtained the ciphertext 0110. The obtained result from the Simplified Grain 4-bit cipher is shown in Figure 4.21.

b. **Simplified grain 4 bit—pair 2:** Here, the given Initialization Vector (IV) is 1111, the Key is 1100, and the Plaintext is 1010. After the cipher's operation, we have obtained the ciphertext 1101. The obtained result from the Simplified Grain 4-bit cipher is shown in Figure 4.22. In the Grover attack, we collect samples from both Pair 1 and Pair 2 listed in Table 4.3. In a single-pair attack, we exclusively utilize Pair 1. However, in a double-pair attack, we make use of data from both pairs.

c. **Grover attack for one Iteration:**

   i. **Single pair method:**

   In the single-pair attack, we provided the Initialization Vector (IV) 1011, plaintext 1001, and ciphertext 0110, resulting in two keys. One key is 0010, and the expected key is 1100, as illustrated in Figure 4.23.

   ii. **Double pair method:**

   In the double pair method, we are given two sets of IV, plaintext, and ciphertext. Set 1 consists of IV$_1$ (1011), Plaintext$_1$ (1001), and Ciphertext$_1$ (0110). Set 2 includes IV$_2$ (1111), Plaintext$_2$ (1010), and

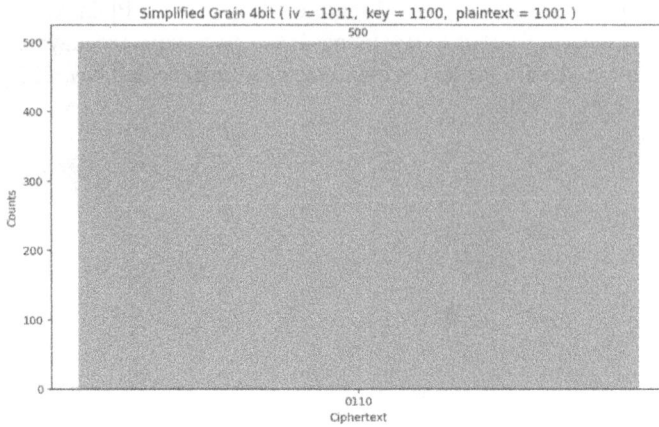

Figure 4.21   Histogram output of simplified grain 4 bit—Test case 3 (Pair 1)

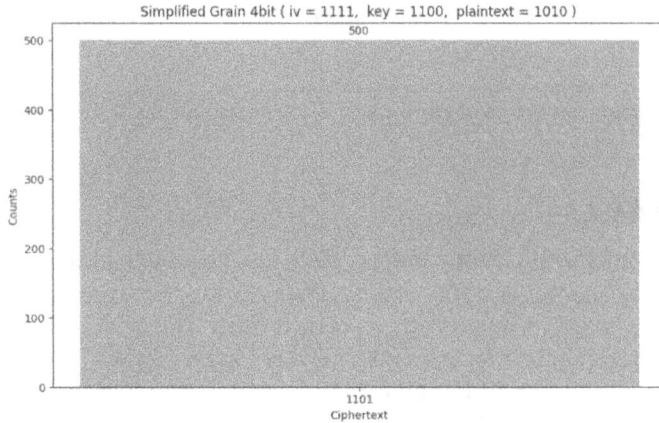

Figure 4.22   Histogram output of simplified grain 4 bit—Test case 3 (Pair 2)

Ciphertext$_2$ (1101). By using these two sets, we have successfully obtained a unique key, which matches the expected key 1100, as shown in Figure 4.24.

4.8.4   TEST CASE 4

a. **Simplified grain 4-bit—Pair 1:** Here, the given Initialization Vector (IV) is 1111, the Key is 0101, and the Plaintext is 0001. After the cipher's operation, we have obtained the ciphertext 0110. The obtained result from the Simplified Grain 4-bit cipher is shown in Figure 4.25.

b. **Simplified grain 4-bit—Pair 2:** Here, the given Initialization Vector (IV) is 0110, the Key is 0101, and the Plaintext is 1010. After the cipher's

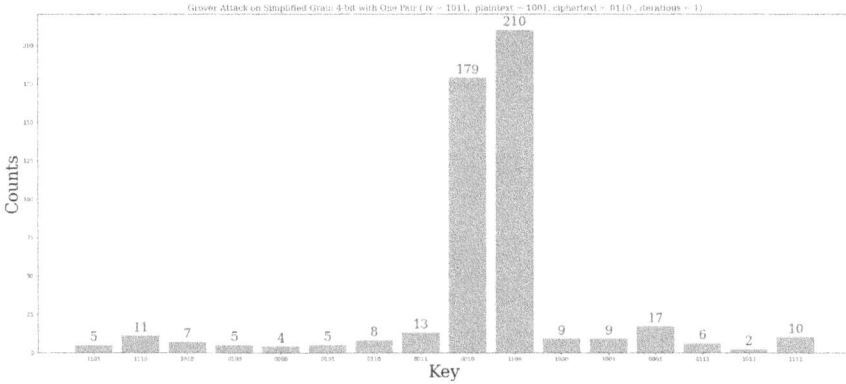

Figure 4.23 Histogram output of Grover attack single pair method—Test case 3

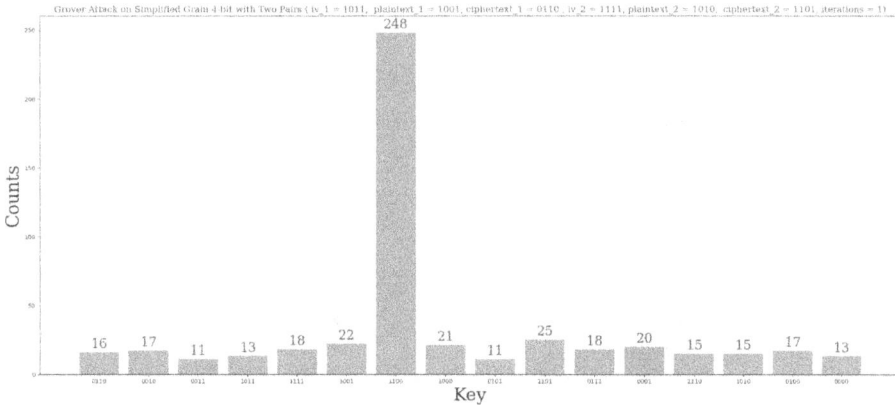

Figure 4.24 Histogram output of Grover attack double pair method—Test case 3

operation, we have obtained the ciphertext 0111. The obtained result from the Simplified Grain 4-bit cipher is shown in Figure 4.26. In the Grover attack, we collect samples from both Pair 1 and Pair 2 listed in Table 4.4. In a single-pair attack, we exclusively utilize Pair 1. However, in a double-pair attack, we make use of data from both pairs.

c. **Grover attack for one iteration:**
  i. **Single pair method:**
     In the single-pair attack, we provided the Initialization Vector (IV) 1111, plaintext 0001, and ciphertext 0110, resulting in three keys. One

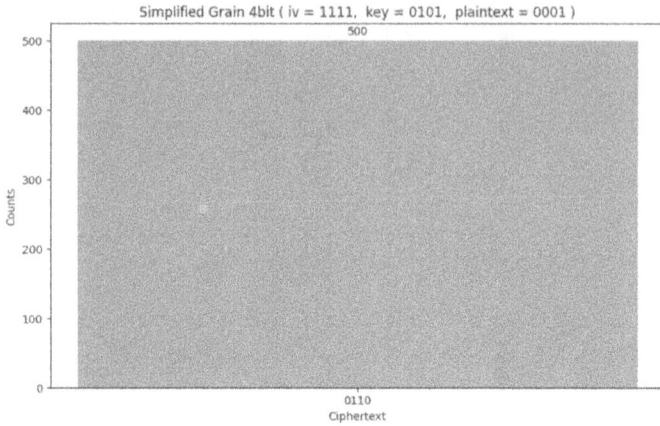

Figure 4.25 Histogram output of simplified grain 4 bit—Test case 4 (Case 1)

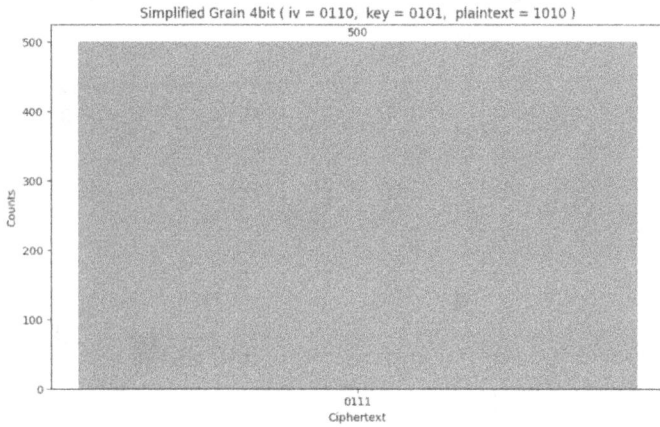

Figure 4.26 Histogram output of simplified grain 4 bit—Test case 4 (Case 2)

Table 4.4

Inputs and outputs of grain 4-bit—Test case 4

Pair	IV (Initialization vector)	Key	Plaintext	Obtained ciphertext
Pair 1	1111	0101	0001	0110
Pair 2	0110	0101	1010	0111

key is 1100, the second key is 0100, and the last one is the expected key 0101, as illustrated in Figure 4.27.

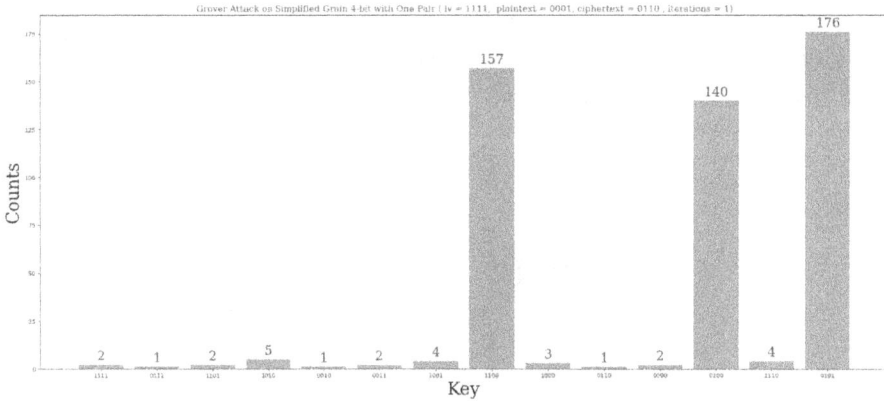

Figure 4.27 Histogram output of Grover attack single pair method—Test case 4

ii. **Double pair method:**
In the double pair method, we are given two sets of IV, plaintext, and ciphertext. Set 1 consists of IV_1 (1111), $Plaintext_1$ (0001), and $Ciphertext_1$ (0110). Set 2 includes IV_2 (0110), $Plaintext_2$ (1010), and $Ciphertext_2$ (0111). By using these two sets, we have successfully obtained a unique key, which matches the expected key 0101, as shown in Figure 4.28.

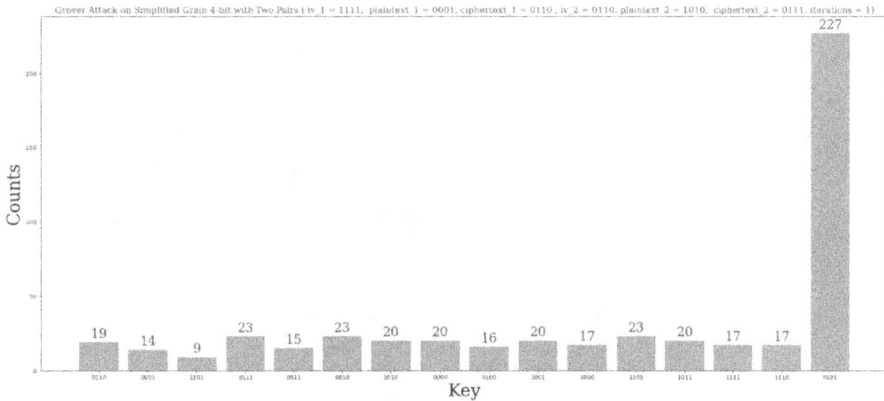

Figure 4.28 Histogram output of Grover attack double pair method—Test case 4

4.8.5 TEST CASE 5

a. **Simplified grain 4-bit—Pair 1:** Here, the given Initialization Vector (IV) is 0100, the Key is 0100, and the Plaintext is 1001. After the cipher's operation, we have obtained the ciphertext 1100. The obtained result from the Simplified Grain 4-bit cipher is shown in Figure 4.29.

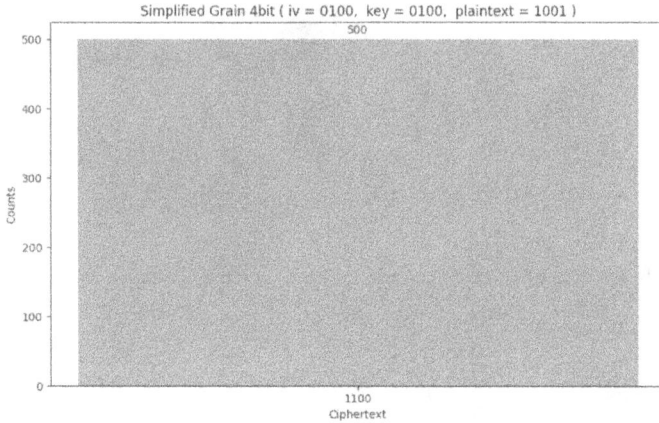

Figure 4.29 Histogram output simplified grain 4 bit—Test case 5 (Pair 1)

b. **Simplified grain 4-bit—Pair 2:** Here, the given Initialization Vector (IV) is 1001, the Key is 0100, and the Plaintext is 0110. After the cipher's operation, we have obtained the ciphertext 0100. The obtained result from the Simplified Grain 4-bit cipher is shown in Figure 4.30.

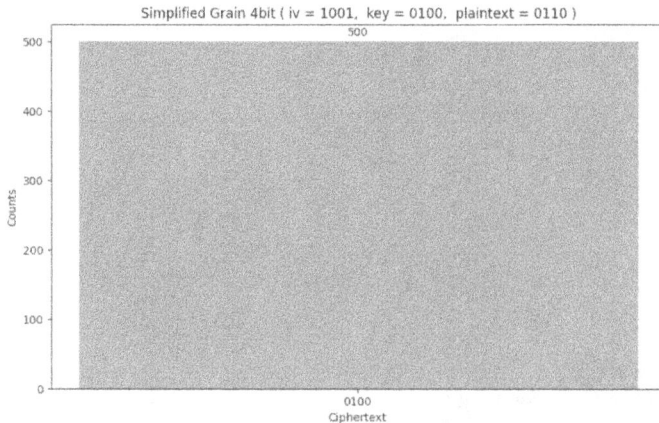

Figure 4.30 Histogram output simplified grain 4 bit—Test case 5 (Pair 2)

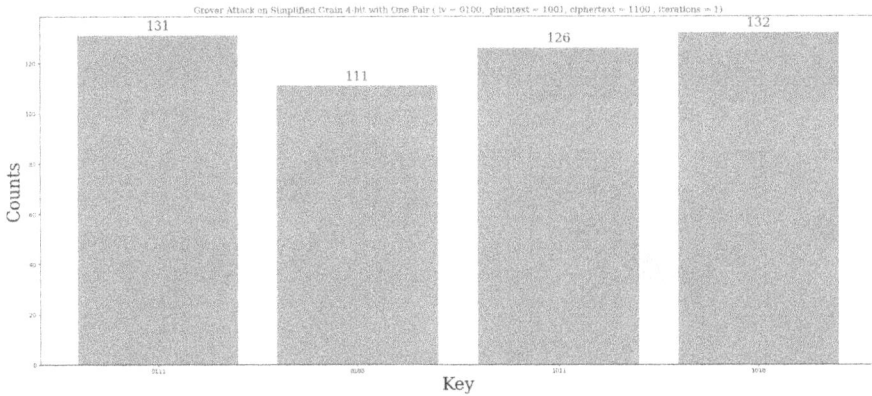

Figure 4.31   Histogram output of Grover attack single pair method—Test case 5

In the Grover attack, we collect samples from both Pair 1 and Pair 2 listed in Table 4.5. In a single-pair attack, we exclusively utilize Pair 1. However, in a double-pair attack, we make use of data from both pairs.

Table 4.5

Inputs and outputs of SGrain 4-bit — Test case 5

Pair	IV (Initialization vector)	Key	Plaintext	Obtained ciphertext
Pair 1	0100	0100	1001	1100
Pair 2	1001	0100	0110	0100

c. **Grover attack for one iteration:**

   i. **Single pair method:** In the single-pair attack, we provided the Initialization Vector (IV) 0100, plaintext 1001, and ciphertext 1100, resulting in four keys: 0111, 1011, 1010, and the expected key, 0100, as illustrated in Figure 4.31.

   ii. **Double pair method:**
   In the double pair method, we are given two sets of IV, plaintext, and ciphertext. Set 1 consists of IV_1 (0100), $Plaintext_1$ (1001), and $Ciphertext_1$ (1100). Set 2 includes IV_2 (1001), $Plaintext_2$ (0110), and $Ciphertext_2$ (0100). By using these two sets, we have successfully obtained a unique key, which matches the expected key 0100, as shown in Figure 4.32.

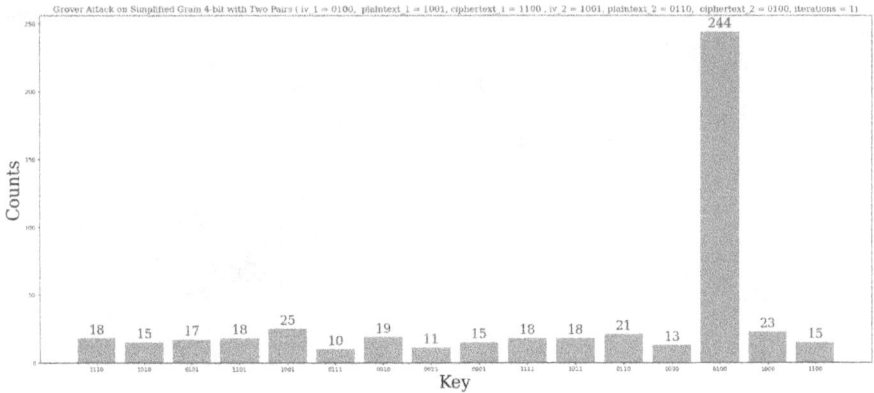

Figure 4.32 Histogram output of Grover attack double pair method—Test case 5

4.8.6   SUMMARY OF TEST CASES

Table 4.6 summarizes the test cases applied to the Simplified Grain 4-bit cipher and the corresponding results of the Grover attack for key recovery. In each case, two sets of data are provided, consisting of an Initialization Vector (IV), a key, a plaintext, and the resulting ciphertext. The Grover attack is then used to attempt key recovery through two methods: the Single Pair Method and the Double Pair Method. The Single Pair Method generally results in multiple recovered keys, ranging from 2 to 4, depending on the test case. This suggests that this method may generate several possible keys for certain pairs of IV, plaintext, and ciphertext, indicating potential vulnerabilities in the cipher. On the other hand, the Double Pair Method consistently recovers only one key in each case, which matches the correct key, demonstrating its accuracy in key recovery. The test cases show that, while the Single Pair Method can produce multiple key candidates, the Double Pair Method provides a more reliable and accurate way to recover the correct encryption key. Overall, the results highlight the varying success rates of each method in recovering keys, with the Double Pair Method being the more effective approach in all test cases.

4.8.7   CLASSICAL COMPUTATION TIME

We have estimated the classical computation time based on the Qiskit MPS simulator, as shown in Table 4.7.

4.8.8   QUANTUM RESOURCE ESTIMATION

We have used a swap gate, which is a combination of three CNOT gates [30], as we can see in Figure 4.33. As in [12], we neglect the NOT gates that depend on the inputs to the Simplified Grain 4-bit cipher, including the Initialization Vector (IV), Key,

Table 4.6
Summary of test cases

Case	Simplified grain 4 bit								Key recovery using Grover attack	
	pair 1				pair 2				Recovered keys	
	IV	key	Plain text	Cipher text	IV	key	Plain text	Cipher text	Single pair method	Double pair series method
1	0111	1111	0001	0010	0110	1111	1001	1010	3 keys	1 key
2	1010	1001	0110	0100	1111	1001	0110	0101	2 keys	1 key
3	1011	1100	1001	0110	1111	1100	1010	1101	2 keys	1 key
4	1111	0101	0001	0110	0110	0101	1010	0111	3 keys	1 key
5	0100	0100	1001	1100	1001	0100	0110	0100	4 keys	1 key

Table 4.7
Classical computation time for Grover attack on SGrain 4-bit

	Key recovery using Grover attack	
Case	Single pair method (seconds)	Double pair method (seconds)
1	1.5	6.5
2	1.5	6.3
3	1.4	6.5
4	1.6	6.6
5	1.5	6.5

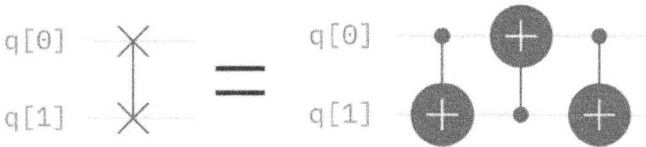

Figure 4.33 Swap gate decomposition

Plaintext, and Ciphertext. The decomposition of the Toffoli (CCNOT) gate shown in Figure 4.34 uses a total of 6 T-gates (including T and T†), along with 8 Clifford gates, and achieves a T-depth of 4. The overall circuit depth is 11, which is calculated based on the number of sequential gate layers acting on the qubits, considering parallelizable operations. Specifically, gates that operate on different qubits and do not interfere can be executed simultaneously, which helps optimize the circuit's depth. This decomposition, as referenced in [23], efficiently balances gate count and depth, which is crucial for fault tolerant quantum computation.

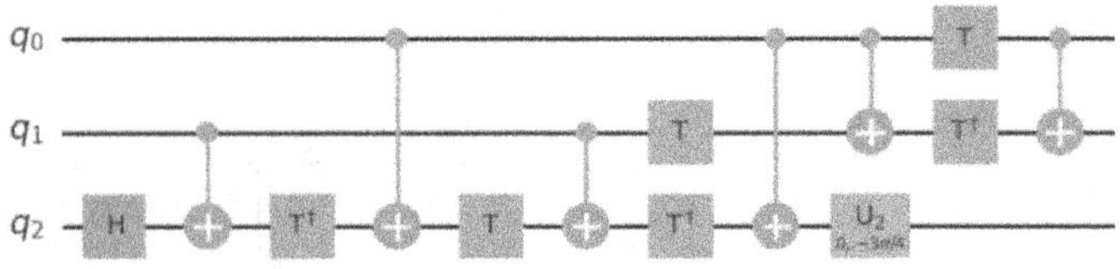

Figure 4.34   Toffoli gate decomposition

4.8.9   COST OF SIMPLIFIED GRAIN 4 BIT

Table 4.8 shows a comparison between the cost of implementing simplified grain 16-bit quantum circuits without reset gates. The parameters considered for the comparison are the number of CNOT gates, Toffoli (CCNOT) gates, circuit depth, and qubit count.

Table 4.8

Cost of simplified grain 4 bit

	CNOT	Toffoli	Depth	Qubits
Count	452	72	318	120

4.8.10   COST OF GROVER ORACLE

Table 4.9 shows the cost of the Grover oracle in terms of Clifford gates, T gates, T depth, full depth, and qubits for the single-pair and double-pair methods.

Table 4.9

Cost of Grover oracle

	Clifford gates	T gates	T-depth	Full depth	Qubits
Single Pair	2139	864	576	1120	121
Double Pair method	6495	2592	1728	3437	122

4.8.11   COST OF EXHAUSTIVE KEY SEARCH

Table 4.10 shows the cost of exhaustive key search in terms of Clifford gates, T gates, T depth, full depth, and qubits for the single-pair and double-pair methods.

Table 4.10

Cost of exhaustive key search

	Clifford gates	T gates	T-depth	Full depth	Qubits
Single Pair	2176	864	576	1145	121
Double Pair method	6532	2592	1728	3462	122

"**The estimation of the cost of an exhaustive key search is based on one iteration, and we should multiply it by the required number of iterations.**"

4.8.12   CLASSICAL RESOURCE ESTIMATION

Table 4.11 shows the estimated classical resources based on the Qiskit MPS simulator.

Table 4.11

Classical resource estimation of Grover attack on Sgrain 4-bit

Pair	Required RAM(GB)
Single Pair	8
Double Pair method	8

4.8.13   REQUIRED PYTHON PACKAGES

You can download Python version 3.11.1 from the official website using the following link: `https://www.python.org/downloads/release/python-3111/` In order to run Jupyter Notebook files in Visual Studio Code, you should install the Python and Jupyter extensions in Visual Studio Code. The required Python packages are shown in Table 4.12.

4.8.14   GROVER ITERATION CALCULATION

We use the general formula to calculate the iterations for Grover's algorithms as follows (Table 4.12):

$$\text{Iterations} = \frac{\pi}{4}\sqrt{\frac{2^k}{s}}$$

Table 4.12

Python packages, versions, and installation commands

Package name	Version	Pip command
qiskit	0.44.1	pip install qiskit==0.44.1
qiskit aer	0.12.1	pip install qiskit aer==0.12.1
matplotlib	3.6.3	pip install matplotlib==3.6.3
pylatexenc	2.10	pip install pylatexenc==2.10
pandas	1.5.3	pip install pandas==1.5.3

Here,

k = Key size
s = Number of solutions

In the Grover algorithm, we generally mark the state we are interested in directly. If we mark one state, we assign "1" to s, and if we mark two states, we assign "2" to s, then calculate the number of iterations. Therefore, s represents the number of states we are interested in.

Due to the possibility of other keys producing the same ciphertext using the same IV and plaintext, the Grover attack aims to discover all the keys that can yield the same ciphertext. Initially, we set the iteration equal to 1, then find keys which produce the same ciphertext using the same IV and plaintext.

In this case, we calculate the number of iterations by setting s as the number of keys obtained in the first iteration. This approach enables us to conduct the Grover attack with the precise number of iterations required for that particular case.

Here, we are considering Case 2 in the test cases of the Grover attack and calculating the exact number of iterations required for this case. In Case 2, the applied inputs to the single pair Grover attack are:

IV = "1010"
Plaintext = "0110"
Ciphertext = "0100"

In the Grover attack for a single pair, we have obtained 2 keys. Therefore, we need to set $s = 2$, and we know that $k = 4$ (the key size), as follows:

$$\text{Iterations} = \frac{\pi}{4}\sqrt{\frac{2^4}{2}}$$

Simplifying this:

$$\text{Iterations} = \frac{3.14}{4}\sqrt{\frac{2^4}{2}} = \frac{3.14}{4}\sqrt{16/2} = \frac{3.14}{4}\sqrt{8} = \frac{3.14}{4} \times 2.828 = 2.2203$$

Thus, the number of iterations is approximately:

$$\text{Iterations} \approx 2$$

4.8.15 RESULTS AND DISCUSSION

In the Grover attack, when working with a single pair of plaintext and ciphertext along with the corresponding Initialization Vector (IV), it is possible to obtain multiple keys due to the probabilistic nature of Grover's search algorithm. However, the primary goal is to determine the correct key, which is the key that successfully encrypts the given plaintext to the corresponding ciphertext under the provided IV. To increase the accuracy of finding the expected key, we enhance the attack by using two pairs of plaintext and ciphertext along with their associated IV. By applying Grover's algorithm to these two pairs, we significantly improve the chances of narrowing down the correct key.

The use of two pairs allows for more robust search through the key space, leveraging the additional data to refine the search process. This method effectively reduces the ambiguity that arises when only a single pair is used, where multiple keys may lead to valid results. As a result, performing the Grover attack with two pairs of plaintext and ciphertext ensures that only one key emerges as the correct one, yielding a unique key that matches the expected key. This approach enhances the reliability and success rate of the Grover attack in key recovery.

This concept is demonstrated in Table 4.6, where we summarize the test cases for the Simplified Grain 4-bit cipher and the corresponding results of the Grover attack. For example, in Case 1, using a single pair of plaintext and ciphertext with their associated IV, we obtained 3 possible keys, but when using the double pair method (two pairs), we successfully recovered 1 unique key. Similarly, in other test cases, the Double Pair Method consistently led to the recovery of a single correct key, highlighting the enhanced accuracy and reliability when using multiple pairs for Grover's attack. This demonstrates how leveraging additional plaintext and ciphertext pairs improves key recovery outcomes and ensures the uniqueness of the key.

4.9 CONCLUSION AND FUTURE ENHANCEMENTS

In this research, we began by designing a simplified version of the Grain cipher, a lightweight stream cipher known for its efficiency in constrained environments. The main goal was to adapt this cipher for quantum analysis, and to that end, we successfully developed a dedicated quantum circuit capable of simulating its operations. This foundational work allowed us to model how the cipher behaves under quantum conditions, providing a basis for deeper cryptographic exploration. The design focused on maintaining the essential features of Grain while simplifying its structure enough to make quantum simulation and attack analysis feasible within current computational limits.

Building upon the cipher's design, we then directed the efforts toward exploring its susceptibility to quantum attacks, specifically employing Grover's algorithm - a powerful quantum search method that offers a quadratic speedup for key-recovery tasks. The investigation covered both the single pair and double pair methods of Grover's attack, giving a comparative view of how different plaintext-ciphertext relationships influence the attack's effectiveness. Through these experiments, we gained critical insight into how varying the number of known plaintext-ciphertext pairs impacts the complexity and success rate of quantum attacks, thus enriching the understanding of the cipher's potential vulnerabilities in a quantum computing era.

Finally, we made significant strides in estimating the quantum resources such as the number of qubits and quantum gates which are required to both implement the cipher and execute Grover's attack against it. These estimations are crucial for evaluating the practical feasibility of quantum attacks on lightweight cryptographic systems. Looking ahead, this research lays a strong groundwork for future expansions, such as increasing the cipher's length to enhance its security or using a larger number of plaintext-ciphertext pairs to better assess its resilience. By opening these pathways, this work not only addresses current quantum threats but also provides a flexible framework for continued cryptographic research in the post-quantum era.

REFERENCES

1. Qiu, D., Luo, L., & Xiao, L. (2024). Distributed Grover's Algorithm. *Theoretical Computer Science*, *993*, 114461.
2. M. Hell, T. Johansson, and W. Meier, "Grain: A Stream Cipher for Constrained Environments," *International Journal of Wireless and Mobile Computing*, vol. 2, no. 1, p. 86, 2007, doi: 10.1504/ijwmc.2007.013798.
3. M. Hell, T. Johansson, A. Maximov, and W. Meier, "A Stream Cipher Proposal: Grain-128," *2006 IEEE International Symposium on Information Theory*, Jul. 2006, doi: 10.1109/isit.2006.261549.
4. A. Maximov, "Cryptanalysis of the 'Grain' Family of Stream Ciphers," *ACM Symposium on Information, Computer and Communications Security (ASIACCS'06)*, 2006, pp. 283–288.
5. V. V. Chepyzhov, T. Johansson, and B. Smeets, "A Simple Algorithm for Fast Correlation Attacks on Stream Ciphers," *Lecture Notes in Computer Science*, pp. 181–195, 2001, doi: 10.1007/3-540-44706-7˙13.
6. T. Johansson and F. Jönsson, "Fast Correlation Attacks Based on Turbo Code Techniques," *Lecture Notes in Computer Science*, pp. 181–197, 1999, doi: 10.1007/3-540-48405-1˙12.
7. N. T. Courtois and W. Meier, "Algebraic Attacks on Stream Ciphers with Linear Feedback," *Advances in Cryptology—EUROCRYPT 2003*, pp. 345–359, 2003, doi: 10.1007/3-540-39200-9˙21.
8. J. J. Hoch and A. Shamir, "Fault Analysis of Stream Ciphers," *Cryptographic Hardware and Embedded Systems—CHES 2004*, pp. 240–253, 2004, doi: 10.1007/978-3-540-28632-5˙18.
9. A. Canteaut and M. Trabbia, "Improved Fast Correlation Attacks Using Parity-Check Equations of Weight 4 and 5," *Lecture Notes in Computer Science*, pp. 573–588, 2000, doi: 10.1007/3-540-45539-6˙40.

10. E. Barkan, E. Biham, and N. Keller, "Instant Ciphertext-Only Cryptanalysis of GSM Encrypted Communication," *Lecture Notes in Computer Science*, pp. 600–616, 2003, doi: 10.1007/978-3-540-45146-4˙35.

11. A. Biryukov and A. Shamir, "Cryptanalytic Time/Memory/Data Tradeoffs for Stream Ciphers," Lecture Notes in Computer Science, pp. 1–13, 2000, doi: 10.1007/3-540-44448-3˙1.

12. R. Anand, A. Maitra, S. Maitra, C. S. Mukherjee, and S. Mukhopadhyay, "Quantum Resource Estimation for FSR Based Symmetric Ciphers and Related Grover's Attacks," *Progress in Cryptology – INDOCRYPT 2021*, pp. 179–198, 2021, doi: 10.1007/978-3-030-92518-5˙9.

13. Hsu, L. Y. (2003). Quantum Secret-Sharing Protocol based on Grover's Algorithm. *Physical Review A, 68*(2), 022306.

14. Zhang, X., Lin, S., & Guo, G. D. (2021). Quantum Secure Multi-party Summation based on Grover's Search Algorithm. *International Journal of Theoretical Physics, 60*(10), 3711-3721.

15. Mandviwalla, A., Ohshiro, K., & Ji, B. (2018, December). Implementing Grover's Algorithm on the IBM Quantum Computers. In *2018 IEEE International Conference on Big Data (Big Data)* (pp. 2531–2537). IEEE.

16. M. Almazrooie, R. Abdullah, A. Samsudin, and K. N. Mutter, "Quantum Grover Attack on the Simplified-AES," *Proceedings of the 2018 7th International Conference on Software and Computer Applications*, Feb. 2018, doi: 10.1145/3185089.3185122.

17. Grassl, M., Langenberg, B., Roetteler, M., & Steinwandt, R. (2016, February). Applying Grover's Algorithm to AES: Quantum Resource Estimates. In *International Workshop on Post-Quantum Cryptography* (pp. 29–43). Springer International Publishing.

18. Stoudenmire, E. M., & Waintal, X. (2024). Opening the Black Box Inside Grover's Algorithm. *Physical Review X, 14*(4), 041029.

19. M. Grassl, B. Langenberg, M. Roetteler, and R. Steinwandt, "Applying Grover's Algorithm to AES: Quantum Resource Estimates," *Lecture Notes in Computer Science*, pp. 29–43, 2016, doi: 10.1007/978-3-319-29360- 8˙3.

20. Feng, M. (2001). Grover Search with Pairs of Trapped Ions. *Physical Review A, 63*(5), 052308.

21. Brassard, G., Høyer, P., & Tapp, A. (1998). Quantum Cryptanalysis of Hash and Claw-Free Functions. In *LATIN'98: Theoretical Informatics* (pp. 163–169). Springer Berlin Heidelberg.

22. Orts, F. J., Ortega, G., Cruz, N., & Garzón, G. E. (2019). Understanding Grover's Search Algorithm through a Simple Case of Study. In *EDULEARN19 Proceedings* (pp. 1730–1737). IATED.

23. R. Anand, A. Maitra, and S. Mukhopadhyay, "Grover on SIMON" *Quantum Information Processing*, vol. 19, no. 9, Sep. 2020, doi: 10.1007/s11128-020-02844-w.

24. Udrescu, M., Prodan, L., & Vlădutiu, M. (2006, May). Implementing Quantum Genetic Algorithms: A Solution based on Grover's Algorithm. In *Proceedings of the 3rd Conference on Computing Frontiers* (pp. 71–82).

25. Quantum Inspire—By QuTech, "*Resetting Qubits*". https://www.quantum-inspire.com/kbase/resetting-qubits/

26. MohanKumar, M., Singh, B., Thamaraimanalan, T., Korada, S. K., Yuvaraj, P., & Jyothikamalesh, S. (2024, March). Quantum Key Recovery Attack on Simplified Grain 4-Bit Cipher Using Grover's Algorithm. In *2024 10th International Conference on Advanced Computing and Communication Systems (ICACCS)* (Vol. 1, pp. 2596–2601). IEEE.

27. Szabłowski, P. J. (2021). Understanding Mathematics of Grover's Algorithm. *Quantum Information Processing*, *20*(5), 191.

28. L. K. Grover, "A Fast Quantum Mechanical Algorithm for Database Search," *Proceedings of the Twenty-Eighth Annual ACM Symposium on Theory of Computing—STOC '96*, 1996, doi: 10.1145/237814.237866.

29. Qiskit Textbook, "*Grover's Algorithm.*" https://learn.qiskit.org/course/ch-algorithms/grovers-algorithm

30. J. C. Garcia-Escartin and P. Chamorro-Posada, "A SWAP Gate for Qudits," Quantum Information Processing, vol. 12, no. 12, pp. 3625–3631, Aug. 2013, doi: 10.1007/s11128-013-0621-x.

31. Roy, A., Pachuau, J. L., Krishna, G., & Saha, A. K. (2024). Applying Grover's Algorithm to Implement Various Numerical and Comparison Operations. *Quantum Studies: Mathematics and Foundations*, *11*(2), 291–306.

Section V

Simon's Algorithm: Collision Finding

5 Simon's Algorithm: Collision Finding

"Simon's algorithm revealed the quantum power to solve problems that were thought to be classically intractable."

— Daniel Simon

SUMMARY

This chapter explains Simon's algorithm, focusing on how it helps in finding collisions. It starts with an overview of how the algorithm works. A literature review is included, covering both Simon's algorithm and its uses in cryptography. The section then introduces Simon's problem, comparing how classical and quantum methods solve it, and explains how to build a quantum circuit for a blackbox function. Different examples of blackbox functions (oracles) are shown, such as 1-to-1 and 2-to-1 mappings, with detailed implementations of Simon's algorithm for both 4-bit and 8-bit cases. The section also looks at a suggested attack method on the Grain-128a cipher, explaining how the key and initialization vector (IV) are set up, how the keystream is generated, and how the authenticated tag is created. It provides a quantum circuit design for the Simon attack on Grain-4a, along with steps for carrying out the attack. The section also presents experimental results from several test cases and quantum resource estimates. It wraps up with a discussion of the results and thoughts on future improvements and developments in using Simon's algorithm for cryptographic attacks.

5.1 OVERVIEW OF SIMON'S ALGORITHM

Simon's algorithm is a pioneering quantum algorithm that marked a significant milestone in the evolution of quantum computing. Proposed by Daniel Simon in 1994, it was one of the first algorithms to demonstrate the superiority of quantum computers over classical counterparts for certain computational problems. The core problem addressed by Simon's algorithm is the "collision finding" problem for a specific type of function. Given a black box function $f : \{0,1\}^n \rightarrow \{0,1\}^n$ that satisfies the promise $f(x) = f(y)$ if and only if $x \oplus y = s$, where s is an unknown binary string, the goal is to determine s. Here, $\oplus$ denotes the bitwise XOR operation. Classically, solving this problem requires an exponential number of queries to the function, making it computationally infeasible for large n.

DOI: 10.1201/9781003606338-5

Simon's algorithm influences the principles of quantum mechanics—specifically, superposition, interference, and measurement—to solve the problem exponentially faster. Using a quantum circuit model, it determines s with high probability in $O(n)$ queries to the black box function, demonstrating an exponential speedup over the classical $O(2^{n/2})$ approach.

The significance of Simon's algorithm lies not only in its efficiency but also in its theoretical implications. It provided the first formal evidence that quantum computing could solve certain problems exponentially faster than classical computing, thus influencing the field's development. Simon's Algorithm has applications in cryptography, particularly in analyzing symmetric-key encryption schemes. It highlights the potential vulnerabilities of classical cryptographic systems in a quantum computing era, emphasizing the need for quantum-resistant cryptographic techniques.

In this section, Simon's algorithm is explored in detail, including its problem formulation, quantum circuit implementation, and the mathematical principles underlying its operation.

5.2 LITERATURE SURVEY

5.2.1 SIMON ALGORITHM

The quantum model of computation presented by D. R. Simon. [1] represents a departure from classical Probabilistic Turing Machines (PTMs), as it incorporates principles observed at the quantum mechanical scale to replace conventional laws of chance. In this literature survey, the author explores the efficient differentiation between two distinct classes of functions within the quantum computational framework, emphasizing a notable contrast in efficiency compared to classical probabilistic methods. By analyzing oracles drawn uniformly from the respective classes, the author presents compelling evidence supporting the assertion that quantum computation exhibits greater complexity theoretic power than PTMs. The survey underscores the transformative potential of quantum computation, exemplified by Shor's groundbreaking work on quantum polynomial-time algorithms for discrete logarithm and integer factoring problems. This research collectively contributes to a comprehensive narrative showcasing the capability of quantum computation to revolutionize complexity theory and algorithmic efficiency.

5.2.2 SIMON'S ALGORITHM APPLICATION TO CRYPTOGRAPHY

Shor's algorithm has prompted concerns regarding the susceptibility of public key cryptography to quantum computers presented by B.M. Zhou et al. [2], leading the cryptographic community to seek quantum-safe alternatives. The author explores the less understood impact of quantum computing on secret key cryptography, specifically examining attacks where an adversary queries a quantum superposition oracle implementing a cryptographic primitive. Despite the adversary's enhanced power, recent results demonstrate the feasibility of constructing secure cryptosystems within this quantum model. By focusing on Simon's algorithm, a basic quantum period finding algorithm, author reveal that it dramatically accelerates classical attacks on symmetric cryptosystems based on collision finding, enabling the identification of collisions with just $O(n)$ queries in the quantum model. These findings result in substantial attacks, exposing the complete vulnerability of widely used authentication and authenticated encryption modes, including Cipher Block Chaining Message Authentication Code (CBC-MAC), Parallelizable Message Authentication Code (PMAC), Galois Message Authentication Code (GMAC), Galois/Counter Mode (GCM), Offset Codebook Mode (OCB), and several Competition for Authenticated Encryption: Security, Applicability, and Robustness (CAESAR) candidates. Additionally, the author highlighted the applicability of Simon's algorithm to slide attacks, exponentially speeding up classical symmetric cryptanalysis techniques within the quantum model.

Simon's algorithm and Symmetric key Crypto Generalizations and Automatized Applications presented by F. Canale et al. [3]. The author presented the application of Simon's algorithm to compromise symmetric key cryptographic primitives. The author employs an automated approach to systematically discover novel attacks, leading to the identification of the first efficient key-recovery vulnerabilities in constructions such as the 5-round MISTY L-FK or 5-round Feistel-FK (with internal permutation) using Simon's algorithm. Simultaneously, the author explores the generalizations of Simon's algorithm, incorporating non-standard Hadamard matrices, with the objective of broadening the quantum symmetric cryptanalysis toolkit beyond periodicity. The key finding suggests that none of these generalizations can achieve this goal. Consequently, the author infers that exploiting non-standard Hadamard matrices with quantum computers for breaking symmetric primitives will necessitate the development of fundamentally new attack strategies.

Using Simon's algorithm to attack symmetric-key cryptographic primitives presented by T. Santoli et al. [4]. The author establishes novel connections between quantum information and classical cryptography, explores instances where Simon's algorithm exposes the insecurity of widely employed cryptographic symmetric-key primitives. The author contributions include a quantum distinguisher for the 3-round Feistel network and a forgery attack on CBC-MAC capable of creating a tag for a chosen-prefix message by querying only other messages of the same length. These findings assume an adversary with quantum-oracle access to the respective classical primitives. The author discoveries cast a fresh perspective on the post-quantum security of cryptographic schemes, emphasizing the imperative need to reevaluate classical security proofs in the face of quantum adversaries.

Quantum Related-Key Attack Based on Simon's algorithm and its applications presented by P. Zhang. [5]. In the backdrop of advancing quantum technology, quantum computing is applying a growing influence on cryptanalysis with notable algorithms like Simon's algorithm, Grover's algorithm, the Bernstein–Vazirani algorithm, Shor's algorithm, and the Grover-meets-Simon algorithm being successively proposed. However, the majority of cryptanalysis focuses on the quantum Chosen-

Plaintext Attack (qCPA) model. This paper shifts its focus to the potent cryptan-alytic model of quantum Related-Key Attack (qRKA), introducing a strategy for qRKAs against symmetric key ciphers employing Simon's algorithm. The author constructs a periodic function designed to efficiently recover the secret key of sym-metric key ciphers when the targeted ciphers adhere to Simon's promise, providing a detailed complexity analysis for specific symmetric ciphers. Applying qRKA to the Even–Mansour cipher and Sum of Even Monsour (SoEM), construction, author suc-cessfully recover their secret keys and present a comparative complexity analysis in distinct attack models. This work holds significance for advancing the qRKA crypt-analysis of existing provably secure cryptographic schemes and informs the design of future quantum-secure cryptographic schemes.

No polynomial classical algorithms can effectively distinguish between the 3-round Feistel cipher with internal permutations and a random permutation, indicat-ing security against classical chosen-plaintext attacks presented by H. Kuwakado et al. [6], the author introduces a polynomial quantum algorithm that achieves this dis-tinction. Consequently, the 3-round Feistel cipher with internal permutations may exhibit vulnerabilities against chosen-plaintext attacks on a quantum computer. This distinguishing problem stands as an instance efficiently solved through quantum par-allelism. Notably, the algorithm proposed in this paper represents the inaugural appli-cation of Simon's algorithm to cryptographic analysis, marking a pioneering progress in leveraging quantum computing for cryptanalysis purposes.

Security on the quantum-type Even-Mansour cipher presented by H. Kuwakado et al. [7], The author explores the security implications of applying quantum cryp-tography to the Even-Mansour cipher which is traditionally resistant to classical at-tacks, demonstrating a notable upgradation from classical security guarantees. While quantum cryptography, exemplified by protocols like BB84, is primarily designed for sharing classical information, this study considers the encryption of quantum in-formation using the quantum circuit of the Even-Mansour cipher. In contrast to the proven exponential time complexity for breaking the classical Even-Mansour cipher using classical algorithms, the paper reveals a vulnerability in the quantum version. Specifically, it demonstrates that the quantum instantiation of the Even-Mansour ci-pher is insecure, permitting the discovery of a key in polynomial time relative to the key length. This example serves as a cautionary illustration that the quantum version of a classically secure cipher may not necessarily ensure quantum security, emphasizing the need for thorough scrutiny when adapting classical cryptographic techniques to the quantum field.

It has been commonly believed that the security of symmetric key schemes is less vulnerable to quantum computers compared to public key schemes presented by A. Hosoyamada et al. [8]. However, research has exposed specific scenarios in which symmetric key schemes can be broken in polynomial time by adversaries em-ploy quantum computers. Notably, these works include a quantum distinguishing attack on 3-round Feistel ciphers and a quantum key recovery attack on the Even-

Mansour cipher by Kuwakado and Morii, along with an independent proposal of a quantum forgery attack on CBC-MAC by Kaplan et al. and by Santoli and Schaffner. The Iterated Even-Mansour cipher, viewed as an idealization of AES, is a critical yet straightforward block cipher. Investigating the existence of an efficient quantum algorithm capable of breaking the Iterated Even-Mansour cipher with independent subkeys is pivotal for analyzing the post-quantum security of block ciphers. While a prior efficient quantum attack on Iterated Even-Mansour cipher by Kaplan et al. applies only when all subkeys are the same, this paper introduces a polynomial time quantum algorithm capable of recovering partial keys in a related-key setting, offering insights into post-quantum security analysis for block ciphers. Despite the somewhat strong related-key condition, their algorithm demonstrates the capability to recover subkeys with two related oracles. Additionally, Author show that their algorithm can recover all keys of the "i"-round iterated Even-Mansour cipher given access to "i" related quantum oracles. To enable quantum related-key attacks, Author extend Simon's quantum algorithm to recover the hidden period of a function that is periodic only up to a constant, employing a technique involving the differential of the target function to create a double periodic function before applying Simon's algorithm.

Tweakable Even–Mansour ciphers, derived from public permutations presented by P. Zhang et al. [9]. The author finds widespread usage in disk sector encryption and data storage encryption. With the rapid advancement of computing power, particularly in quantum computing technology, there arises a need to assess and study the quantum security of tweakable Even–Mansour ciphers. This paper explores into the quantum security analysis of tweakable Even–Mansour ciphers, with a focus on one-round, two-round, and generalized r-round scenarios. For the one-round case, Author provide the quantum circuit, present a polynomial-time quantum key recovery attack utilizing Simon's algorithm, and detail the associated resource estimation. In the case of a two-round tweakable Even–Mansour cipher, author introduce a superior quantum key recovery attack employing the Brassard-Hoyer-Tapp (BHT)-meets-Simon algorithm compared to the Grover-meets-Simon algorithm, offering a new perspective on variable tweaks and providing concrete resource estimates. Extending their analysis to r-round tweakable Even–Mansour ciphers, author propose a quantum key recovery attack by combining Grover's algorithm and Simon's algorithm. This work is highly significant, introducing the BHT-meets-Simon algorithm for achieving more efficient quantum key recovery attacks than the Grover-meets-Simon algorithm for the first time.

Beyond Quadratic Speedups in Quantum Attacks on Symmetric key schemes, presented by Bonnetain et al. in ASIACRYPT [10]. The author introduced the offline-Simon algorithm which demonstrates its efficacy in attacking the 2XOR-Cascade construction within a quantum time complexity of $O(2^n)$, resulting in a notable 2.5 quantum speedup over the best classical attack. Additionally, the paper challenges the conventional assumption in post-quantum security that doubling the key size for protection, highlighting how certain symmetric key constructions, such as the

2XOR-Cascade, can go beyond the quadratic speedup limit imposed by Grover's quantum search algorithm. The authors provide a groundbreaking example of a more than quadratic speedup in a symmetric cryptanalytic attack within the classical query model, refuting the widely held belief that doubling key sizes guarantees safety against quantum threats. Notably, they emphasize the necessity for meticulous scrutiny of generic key-length extension techniques, exemplified by the ineffectiveness of the 2XOR Cascade in sustaining security against quantum adversaries. Finally, the paper acknowledges remaining questions regarding the potential expansion of this gap, hinting at the limitations of the offline-Simon algorithm and the uncertainty surrounding the existence of polynomial relations in the general context of the problems at hand.

Breaking Symmetric Cryptosystems Using Quantum Period Finding presented by M. Kaplan et al. [11]. The author explores the profound impact of quantum computing on both public key and secret key cryptography. It highlights the well-known threat posed by Shor's algorithm to public key cryptography, which has induced the cryptographic community to seek quantum-safe solutions. In contrast, the implications of quantum computing on secret key cryptography remain less understood. The authors focus on attacks where adversaries can query an oracle implementing a cryptographic primitive in a quantum superposition of different states, granting significant power to the adversary. Despite this forbidding challenge, some findings indicate the feasibility of constructing secure cryptosystems within this model. Specifically, the paper investigates the application of Simon's algorithm, the simplest quantum period-finding algorithm, to attack symmetric cryptosystems in this context. By leveraging Simon's algorithm, classical attacks based on collision finding can be dramatically accelerated, enabling the identification of collisions with hidden periodicity using significantly fewer queries in the quantum model compared to the classical setting.

Anand et al. [12] analyze the IND-qCPA (Indistinguishability under quantum Chosen-Plaintext Attack) security of several widely used block cipher modes of operation—namely CBC, CFB, OFB, CTR, and XTS—in the presence of quantum adversaries capable of making queries in superposition. The study reveals that the OFB and CTR modes retain security assuming the underlying block cipher behaves as a standard secure pseudorandom function (PRF) secure against classical queries. However, the authors present counterexamples showing that CBC, CFB, and XTS modes do not preserve security under the same assumption. Notably, the paper provides formal security proofs for the CBC and CFB modes when the block cipher is a quantum-secure PRF, indicating that these constructions can remain secure even against quantum superposition queries. This work highlights the differential impact of quantum capabilities on symmetric cryptographic modes and emphasizes the need to adopt quantum-secure primitives to ensure robust post-quantum cryptographic protection.

G. Brassard et al. (2016) [13] introduced a groundbreaking quantum algorithm for solving the collision problem, significantly outperforming classical counterparts. The algorithm achieves collision detection with an expected evaluation complexity of $O(\sqrt[3]{N/r})$, even when probabilistic approaches are considered. Furthermore, the authors extended this algorithm to efficiently identify collisions in pairs of functions, demonstrating its versatility and broad applicability. Notably, the paper emphasizes the space-time trade-off inherent in the proposed technique and highlights the innovative use of Grover's quantum search algorithm to address fundamental challenges in cryptography. This development underscores the algorithm's potential impact on both theoretical and practical aspects of quantum computing.

W. Liu et al. (2023) [14] proposed quantum forgery attacks against OTR (One-Time-Randomized) structures by leveraging Simon's algorithm to overcome the inherent limitations of classical forgery methods, which typically rely on restrictive conditions and yield low success rates. Their quantum attack targets intercepted ciphertext-tag pairs (C, T) transmitted between sender and receiver in OTR communications. By exploiting Simon's algorithm to identify the period of the tag generation function, the attacker can forge a distinct ciphertext $C' \neq C$ that still maps to the same tag T. Additionally, the paper presents a universal forgery attack on a variant of OTR, namely the Prost-OTR-Even-Mansour structure. This attack allows the generation of valid tags for arbitrary messages by altering a single block. The attacker first recovers the secret parameter L using Simon's algorithm, and subsequently derives the keys K_1 and K_2, which enable forging of modified ciphertexts. Remarkably, the attack requires only a few plaintext blocks to obtain these keys, significantly enhancing efficiency. The authors report a query complexity of $O(n)$ and a success probability approaching 1, demonstrating the high effectiveness of their attack strategy on OTR-based cryptographic constructions.

Even and Mansour [15] proposed a novel block cipher construction based on a single pseudorandom permutation, offering a streamlined alternative to traditional cipher designs that rely on multiple permutations or complex key schedules. In this scheme, a randomly chosen permutation F is used along with a key composed of two blocks, K_1 and K_2. The encryption process involves first XORing the plaintext block with K_1, applying the permutation F, and then XORing the output with K_2 to produce the ciphertext. This minimalist design is shown to provide provable security guarantees when F behaves as a random or pseudorandom permutation. The construction significantly simplifies implementation by eliminating the need for storing or generating multiple permutations, thereby enhancing both efficiency and practicality in cryptographic applications.

A flexible authenticated lightweight cipher using Even-Mansour construction presented by E. Marsola do Nascimento et al. [16]. The author introduces a novel approach to address the challenge of integrating authentication directly into lightweight ciphers for IoT environments. The proposed Flexible Authenticated Encryption (AE) cipher, based on the Even-Mansour construction and the Integrity Aware

Parallelizable Mode (IAPM), offers authentication as an integral part of its operation, eliminating the need for external authentication mechanisms and simplifying implementation while ensuring security. By supporting variable block sizes and utilizing an initialization vector (IV) to generate different ciphertexts for the same plaintext and key pair, the cipher provides flexibility and resistance against plaintext correlation and replay attacks. Extensive statistical tests using the NIST Statistical Test Suite tool validate the cipher's randomness, while differential cryptanalysis demonstrates its resilience against such attacks. While further research is needed to explore other cryptanalytic techniques, the Flexible AE cipher represents a promising advancement in the development of secure and efficient cryptographic solutions tailored for IoT applications.

Zhang and Yuan [17] address the challenge of minimizing key material in the Even–Mansour cipher while preserving its strong security guarantees an essential requirement for resource-constrained environments such as smart homes, smart transportation systems, and the IoT. The authors propose four novel short-key variants of the Even–Mansour cipher and employ Patarin's H-coefficients technique to formally establish their security against up to $O\left(\frac{2^k}{\mu}\right)$ adversarial queries, where k denotes the key bit length and μ the maximal multiplicity. These variants are applied to lightweight authenticated encryption modes, demonstrating resistance to adversaries making up to approximately $\min\left(\frac{b}{2}, c, k - \log \mu\right)$-bit queries, where b is the permutation size and c is its capacity. The paper also outlines an open problem concerning the security of the t-round iterated Even–Mansour cipher when short keys are used, inviting further research in this domain. These short-key constructions offer key benefits such as on-the-fly computation, elimination of key schedule overhead, and minimized hardware footprint, making them particularly well-suited for lightweight and embedded cryptographic applications.

5.3   SIMON'S PROBLEM

We are handed a black box function, labeled as f, and we know for certain that it falls into one of two categories:

1. It's a one-to-one (1:1) function, meaning each input corresponds to a unique output, (or)
2. It's a two-to-one (2:1) function, where every output has exactly two corresponding inputs.

In the one-to-one scenario, a function with 4 inputs might look like this:

$$f(x_1) \to A, \quad f(x_2) \to B, \quad f(x_3) \to C, \quad f(x_4) \to D$$

On the other hand, a two-to-one function with the same set of inputs could be:

$$f(x_1) \to A, \quad f(x_2) \to B, \quad f(x_3) \to A, \quad f(x_4) \to B$$

where (x_1, x_2, x_3, x_4) are 2-bit inputs and A, B, C, D are the 2-bit outputs.

The two-to-one mapping is influenced by a hidden 2-bit string b, and it follows the rule:

$$f(x_1) = f(x_3), \quad f(x_2) = f(x_4)$$

Then, the following equations hold:

$$x_1 \oplus x_3 = b, \quad x_2 \oplus x_4 = b$$

The challenge is to determine how quickly we can figure out whether f is one-to-one or two-to-one. If it turns out to be two-to-one, how fast can we uncover the bit string b. Surprisingly, both situations come down to the same challenge of identifying b, where a bit string $b = 00$ signals that f is one-to-one.

5.3.1   CLASSICAL SOLUTION

In the classical context, if we aim to definitively discern the bit string b for a given function f, we are confronted with the challenge of examining up to $2^{(n-1)} + 1$ inputs, where n represents the number of bits in the input. This means that we must investigate just beyond half of all possible inputs until we encounter two instances yielding the same output. This scenario is similar to the Deutsch-Jozsa problem, where a stroke of luck might lead to solving the problem in the initial attempts. However, if we encounter a one-to-one function or, less favorably, a two-to-one function, we find ourselves obligated to evaluate the complete $2^{(n-1)} + 1$ input range.

5.3.2   QUANTUM SOLUTION

The quantum circuit that implements Simon's algorithm is shown in Figure 5.1. In the quantum context, the query function Q_f acts on two quantum registers as:

$$|x\rangle |a\rangle \xrightarrow{Q_f} |x\rangle |a \oplus f(x)\rangle$$

In the specific case where the second register is initially in the state $|0\rangle = |00 \dots 0\rangle$, the transformation looks like:

$$|x\rangle |0\rangle \xrightarrow{Q_f} |x\rangle |f(x)\rangle$$

The algorithm involves the following steps:

Step 1: Initialize the two n qubit input registers to the zero state:

$$|\psi_1\rangle = |0\rangle^{\otimes n} |0\rangle^{\otimes n}$$

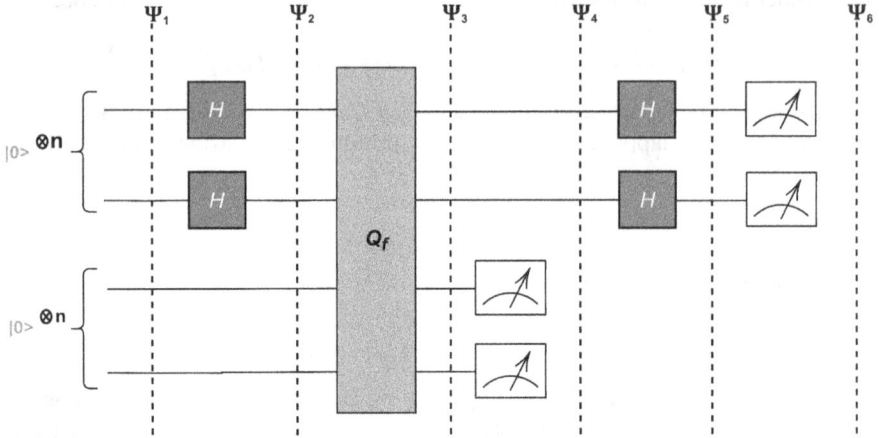

Figure 5.1   Quantum circuit of Simon's algorithm

Step 2: Apply a Hadamard transform to the first register:

$$|\psi_2\rangle = \frac{1}{\sqrt{2^n}} \sum_{x \in \{0,1\}^n} |x\rangle |0\rangle^{\otimes n}$$

Step 3: Apply the query function Q_f:

$$|\psi_3\rangle = \frac{1}{\sqrt{2^n}} \sum_{x \in \{0,1\}^n} |x\rangle |f(x)\rangle$$

Step 4: Measure the second register. A certain value of $f(x)$ will be observed.
If the function is One-to-One: The observed value $f(x)$ could correspond to a unique input x, therefore, the first register becomes:

$$|\psi_4\rangle = |x\rangle$$

If the function is Two-to-One: The observed value $f(x)$ could correspond to two possible inputs x and $y = x \oplus b$. Therefore, the first register becomes:

$$|\psi_4\rangle = \frac{1}{\sqrt{2}} (|x\rangle + |y\rangle)$$

where we omit the second register, as it has been measured.

Step 5: Apply a Hadamard transform to the first register:
If the function is One-to-One:

$$|\psi_5\rangle = \frac{1}{\sqrt{2^n}} \sum_{z \in \{0,1\}^n} (-1)^{x \cdot z} |z\rangle$$

If the function is Two-to-One:

$$|\psi_5\rangle = \frac{1}{\sqrt{2^{n+1}}} \sum_{z \in \{0,1\}^n} \left[(-1)^{x \cdot z} + (-1)^{y \cdot z}\right] |z\rangle$$

$$|\psi_5\rangle = \frac{1}{\sqrt{2^{n+1}}} \sum_{z \in \{0,1\}^n} \left[(-1)^{x \cdot z} + (-1)^{(x \oplus b) \cdot z}\right] |z\rangle$$

Step 6: Measure the first register.
If the function is One-to-One: The measurement will return a random bit string z, uniformly chosen from $\{0,1\}^n$.

If the function is Two-to-One: The measurement will return a random bit string z such that:

$$(-1)^{x \cdot z} = (-1)^{y \cdot z}$$

This implies:

$$x \cdot z = y \cdot z$$
$$x \cdot z = (x \oplus b) \cdot z$$
$$x \cdot z = x \cdot z \oplus b \cdot z$$
$$b \cdot z = 0$$

Thus, after repeating the algorithm approximately n times, we will obtain n different values of z, from which we can write the following system of equations:

$$b \cdot z_1 = 0$$
$$b \cdot z_2 = 0$$
$$\vdots$$
$$b \cdot z_n = 0$$

From this, b can be determined by Gaussian elimination.

5.3.3 CONSTRUCTING A CIRCUIT FOR THE BLACK BOX FUNCTION

We now detail the construction of the 1-to-1 and 2-to-1 permutation circuit of the Black box function. Let us assume the Black box function receives the input $|x\rangle|0\rangle$. With respect to a predetermined b, the Black box function writes its output to the second register, so that it transforms the input to $|x\rangle|f_b(x)\rangle$ such that $f(x) = f(x \oplus b)$ for all $x \in \{0,1\}^n$.

Such a Black box function can be realized by the following procedures:

STEPS TO CONSTRUCT THE BLACK BOX FUNCTION:

The following are the steps involved in the construction of a black box.

Step 1: Copy the content of the first register to the second register: $|x\rangle|0\rangle \to |x\rangle|x\rangle$

Step 2: Creating 1-to-1 or 2-to-1 mapping based on b: If b is not all-zero, then there is the least index j such that $b_j = 1$. $x_j = 0$, then XOR the second register with b. Otherwise, leave the second register unchanged.

$$|x\rangle|x\rangle \to |x\rangle|x \oplus b\rangle$$

Step 3: Creating a random permutation (Optional): Randomly permute and flip the qubits of the second register (this is not strictly necessary for the function's operation but could be added if needed for randomness).

$$|x\rangle|y\rangle \to |x\rangle|f_b(y)\rangle$$

5.4   EXAMPLE BLACK BOX(ORACLE) FOR 1-TO-1 FUNCTION

A 1-to-1 function is one where each input maps uniquely to a single output. Here's how the given quantum circuit operates as an oracle for such a function shown in Figure 5.2.

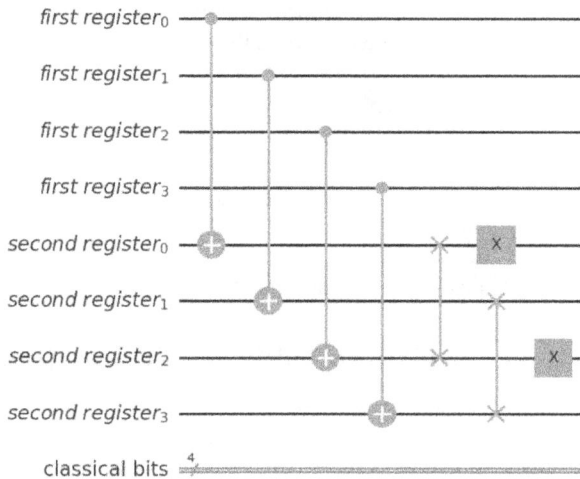

Figure 5.2   Quantum Black box(oracle) of 1-to-1 function

Components of the Circuit

Registers:

First register (Input): Consists of qubits labeled `first register`$_0$ to `first register`$_3$. These qubits store the input values for the function f.

Second register (Ancillary/Output): Consists of qubits labeled `second register`$_0$ to `second register`$_3$. These qubits are used to store the output of the function or intermediate computational results.

Quantum gates:

Controlled-NOT (CNOT) Gates: These gates are crucial for creating entanglement between qubits. In the circuit, CNOT gates are applied between qubits from the first and second registers. They are typically depicted as lines connecting a dot (control qubit) to a plus sign (target qubit).

Pauli-X gates: These gates flip the state of a qubit from $|0\rangle$ to $|1\rangle$ or vice versa and are represented in the diagram by green squares with an "X". Pauli-X gates are applied to `second register`$_2$ and `second register`$_3$.

Measurements: The classical bits shown at the bottom of the circuit indicate that the quantum states are measured at the end of computation, and the outcomes are stored as classical bits.

Quantum registers:

First register (Input register): This register consists of qubits labeled `first register`$_0$ through `first register`$_3$. These qubits represent the input x to the function $f(x)$ and are involved in generating the superposition over all possible inputs.

Second register (Output/Ancillary Register): This register includes qubits labeled `second register`$_0$ to `second register`$_3$. These qubits hold the output $f(x)$ and facilitate the evaluation of the function within the oracle.

Quantum gates:

Controlled-NOT (CNOT) Gates: These gates are used to encode the function $f(x)$ by creating entanglement between the input and output qubits. In the diagram, the qubits from the first register (control qubits) to the second register (target qubits) are connected, enabling function evaluation in superposition.

Pauli-X gates: These gates flip the state of the qubit (i.e., $|0\rangle \leftrightarrow |1\rangle$) and are typically used to set specific output values for the function. In the circuit, Pauli-X gates are applied to `second register`$_2$ and `second register`$_3$ to prepare or modify their state before or after function evaluation.

Measurement: At the end of the circuit, measurement operations are applied to the first register (and sometimes the second, depending on implementation). The classical bits shown at the bottom represent the measurement outcomes, which are then used to extract information about the hidden string s in Simon's problem.

How the circuit works:

Initialization: The first register is initialized to the state $|0\rangle^{\otimes n}$, and Hadamard gates are applied to place it into an equal superposition over all possible n-bit strings. The second register is initialized to $|0\rangle^{\otimes n}$, the all-zero state.

Oracle application: A quantum oracle (black-box function) implements the transformation $|x\rangle|0\rangle \rightarrow |x\rangle|f(x)\rangle$, where f hides a secret string s such that $f(x) = f(x \oplus s)$. This step entangles the input and output registers based on the function f.

Interference and measurement Preparation: After the oracle, Hadamard gates are applied again to the first register. This step exploits quantum interference to extract information about the hidden string s, encoding it in the amplitudes of the quantum state.

Measurement: The first register is measured, collapsing it to a classical bitstring y such that $y \cdot s = 0 \mod 2$. Repeating the process multiple times yields enough linear equations to solve for the secret string s.

5.5 EXAMPLE BLACK BOX(ORACLE) FOR 2-TO-1 (HIDDEN BIT STRING 1001)

A black box (oracle) implementation for a 2-to-1 oracle with the hidden bit string 1001 is shown in Figure 5.3.

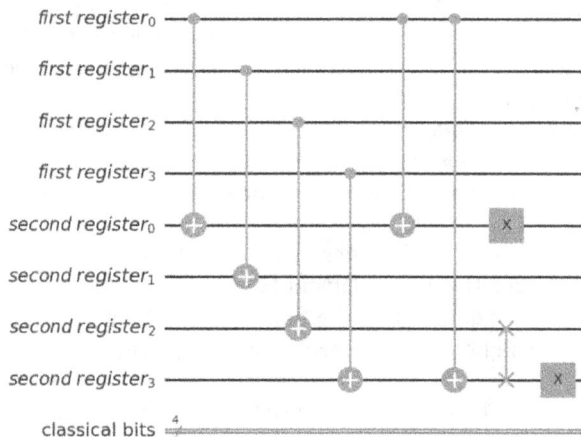

Figure 5.3 Quantum Black box(oracle) of 2-to-1 function

Components of the Circuit

Registers:

first register (Input): Consists of qubits labeled first register$_0$ to first register$_3$. These qubits store input values x to the function f and are later measured to reveal information about the hidden string.

second register (Output): Consists of qubits labeled `second register₀` to `second register₃`. These qubits are initialized to the $|0\rangle$ state and are used to hold the output $f(x)$ after the oracle transformation.

Quantum gates:

Controlled-NOT (CNOT) gates: These gates entangle qubits from the first and second registers. Each line with a dot (control) and a plus sign (target) represents a CNOT operation, mapping part of the function $f(x)$ based on Simon's oracle.

Pauli-X gates: Represented by green squares with "X", these gates flip the state of the target qubit. In the diagram, they are applied to `second register₂` and `second register₃`, encoding a constant offset in the oracle's output.

Measurements: After applying the quantum operations, the qubits in the first register are measured. The outcomes are stored as classical bits and used to extract equations that are linearly orthogonal to the hidden string s.

How the circuit works:

Initialization: The first register and second register are initialized to $|0\rangle^{\otimes 4}$.

Oracle application: The circuit implements the oracle U_f for Simon's problem. The configuration of CNOT and Pauli-X gates represents a specific function f that satisfies Simon's promise (i.e., $f(x) = f(x \oplus s)$ for a hidden s). The exact structure of the hidden string s depends on which input qubits control which output qubits.

Pauli-X gates: The Pauli-X gates introduce fixed output bits in certain positions (in this case, on the third and fourth qubits of the second register), effectively modifying the function output $f(x)$. They simulate parts of the oracle's internal logic.

Measurement: After applying Hadamard gates again (on the first register, not shown here), the qubits are measured. Each measurement provides a bitstring orthogonal to the hidden string s. Repeating the process multiple times allows recovery of s via solving a system of linear equations.

5.6   SIMON ALGORITHM IMPLEMENTATION FOR 4 BIT (TWO TO ONE)

Let's now see an example of Simon's algorithm for 4 qubits. Our secret bit string b in this case is 1001. The circuit shown in Figure 5.4 represents a complete implementation of Simon's algorithm for a 4-bit input. The algorithm is designed to determine a hidden bit string s such that for a given black-box function $f : \{0,1\}^n \rightarrow \{0,1\}^n$, the promise $f(x) = f(x \oplus s)$ holds. The circuit consists of the following six stages, labeled as ψ_1 through ψ_6:

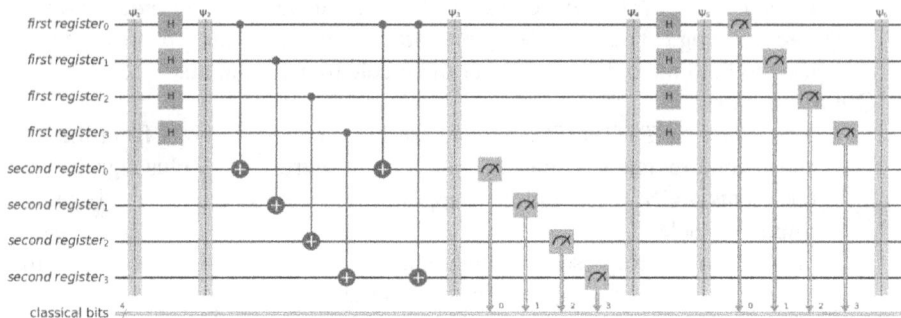

Figure 5.4   Quantum circuit of Simon's algorithm for hidden bit string "1001"

Stage ψ_1: Initialization
All qubits in the first and second registers are initialized to the state $|0\rangle$. The state of the system is:

$$|0\rangle^{\otimes n} \otimes |0\rangle^{\otimes n}$$

Stage ψ_2: Hadamard Gates on the first register
Hadamard gates (H) are applied to each qubit in the first register, creating a uniform superposition over all possible input states:

$$\frac{1}{\sqrt{2^n}} \sum_{x \in \{0,1\}^n} |x\rangle|0\rangle$$

Stage ψ_3: Oracle Query U_f
The oracle U_f maps $|x\rangle|0\rangle \rightarrow |x\rangle|f(x)\rangle$. It is implemented using CNOT gates where qubits from the first register control corresponding target qubits in the second register. The result is:

$$\frac{1}{\sqrt{2^n}} \sum_{x \in \{0,1\}^n} |x\rangle|f(x)\rangle$$

Stage ψ_4: Measurement of the Second Register
The second register is measured, collapsing it to a specific value $f(x)$. This projects the first register into a superposition of all x such that $f(x) = f(x \oplus s)$, creating a correlated quantum state between such inputs.

Stage ψ_5: Hadamard Gates on the First Register (again)
Another round of Hadamard gates is applied to the first register. This transforms the state into a superposition that encodes information orthogonal to the hidden string s. The measurement outcomes will satisfy:

$$y \cdot s = 0 \quad (\text{mod } 2)$$

where y is the output from measuring the first register.

Stage ψ_6: Measurement of the First Register

Measuring the first register gives a bit string y. Repeating the entire circuit multiple times produces several linearly independent equations of the form $y \cdot s = 0$, from which the hidden bit string s can be solved using classical post-processing via Gaussian elimination.

In Table 5.1, the all-possible inputs and the corresponding outputs are summarized.

Table 5.1

Table of inputs and corresponding outputs for $f(x)$ and $f(y)$

Inputs		Outputs $f(x)=f(y)$
x	y	
0000	1001	0000
0001	1000	0001
0010	1011	0010
0011	1010	0011
0100	1101	0100
0101	1100	0101
0110	1111	0110
0111	1110	0111

Step-by-Step procedure for determining the hidden bit string $b = 1001$

Step 1: Initialization

We begin with two 4-qubit registers initialized in the state:

$$|\psi_1\rangle = |0000\rangle \otimes |0000\rangle$$

Step 2: Applying Hadamard Gates to the first register

Hadamard gates are applied to each qubit in the first register to create a uniform superposition:

$$|\psi_2\rangle = \frac{1}{\sqrt{2^4}} \sum_{x \in \{0,1\}^4} |x\rangle \otimes |0000\rangle$$

Expanded, the state becomes:

$$|\psi_2\rangle = \frac{1}{4} (|0000\rangle + |0001\rangle + \cdots + |1111\rangle) \otimes |0000\rangle$$

Step 3: Oracle Application

The oracle maps $|x\rangle|0\rangle \rightarrow |x\rangle|f(x)\rangle$. After applying the oracle:

$$|\psi_3\rangle = \frac{1}{4}\sum_{x\in\{0,1\}^4}|x\rangle\otimes|f(x)\rangle$$

Using a pre-defined mapping (see Table 5.1), we get:

$$|\psi_3\rangle = \frac{1}{4}[|0000\rangle|0000\rangle + |0001\rangle|0001\rangle + \cdots + |1111\rangle|0110\rangle]$$

Step 4: Measurement of the second register

Measuring the second register collapses it to a value $|f(x)\rangle$. The first register is projected into an equal superposition of the two inputs x and $x\oplus b$ that map to the same output:

$$|\psi_4\rangle = \frac{1}{\sqrt{2}}(|x\rangle + |x\oplus b\rangle)$$

For example, if the outcome of the measurement is $|0110\rangle$, then:

$$|\psi_4\rangle = \frac{1}{\sqrt{2}}(|0110\rangle + |0110\oplus 1001\rangle) = \frac{1}{\sqrt{2}}(|0110\rangle + |1111\rangle)$$

Step 5: Applying Hadamard gates to the first register

We now apply Hadamard gates to each qubit of the first register:

$$|\psi_5\rangle = H^{\otimes 4}\left(\frac{1}{\sqrt{2}}(|x\rangle + |x\oplus b\rangle)\right)$$

Using the identity for the Hadamard transform on n-qubits:

$$H^{\otimes n}|x\rangle = \frac{1}{\sqrt{2^n}}\sum_{z\in\{0,1\}^n}(-1)^{x\cdot z}|z\rangle$$

We get:

$$|\psi_5\rangle = \frac{1}{\sqrt{2}}\cdot\frac{1}{\sqrt{2^n}}\sum_{z\in\{0,1\}^n}\left[(-1)^{x\cdot z} + (-1)^{(x\oplus b)\cdot z}\right]|z\rangle$$

Using the identity:

$$(x\oplus b)\cdot z = x\cdot z + b\cdot z \mod 2$$

we can write:

$$|\psi_5\rangle = \frac{1}{\sqrt{2^{n+1}}}\sum_{z\in\{0,1\}^n}(-1)^{x\cdot z}\left[1 + (-1)^{b\cdot z}\right]|z\rangle$$

Now analyze the amplitude:

$$1+(-1)^{b\cdot z} = \begin{cases} 2 & \text{if } b\cdot z = 0 \\ 0 & \text{if } b\cdot z = 1 \end{cases}$$

So the resulting state is:

$$|\psi_5\rangle = \frac{2}{\sqrt{2^{n+1}}} \sum_{\substack{z\in\{0,1\}^n \\ b\cdot z=0}} (-1)^{x\cdot z}|z\rangle$$

This means:
- Only those $z \in \{0,1\}^n$ for which $b\cdot z = 0 \mod 2$ will have non-zero amplitudes.
- Therefore, each measurement outcome z satisfies a linear equation of the form $b\cdot z = 0$.

For the specific case $x = 0110$, $b = 1001$, the output state is:

$$|\psi_5\rangle = \frac{1}{\sqrt{2^5}} (|0000\rangle - |0010\rangle - |0100\rangle + |0110\rangle + |1001\rangle - |1011\rangle - |1101\rangle + |1111\rangle)$$

Each of the output basis states (such as $|0010\rangle, |0100\rangle, |1001\rangle, \ldots$) satisfies:

$$b\cdot z = 0 \mod 2$$

Thus, after measuring the first register, we obtain a string z orthogonal to the hidden string b. Repeating this process yields enough linearly independent equations to recover b.

Step 6: Determining the Hidden Bit String

We collect the measured values of z for which $b\cdot z = 0$. Let's assume we obtain three linearly independent bit strings:

$$z_1 = 0010, \quad z_2 = 0100, \quad z_3 = 1001$$

For each z_i, we write the equation:

$$z_i^T \cdot b = 0 \quad (\text{mod } 2)$$

Writing the system as a matrix:

$$\begin{bmatrix} 0 & 0 & 1 & 0 \\ 0 & 1 & 0 & 0 \\ 1 & 0 & 0 & 1 \end{bmatrix} \begin{bmatrix} b_1 \\ b_2 \\ b_3 \\ b_4 \end{bmatrix} = \begin{bmatrix} 0 \\ 0 \\ 0 \end{bmatrix}$$

We augment with a zero row (optional, for 4x4 form), and perform row operations:

$$\Rightarrow \begin{bmatrix} 1 & 0 & 0 & 1 \\ 0 & 1 & 0 & 0 \\ 0 & 0 & 1 & 0 \\ 0 & 0 & 0 & 0 \end{bmatrix} \begin{bmatrix} b_1 \\ b_2 \\ b_3 \\ b_4 \end{bmatrix} = \begin{bmatrix} 0 \\ 0 \\ 0 \\ 0 \end{bmatrix}$$

From this system:

$$b_2 = 0$$
$$b_3 = 0$$
$$b_1 + b_4 = 0 \Rightarrow b_1 = b_4$$

Let $b_4 = 1 \Rightarrow b_1 = 1$. Thus, the hidden string is:

$$\boxed{b = 1001}$$

5.7   SIMON ALGORITHM IMPLEMENTATION FOR 4 BIT (ONE TO ONE)

Let's now see an example of Simon's algorithm for 4 qubits. Our secret bit string b in this case is 0000. The quantum circuit for this example is shown in Figure 5.5.

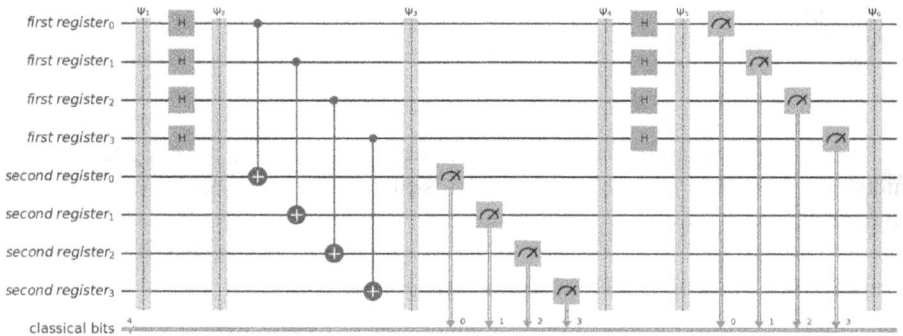

Figure 5.5   Quantum circuit of Simon's algorithm for hidden bit string "0000"

In Table 5.2, we have summarized the all-possible inputs and the corresponding outputs.

Step-by-Step procedure for determining the hidden bit string $b = 0000$

Step 1: Initialization

Two 4-qubit registers are initialized to the input state $|\psi_1\rangle = |0000\rangle|0000\rangle$.

$$|\psi_1\rangle = |0000\rangle|0000\rangle$$

Step 2: Applying Hadamard gates to the first register

Hadamard gates are applied to the first register only. The resulting state is:

Table 5.2

Corresponding outputs for all possible inputs of hidden bit string "0000"

S. No	Inputs (x)	Outputs $f(x)$
1	0000	0000
2	0001	0001
3	0010	0010
4	0011	0011
5	0100	0100
6	0101	0101
7	0110	0110
8	0111	0111
9	1000	1000
10	1001	1001
11	1010	1010
12	1011	1011
13	1100	1100
14	1101	1101
15	1110	1110
16	1111	1111

$$|\psi_2\rangle = \frac{1}{\sqrt{2^4}} \sum_{x \in \{0,1\}^4} |x\rangle |0000\rangle$$

Which expands as:

$$|\psi_2\rangle = \frac{1}{4} \left(|0000\rangle + |0001\rangle + |0010\rangle + |0100\rangle + \cdots + |1111\rangle \right) \otimes |0000\rangle$$

Step 3: Oracle application

Now this state $|\psi_2\rangle$ passes through the oracle and the resulting state is:

$$|\psi_3\rangle = \frac{1}{4} \sum_{x \in \{0,1\}^4} |x\rangle |f(x)\rangle$$

Here the oracle outputs for all possible inputs are shown in Table 5.2. The corresponding output for all possible inputs is:

$$|\psi_3\rangle = \frac{1}{4} \left[|0000\rangle |0000\rangle + |0001\rangle |0001\rangle + |0010\rangle |0010\rangle + \cdots + |1111\rangle |1111\rangle \right]$$

Step 4: Measurement of the second register

Now we measure our second register. For each measured state on the second register, there will be only one corresponding state on the first register. For example, if the second register is measured to be 0010, then:

$$|\psi_4\rangle = |0010\rangle \otimes |0010\rangle$$

After measurement, the second register is ignored, and we are left with the state:

$$|\psi_4\rangle = |0010\rangle$$

Step 5: Applying Hadamard gates to the first register

A Hadamard gate is applied to the first register and the resulting state is given by:

$$|\psi_5\rangle = \frac{1}{\sqrt{2^4}} \sum_{z \in \{0,1\}^4} (-1)^{x \cdot z} |z\rangle$$

which can also be written as:

$$|\psi_5\rangle = H^{\otimes 4}|0010\rangle$$

Step 6: Determining the hidden bit string

After applying the Hadamard gate and doing further simplifications, we get:

$$|\psi_5\rangle = \frac{1}{4}(|0000\rangle - |0001\rangle - |0010\rangle + |0011\rangle + |0100\rangle - |0101\rangle - |0110\rangle + |0111\rangle$$

$$+|1000\rangle - |1001\rangle - |1010\rangle + |1011\rangle + |1100\rangle - |1101\rangle - |1110\rangle + |1111\rangle)$$

If the function is two-to-one, we won't obtain all possible states. Therefore, since the function is one-to-one, we can conclude that the secret bit-string b is:

$$\boxed{0000}$$

5.8   PROPOSED ATTACK METHOD

5.8.1   GRAIN 128A CIPHER

In terms of cryptographic security research, the authentication encryption algorithm can realize the confidentiality and integrity verification of information at the same time, and it has been widely used in various network security systems. The authentication encryption working mode is a cryptographic scheme that encrypts messages to generate ciphertext and calculates authentication labels to solve practical problems such as privacy and authenticity of user information.

At present, a large amount of information not only needs to be kept confidential during the transmission process, but also needs to be authenticated after the receiver receives the information to ensure the confidentiality, integrity, and authenticity of the information during the transmission process [18]. Therefore, it is very necessary to design and study the authentication encryption algorithm.

The Grain 128a stream cipher was first proposed at the Symmetric Key Encryption Workshop (SKEW) in 2011 as an enhancement of its predecessor Grain-128 by Martin Ågren, Martin Hell, Thomas Johansson, and Willi Meier [19]. This improved version introduced security enhancements and an optional message authentication mechanism using the Encrypt-and-MAC approach. One of the key advantages of the Grain cipher family is its flexibility, where throughput can be significantly increased at the cost of additional hardware resources [20].

5.8.2 DESIGN DETAILS OF SIMPLIFIED GRAIN-4A CIPHER

As a simplified version of Grain 128a, we propose a reduced version, known as SGrain 4a. While its parameters are smaller, it has the same structure as Grain 128a. The cipher consists of three main building blocks, namely a Linear Feedback Shift Register (LFSR), Nonlinear Feedback Shift Register (NFSR), and an output function [1].

The LFSR bits are denoted by x_1, x_2, x_3, and x_4. Similarly, NFSR bits are denoted by y_1, y_2, y_3, and y_4. The feedback polynomial of the LFSR, denoted $f(x)$, is a primitive polynomial of degree 4. It is defined as:

$$f(x) = 1 + x + x^4$$

The nonlinear feedback polynomial of the NFSR, $g(x,y)$, is defined as:

$$g(x,y) = 1 + y_1 y_3 + y_2 y_4 + y_2 + y_4 + x_4$$

The 8 memory elements in the two shift registers represent the state of the cipher. From this state, all 8 variables are taken as input to a Boolean function, $h(x,y)$. It is defined as:

$$h(x,y) = x_1 y_1 + x_2 y_2 + x_3 y_3 + x_4 y_4$$

5.8.3 KEY AND IV INITIALIZATION

Before the keystream is generated, the cipher must be initialized with the key and the Initialization Vector (IV). The NFSR elements are loaded with the key bits. This means each bit of the key is sequentially placed into each flip-flop or register element of the NFSR, and the LFSR elements are loaded with the IV bits, filling the corresponding elements of the LFSR in the same manner. After loading the key and IV bits, the cipher is clocked 8 times without producing any keystream [1]. The output function is XORed with the y_4 input of the NFSR, and it is fed back to both the LFSR and the NFSR as shown in Figure 5.6.

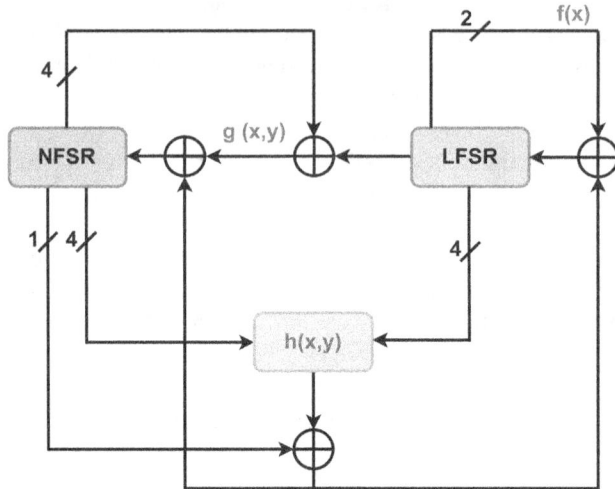

Figure 5.6 Key Initialization of SGrain 4a

5.8.4 KEYSTREAM GENERATION

Figure 5.7 illustrates the classical keystream generation architecture of the SGrain 4a stream cipher, which is composed of two main components: a NFSR and a LFSR. After the key and Initialization Vector (IV) are loaded into the NFSR and LFSR respectively, the cipher transitions into keystream generation mode. The LFSR updates its state using a linear feedback function $f(x)$, while the NFSR evolves using a nonlinear feedback function $g(x,y)$, which introduces nonlinearity by taking inputs from both the LFSR and NFSR. Furthermore, a Boolean function $h(x,y)$ combines selected bits from both registers, and the output of this function is XORed with a specific NFSR bit to produce each keystream bit. This architectural design effectively balances linear and nonlinear transformations to enhance cryptographic strength by achieving good confusion and diffusion properties. After the completion of 8 clocks in key initialization process, the 8-bit keystream bits are generated. Then the keystream is XORed with the plaintext to produce the ciphertext.

5.8.5 AUTHENTICATED TAG GENERATION

After generating the keystream bits, both the ciphertext and authentication tag are derived in a structured manner. The even-positioned bits of the keystream are XORed with the 4-bit plaintext to produce the 4-bit ciphertext. Meanwhile, the entire keystream is consecutively loaded into an 8-bit shift register. To generate the tag, the odd-positioned bits of this shift register are taken and ANDed with the 4-bit plaintext. The resulting 4-bit output serves as the authentication tag, which is then stored in the accumulator. This process, illustrated in Figure 5.8, ensures that both

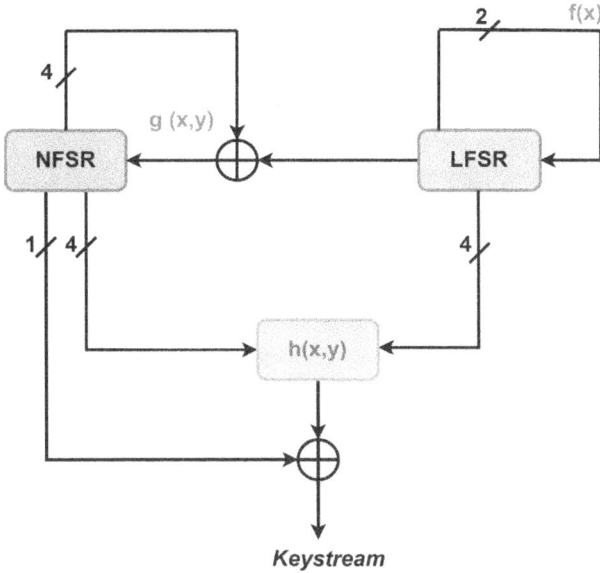

Figure 5.7   Keystream generation of SGrain 4a

the ciphertext and tag are closely tied to the internal state and plaintext, providing confidentiality and integrity.

5.8.6   SIMON ATTACK ON SGRAIN 4A

Simon's algorithm provides an efficient quantum approach to identify hidden linear structures in a function, specifically distinguishing between a one-to-one and a two-to-one function. In the context of SGrain 4a, this distinction becomes critical in evaluating its security. If the cipher's internal function behaves as a two-to-one mapping (i.e., two distinct plaintexts or internal states map to the same output tag), it indicates the presence of a hidden XOR mask or symmetry. Such behavior can be efficiently exploited by Simon's algorithm to recover the hidden period (or mask) in polynomial time, something infeasible with any known classical algorithm.

To apply Simon's algorithm, we model the SGrain 4a keystream generation or authentication tag function as a black-box oracle [24]. This requires constructing a quantum circuit representation of SGrain 4a, which takes quantum superposition inputs and returns outputs based on the cipher's logic. The quantum circuit serves as the Simon oracle, enabling the quantum algorithm to query the cipher with superpositions of input states.

By repeatedly running Simon's algorithm and analyzing the output vectors (which form a basis of the orthogonal complement of the hidden period), we can determine

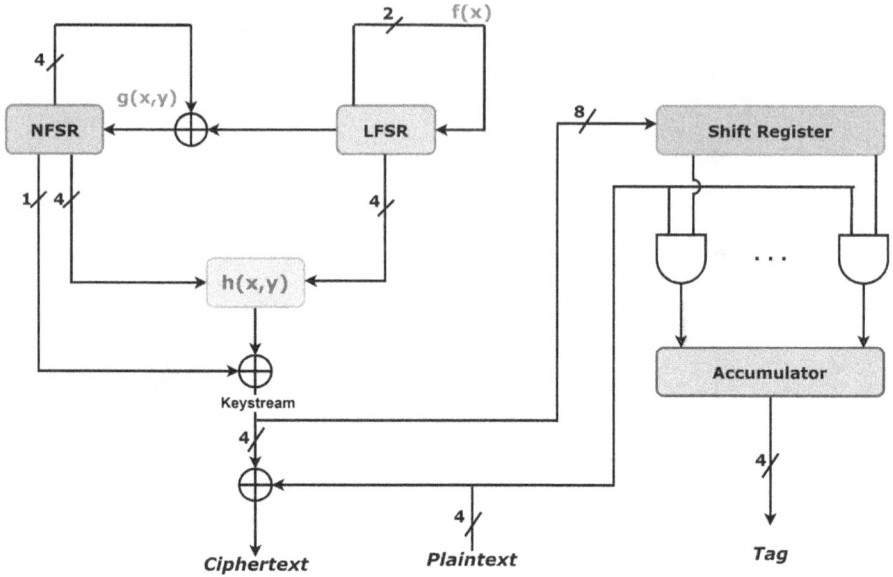

Figure 5.8 Block diagram of SGrain 4a—classical

whether a hidden XOR mask exists implying a two-to-one mapping. If such a mask is found, it suggests potential vulnerabilities in the cipher's design. Conversely, if no such structure exists, the function behaves as one-to-one, implying stronger resistance to this type of quantum attack.

5.8.6.1 Quantum Circuit Development of SGrain 4a

For the quantum circuit development of key initialization, it requires a total of 80 qubits. Four of these qubits are designated for the LFSR, denoted as "lfsr˙iv˙x". Another four qubits are allocated for the NFSR, referred to as "nfsr˙key˙y". The remaining 72 qubits are assigned as ancilla qubits or work qubits.

Step 1: Executing the Feedback Polynomial $f(x)$

The first operation is to execute the feedback polynomial $f(x) = 1 + x + x^4$ for the LFSR. To achieve this:

1. A Controlled-NOT (CNOT) gate is applied, functioning as a classical XOR gate. This gate transfers the value of the fourth bit of the LFSR (lfsr qubit 3) to the ancilla qubit 0.

2. Another CNOT gate performs an XOR operation between the LFSR's first bit (lfsr qubit 0) and the ancilla qubit 0.

This process effectively computes the feedback polynomial $f(x)$, and its result is stored in the ancilla qubit 0, as depicted in Figure 5.9.

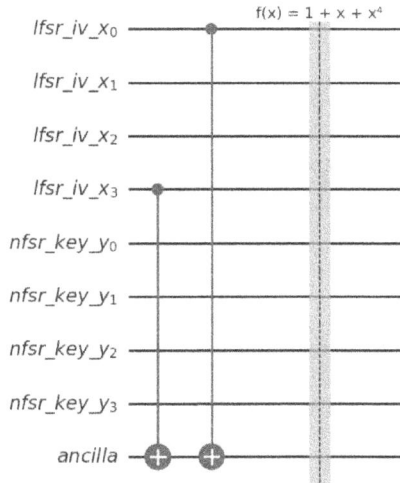

Figure 5.9   Quantum circuit development of key initialization of SGrain 4a—step 1

Step 2: Executing the Feedback Polynomial $g(x, y)$

The next operation is to execute the feedback polynomial $g(x, y) = 1 + y_1 y_3 + y_2 y_4 + y_2 + y_4 + x_4$ for the NFSR. To achieve this, we start by using a Controlled-Controlled-Not (CCNOT) gate, which acts as a classical AND gate when the target qubit is in the zero state.

The first step of $g(x, y)$ involves performing an AND operation between the fourth bit of the NFSR (NFSR qubit 3) and the second bit of the NFSR (NFSR qubit 1). This is achieved using the CCNOT gate, and the output is stored in ancilla qubit 1.

Next, we perform another AND operation, this time between the first bit of the NFSR (NFSR qubit 0) and the third bit of the NFSR (NFSR qubit 2), using another CCNOT gate. The result of this operation is stored in ancilla qubit 2. By XORing the values in ancilla qubits 1 and 2, we obtain $y_1 y_3 + y_2 y_4$, and this value is retained in ancilla qubit 2.

Continuing, we XOR the third bit of the NFSR (NFSR qubit 2) with ancilla qubit 2. This step results in $y_1 y_3 + y_2 y_4 + y_2$, and the output is saved in ancilla qubit 2. Further, we XOR the first bit of the NFSR (NFSR qubit 0) with ancilla qubit 2, yielding $y_1 y_3 + y_2 y_4 + y_2 + y_4$, and ancilla qubit 2 maintains this output.

Finally, we XOR the first bit of the LFSR (LFSR qubit 0) with ancilla qubit 2, resulting in $y_1y_3 + y_2y_4 + y_2 + y_4 + x_4$. At this point, ancilla qubit 2 holds the value of the feedback polynomial $g(x,y)$ as shown in Figure 5.10.

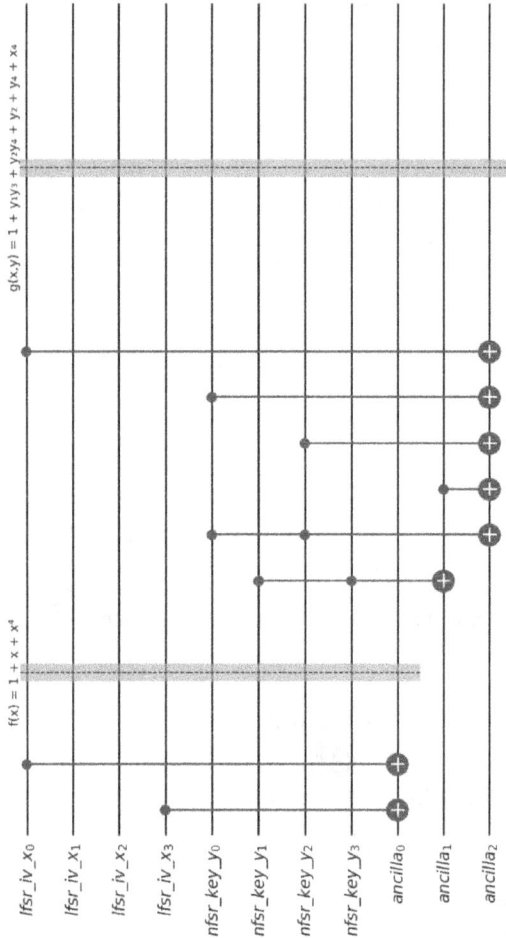

Figure 5.10 Quantum circuit development of Key initialization of SGrain 4a—step 2

Step 3: Executing the Boolean Function $h(x,y)$

In this step, we perform the execution of the Boolean function $h(x,y) = x_1y_1 + x_2y_2 + x_3y_3 + x_4y_4$. We initiate the process by utilizing a Controlled-Controlled-Not gate. This gate operates on the fourth bit of the LFSR, specifically LFSR qubit 3, and the corresponding fourth bit of the Nonlinear Feedback Shift Register (NFSR), specifically NFSR qubit 3. The outcome of this operation is then stored in the ancilla qubit 3.

Subsequently, we replicate this process for the third bit of the LFSR (LFSR qubit 2) and the third bit of the NFSR (NFSR qubit 2), with the result being stored in ancilla qubit 4. Likewise, we repeat the procedure for the second bit of the LFSR (LFSR qubit 1) and the second bit of the NFSR (NFSR qubit 1), and the output is stored in ancilla qubit 5.

This process is also applied to the first bit of the LFSR (LFSR qubit 0) and the corresponding first bit of the NFSR (NFSR qubit 0), with the result being maintained in ancilla qubit 6.

Moving forward, we perform an XOR operation between ancilla qubits 3 and 4. This results in the expression $x_1y_1 + x_2y_2$, which is preserved by ancilla qubit 4. Subsequently, we perform an XOR operation between ancilla qubits 4 and 5. This yields the expression $x_1y_1 + x_2y_2 + x_3y_3$, and the result is stored using ancilla qubit 5.

Lastly, we perform an XOR operation between ancilla qubit 5 and ancilla qubit 6. This culminates in the final form of the Boolean function $h(x,y)$, specifically:

$$h(x,y) = x_1y_1 + x_2y_2 + x_3y_3 + x_4y_4$$

and the output is maintained by ancilla qubit 6 as shown in Figure 5.11.

Step 4: XORing the Fourth Bit of NFSR with the Boolean Function $h(x,y)$

In this step, we perform an XOR operation between the first bit of the NFSR, specifically NFSR qubit 0, and ancilla qubit 6 that holds the output of the Boolean function $h(x,y)$. This operation yields the first key bit of our keystream, which is then retained by ancilla qubit 6 as shown in Figure 5.12.

Step 5: XORing the Keystream Bit with $f(x)$ and $g(x,y)$

In this step, an XOR operation is executed between ancilla qubit 6, which contains the first bit of the keystream, and ancilla qubit 0 (i.e., ancilla qubit 0 holds the feedback polynomial $f(x)$). As a result, ancilla qubit 0 now holds the conclusive feedback state for the LFSR.

In a similar manner, we conduct another XOR operation. This time, the operation takes place between ancilla qubit 6 and ancilla qubit 2 (i.e., ancilla qubit 2 holds the feedback polynomial $g(x,y)$). The outcome of this operation is once again saved in ancilla qubit 2, denoting the ultimate feedback for the NFSR, as shown in Figure 5.13.

Step 6: Shifting the Bits of LFSR and NFSR and Providing Feedback to These Shift Registers

In this step, we perform the shift operation on both the LFSR and the NFSR. The shifting process involves the use of three SWAP gates for each shift register.

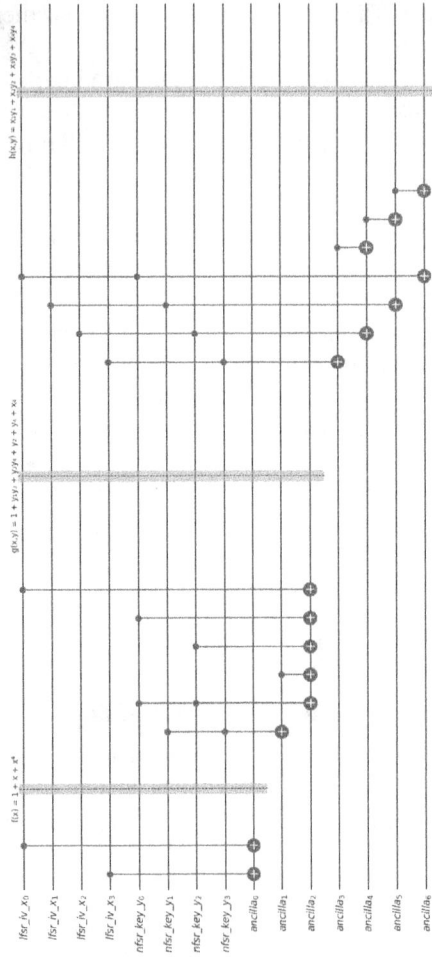

Figure 5.11   Quantum circuit development of key initialization of SGrain 4a—step 3

However, when using SWAP gates, the last bit ends up in the first bit position. To ensure the correct feedback mechanism, the first bit needs to be initialized to zero. This is achieved using two additional ancilla qubits. The states of these ancilla qubits are swapped to the first bit position of both the LFSR and NFSR, ensuring the first bit is set to zero.

After the initialization, feedback is provided to both the LFSR and NFSR by using one CNOT gate for each shift register. This completes the bit shifting and feedback process for key initialization, as depicted in Figure 5.14.

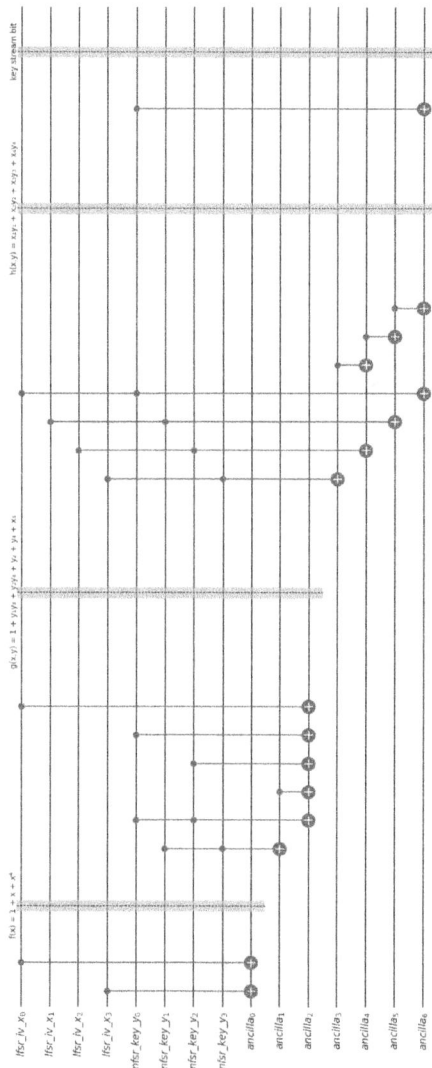

Figure 5.12 Quantum circuit development of key initialization of SGrain 4a—step 4

Ancilla Qubits Management

Since the once-used ancilla qubits are in specific states and cannot be reused for the next cycle, a new set of 9 ancilla qubits is allocated for each subsequent clock cycle. In total, 8 clock cycles are involved in the key initialization process.

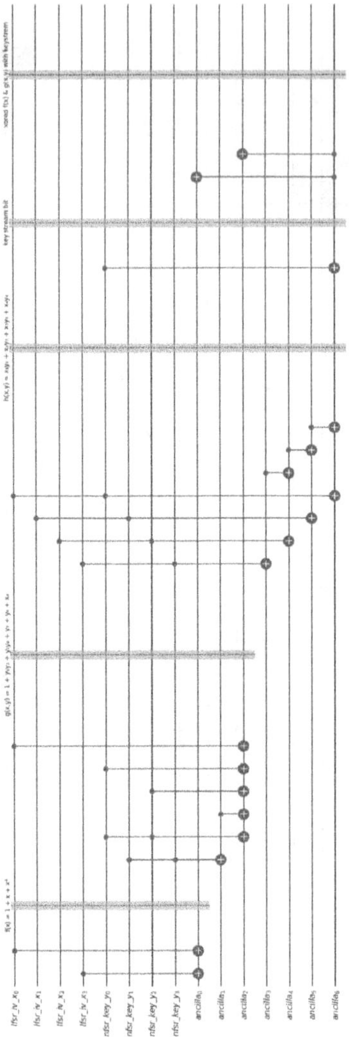

Figure 5.13   Quantum circuit development of key initialization of SGrain 4a—step 5

Keystream Generation

In the Keystream Generation process, the entire procedure is essentially the same as that executed in the Key Initialization process. The only difference is that we do not perform XOR operations with the keystream bit and the functions $f(x)$ and $g(x,y)$. In total, there are 8 clock cycles in the Keystream Generation process, resulting in an 8-bit keystream. Ancilla qubits 6, 15, 24, 33, 42, 51, 60, and 69 hold the 8-bit keystream. The quantum circuit of keystream generation for one clock is shown in Figure 5.15.

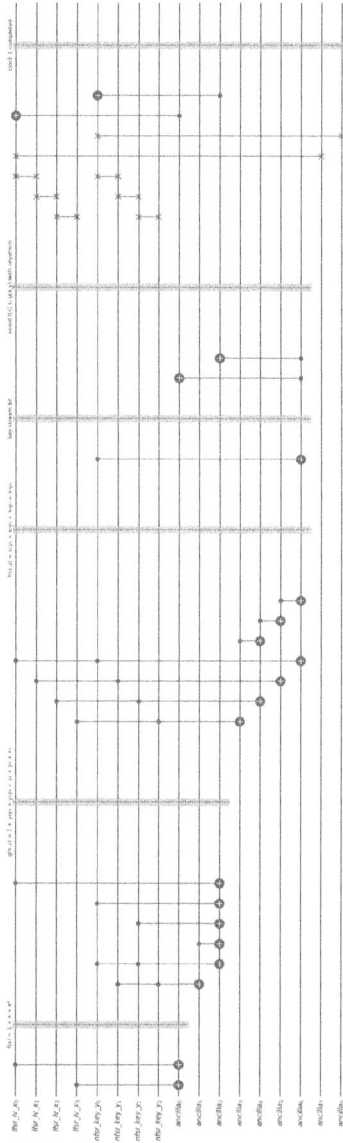

Figure 5.14 Quantum circuit of key initialization of SGrain 4a

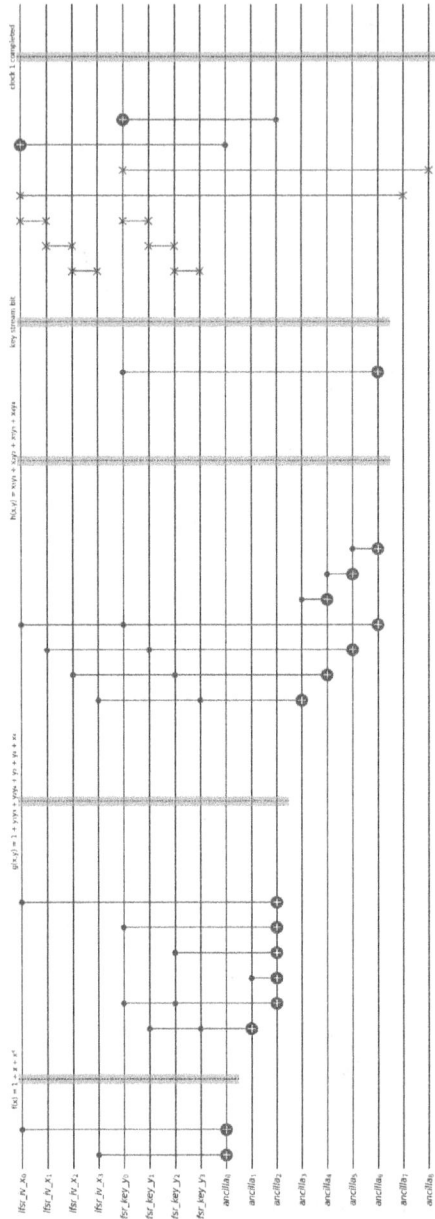

Figure 5.15　Quantum circuit of keystream generation of Grain 4a

Simplified Grain-4a Cipher

We use subcircuits, such as key initialization and keystream generation, as building blocks to construct a simplified Grain-4a cipher. It requires a total of 164 qubits, allocated as follows:

Four qubits allocated for the LFSR,
Four qubits allocated for the NFSR,
72 qubits for implementing key initialization as ancilla,
Another 72 qubits for implementing keystream generation as ancilla,
Four qubits for plaintext,
Four qubits for storing ciphertext,
Four qubits for storing the tag.

First, we load the inputs such as the initialization vector (IV), key, and plaintext into their respective qubits. Afterwards, we apply the key initialization circuit to the qubits representing IV, key, and ancilla for key initialization. Then, we apply the keystream generation circuit to the IV, key, and ancilla for keystream generation.

Generating Ciphertext and Tag

1. **Ciphertext Generation:** Even bits of the keystream are XORed with the 4-bit plaintext to produce the 4-bit ciphertext. The result is stored in the first four ancilla qubits.
2. **Tag Generation:** An AND operation is performed between the odd bits of the keystream and the 4-bit plaintext. This produces the 4-bit tag, which is stored in the second set of four ancilla qubits.

The block diagram for such a quantum circuit is shown in Figure 5.16.

5.8.7 QUANTUM CIRCUIT DEVELOPMENT OF SIMON ATTACK ON GRAIN-4A

It requires a total of 160 qubits, with four allocated for plaintext, four allocated for the tag, and the remaining 152 qubits assigned as ancilla. First, we apply Hadamard on the plaintext qubits to obtain all possible combinations of 4-bit plaintext. Then, we apply Grain-4a on the plaintext, ancilla, and tag qubits. Afterward, we measure the tag qubits. Following this, we apply Hadamard again on the plaintext qubits, and finally, we measure the plaintext qubits. These are the steps implemented in the Simon attack circuit as shown in Figure 5.17. we omit the generating ciphertext part of Grain-4a.

5.8.8 SIMON ATTACK ON SGRAIN 4A ALGORITHM STEPS

The Simon attack on a symmetric encryption system like Grain-4a focuses on analyzing weaknesses in stream ciphers, particularly how the key and state influence outputs.

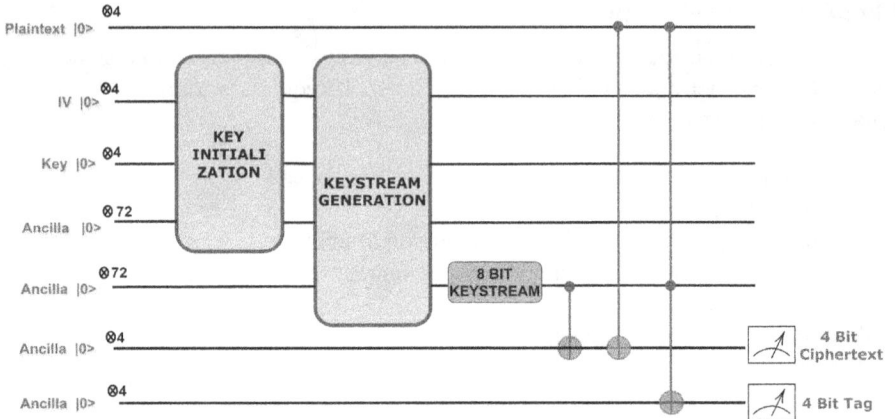

Figure 5.16 Block diagram of SGrain 4a quantum circuit

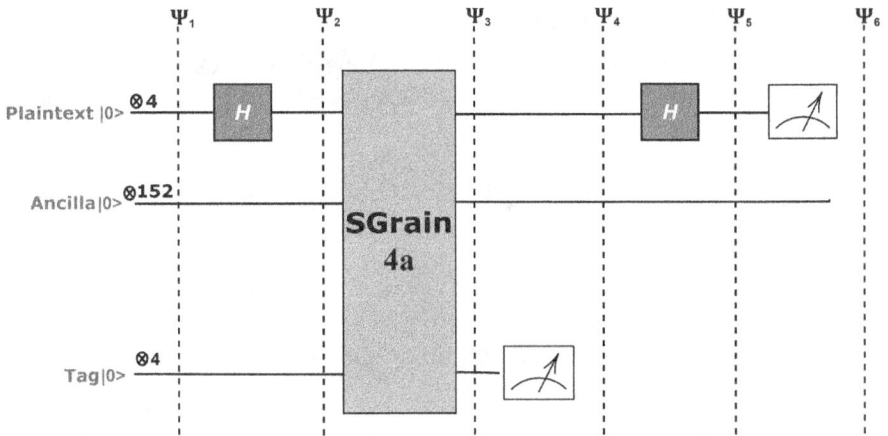

Figure 5.17 Block diagram of Simon attack on SGrain-4a Quantum circuit

Step 1: Three sets of input registers are initialized to the zero state with different counts.

$$|\psi_1\rangle = |0\rangle^{\otimes 4}|0\rangle^{\otimes 152}|0\rangle^{\otimes 4}$$

Step 2: Apply Hadamard to the first register:

$$|\psi_2\rangle = \frac{1}{\sqrt{2^4}} \sum_{p\in\{0,1\}^4} |p\rangle|0\rangle^{\otimes 152}|0\rangle^{\otimes 4}$$

We consider the first register as the plaintext.

Step 3: Apply the Grain-4a to the state $|\psi_2\rangle$, we get the following state as a result:

$$|\psi_3\rangle = \frac{1}{4} \sum_{p \in \{0,1\}^4} |p\rangle |\text{garbage}\rangle^{\otimes 152} |f(p)\rangle$$

We consider the third register as the output of Grain-4a, which is the tag generated by using all the possible plaintexts.

Step 4: Measure the third register. A certain value of $f(p)$ will be observed.

If the Grain-4a function is One-to-One:
The observed value $f(p)$ could correspond to one possible input assumed as p. Therefore, the first register becomes:

$$|\psi_4\rangle = |p\rangle$$

If the Grain-4a function is Two-to-One:
The observed value $f(p)$ could correspond to two possible input states assumed as p and $q = p \oplus b$, where b is the hidden bit string of Grain-4a. Therefore, the first register becomes:

$$|\psi_4\rangle = \frac{1}{\sqrt{2}}(|p\rangle + |q\rangle)$$

where we omitted the third register since it has been measured, and also the second register since it contains garbage values.

Step 5: Apply Hadamard on the first register:

If the function is One-to-One:

$$|\psi_5\rangle = \frac{1}{\sqrt{2^4}} \sum_{z \in \{0,1\}^4} (-1)^{p \cdot z} |z\rangle$$

If the function is Two-to-One:

$$|\psi_5\rangle = \frac{1}{\sqrt{2^{4+1}}} \sum_{z \in \{0,1\}^4} [(-1)^{p \cdot z} + (-1)^{q \cdot z}] |z\rangle$$

$$|\psi_5\rangle = \frac{1}{\sqrt{2^{4+1}}} \sum_{z \in \{0,1\}^4} [(-1)^{p \cdot z} + (-1)^{(p \oplus b) \cdot z}] |z\rangle$$

Step 6: Measure the first register.

If the function is One-to-One, measurements return a random bit string z uniformly chosen from $\{0,1\}^4$.

If the function is Two-to-One, measurements return a random bit string z such that:

$$(-1)^{p \cdot z} = (-1)^{q \cdot z}$$

Which means:

$$p \cdot z = q \cdot z$$
$$p \cdot z = (p \oplus b) \cdot z$$
$$p \cdot z = p \cdot z \oplus b \cdot z$$
$$b \cdot z = 0 \quad \mod 2$$

A string z will be measured, whose inner product with $b = 0$. Thus, repeating the algorithm approximately n times, we will obtain n different values of z, and the following system of equations can be written:

$$\begin{cases} b \cdot z_1 = 0 \\ b \cdot z_2 = 0 \\ \vdots \\ b \cdot z_n = 0 \end{cases}$$

From which b can be determined by Gaussian elimination. If we get the bit string 0000 from Gaussian elimination, we conclude that the Grain-4a is One-to-One. If we get a string other than 0000, we conclude that the SGrain 4a is Two-to-One.

5.9   EXPERIMENTAL RESULTS

We conducted these attacks using own custom-built simulator, which is based on the Qiskit Matrix Product State (MPS) simulator., A tensor-network simulator that uses a MPS representation for states.

We have summarized the test cases and the outputs for both SGrain 4a and Simon attack on SGrain 4a. The following implementations are implemented on a system with the following specifications shown in Table 4.1.

Firstly, we give the specified IV and key to the SGrain 4a, which generates the keystream, tag, and ciphertext as outputs. Odd bits of the keystream are used to generate the tag by performing an AND operation with the plaintext. Even bits of the keystream are used to generate the ciphertext by performing an XOR operation with the plaintext. We apply a Simon attack on this SGrain 4a and got set of states as outputs. From those states, we obtain the hidden bit string using Gaussian elimination. With the hidden bit string, we conclude whether the function is one-to-one or two-to-one.

The experimental implementation of the Simon attack, including the quantum circuit design and simulation scripts, is publicly available at the following GitHub repository: github.com/mohanyaso/Simon.git. This repository contains the Qiskit-based code used for generating the histograms, executing quantum simulations on the MPS backend, and performing Gaussian elimination to extract hidden bit strings.

Table 5.3
Test case 1

Sl. No.	Plaintext	Tag	Ciphertext	Simon Attack Output {'state': probability}	Hidden Bit String
1	0000	0000	1101		
2	0001	0001	1100		
3	0010	0000	1111		
4	0011	0001	1110		
5	0100	0100	1001	{'0011': 128,	
6	0101	0101	1000	'1000': 138,	
7	0110	0100	1011	'1001': 123,	
8	0111	0101	1010	'1011': 115,	
9	1000	1000	0101	'1010': 135,	0010
10	1001	1001	0100	'0001': 118,	
11	1010	1000	0111	'0000': 141,	
12	1011	1001	0110	'0010': 126}	
13	1100	1100	0001		
14	1101	1101	0000		
15	1110	1100	0011		
16	1111	1101	0010		

5.9.1 TEST CASE 1

In Test Case 1, the cipher SGrain 4a is initialized with the IV "0100" and key "1111", resulting in the 8-bit keystream "11110011". This keystream is divided into odd bits ("1101") and even bits ("1101") for further processing. As shown in Table 5.3, each possible 4-bit plaintext (from 0000 to 1111) is encrypted using the even bits of the keystream through XOR, producing the corresponding ciphertexts.

Simultaneously, the tags are generated by performing a bitwise AND operation between the plaintext and the odd keystream bits. These ciphertext-tag pairs reflect the deterministic output behavior of SGrain-4a under a fixed key-IV setup. To analyze the cryptographic structure, a Simon attack is conducted using a custom-built simulator based on Qiskit's MPS backend. The resulting quantum measurement outputs are tabulated, showing the frequency of each observed 4-bit state. From these results, Gaussian elimination is applied to extract the hidden period or bit string, which is found to be "0010". The measurement frequencies are further visualized in Figure 5.18, a histogram that illustrates the distribution of outcomes and supports the successful execution of the Simon attack.

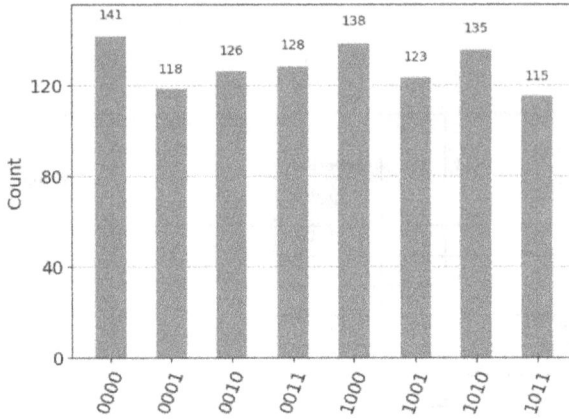

Figure 5.18 Histogram output of Simon attack—Test case 1

5.9.2 TEST CASE 2

In Test Case 2, the cipher SGrain 4a is initialized with the IV "0101" and key "1110", resulting in the 8-bit keystream "11101000". This keystream is split into odd bits ("1110") and even bits ("1000") for further processing. As shown in Table 5.4, each possible 4-bit plaintext (from 0000 to 1111) is encrypted using the even bits of the keystream through XOR, yielding the corresponding ciphertexts. In parallel, the tags are computed by applying a bitwise AND operation between the plaintext and the odd keystream bits. These ciphertext-tag pairs represent the consistent behavior of SGrain-4a under the specified key and IV. To further analyze its structure, a Simon attack is executed using a custom-built simulator based on Qiskit's MPS backend. The simulator collects quantum measurement outputs, which are then recorded along with their respective frequencies. Using Gaussian elimination, the hidden bit string is determined to be "0001", indicating a period in the cipher's behavior. These outcomes are graphically depicted in Figure 5.19, where a histogram shows the frequency distribution of the quantum states, supporting the validity and effectiveness of the Simon attack.

5.9.3 TEST CASE 3

In Test Case 3, the cipher SGrain 4a is initialized with the IV "1000" and key "0001", resulting in the 8-bit keystream "11110011". This keystream is divided into odd bits ("1101") and even bits ("1101") for subsequent processing. As detailed in Table 5.5, each 4-bit plaintext value (ranging from 0000 to 1111) is encrypted using the even keystream bits via XOR to produce the corresponding ciphertexts. Simultaneously, the tags are generated by applying a bitwise AND operation between the plaintext and the odd bits of the keystream. These resulting ciphertext-tag pairs demonstrate the deterministic nature of the cipher under the fixed IV and key inputs. A Simon

Table 5.4

Test case 2

Sl. No.	Plaintext	Tag	Ciphertext	Simon Attack Output {'state': probability}	Hidden Bit String
1	0000	0000	1000		
2	0001	0000	1001		
3	0010	0010	1010		
4	0011	0010	1011		
5	0100	0100	1100	{'0111': 109,	
6	0101	0100	1101	'0011': 142,	
7	0110	0110	1110	'0001': 141,	
8	0111	0110	1111	'0100': 115,	0001
9	1000	1000	0000	'0110': 121,	
10	1001	1000	0001	'0010': 126,	
11	1010	1010	0010	'0000': 123,	
12	1011	1010	0011	'0101': 147}	
13	1100	1100	0100		
14	1101	1100	0101		
15	1110	1110	0110		
16	1111	1110	0111		

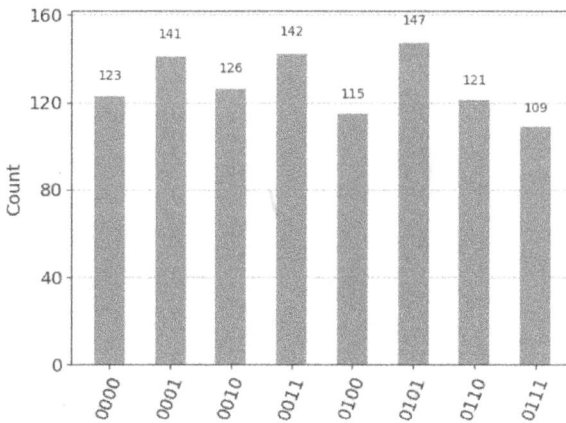

Figure 5.19   Histogram output of Simon attack—Test case 2

attack is then performed using a custom-designed simulator built on Qiskit's MPS backend. The quantum outputs from this simulation are collected and analyzed, with frequencies of each measured state documented. Applying Gaussian elimination on

Table 5.5

Test case 3

Sl. No.	Plaintext	Tag	Ciphertext	Simon Attack Output {'state': probability}	Hidden Bit String
1	0000	0000	1101		
2	0001	0001	1100		
3	0010	0000	1111		
4	0011	0001	1110	{'1001': 124,	
5	0100	0100	1001	'1011': 124,	
6	0101	0101	1000	'1010': 123,	
7	0110	0100	1011	'0010': 128,	
8	0111	0101	1010	'0000': 136,	
9	1000	1000	0101	'0011': 124,	0010
10	1001	1001	0100	'1000': 122,	
11	1010	1000	0111	'0001': 143}	
12	1011	1001	0110		
13	1100	1100	0001		
14	1101	1101	0000		
15	1110	1100	0011		
16	1111	1101	0010		

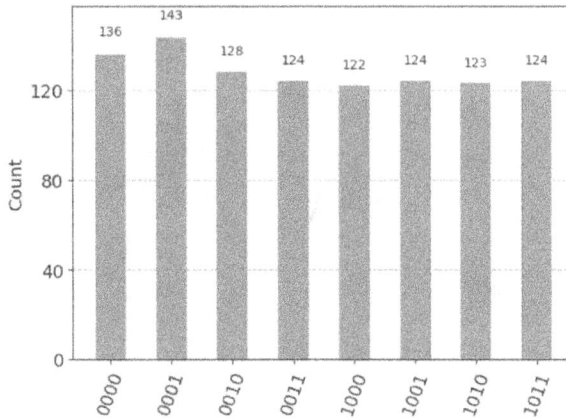

Figure 5.20   Histogram output of Simon attack—Test case 3

these results reveals the hidden bit string "0010". The corresponding histogram in Figure 5.20 visualizes the frequency distribution of the quantum states and reinforces the correctness of the Simon attack execution.

5.10   QUANTUM RESOURCE ESTIMATION

In order to assess the practicality of executing quantum cryptanalysis on near-term quantum devices, a comprehensive quantum resource estimation has been carried out. The evaluation focuses on both the implementation of a SGrain 4a stream cipher and the corresponding Simon's algorithm-based quantum attack. All simulations and circuit optimizations were performed using the Qiskit MPS simulator [21, 22]. The MPS backend was selected for its efficiency in handling quantum circuits with limited entanglement, making it especially suitable for simulating algorithms like Simon's, which primarily involve a hidden structure rather than deep quantum correlations.

5.10.1   GATE DECOMPOSITION AND OPTIMIZATION

Swap Gate Decomposition

As shown in Figure 5.21, a SWAP gate [25], which exchanges the states of two qubits, is implemented using three consecutive CNOT gates. This gate decomposition is standard in quantum computing, as it simplifies hardware requirements and ensures compatibility with architectures that support only nearest-neighbor interactions. Each SWAP gate used in the cipher or attack circuit is therefore mapped to three CNOT gates, which are part of the Clifford group.

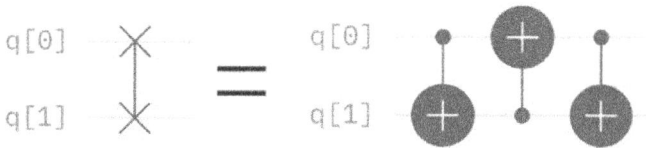

Figure 5.21   Swap gate decomposition

Toffoli (CCNOT) Gate Decomposition

Figure 5.22 illustrates the breakdown of the Toffoli gate, a crucial three-qubit gate used to implement classical logic in quantum circuits into elementary single and two qubit gates. In our decomposition strategy, each Toffoli gate is replaced by 6 T gates, 8 Clifford gates, a T-depth of 4, and a full circuit depth of 11. These parameters follow the decomposition guidelines described in [23]. The T and $T^\dagger$ gates (T inverse) are collectively counted as T gates for estimating fault-tolerant quantum costs. Notably, the initialization related NOT gates controlled by the Initialization Vector (IV) and Key are excluded from the cost model, as they do not contribute to the complexity of reversible computation or entanglement.

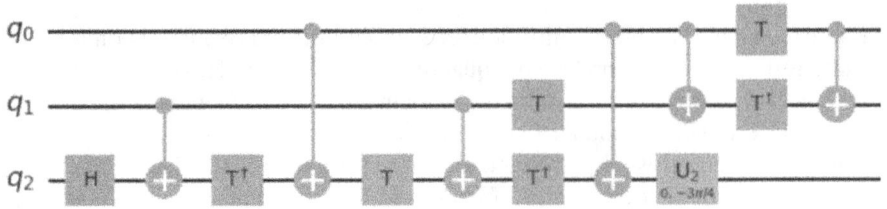

Figure 5.22   Toffoli gate decomposition

5.10.2   QUANTUM RESOURCE COST ANALYSIS

SGrain 4a Implementation

Table 5.6 summarizes the quantum resource requirements for implementing the SGrain 4a cipher. This includes 1,404 Clifford gates, 600 T gates, and a T-depth of 400. The full circuit depth which includes Clifford and non-Clifford gates is 667. A total of 164 qubits are needed to represent the various internal states of the cipher, including the LFSR, NFSR, IV, key, and intermediate ancilla qubits. This resource estimation provides a baseline understanding of the cipher's quantum footprint and forms the foundation for comparing it with quantum attack costs.

Table 5.6

Quantum resource cost for SGrain 4a cipher

Clifford gates	T gates	T-depth	Full depth	Qubits
1404	600	400	667	164

Simon's Attack on SGrain 4a

Table 5.7 presents the resource estimation for the Simon attack on the simplified cipher. The quantum circuit designed to extract the hidden bit string using Simon's algorithm comprises 1,400 Clifford gates, 600 T gates, and has the same T-depth of 400 as the cipher implementation. The full depth is slightly higher at 669, due to the additional post-processing steps needed to implement the oracle and compute the period of the hidden function. The number of qubits required is 160, slightly fewer than in the cipher model, as the structure of the oracle allows for reuse of ancilla and omits some state-preserving steps.

Table 5.7

Quantum resource cost of Simon attack on SGrain 4a

Clifford gates	T gates	T-depth	Full depth	Qubits
1400	600	400	669	160

5.11 CONCLUSION

This study explores the quantum cryptanalysis of the SGrain 4a stream cipher using Simon's algorithm. The entire experiment was conducted in two distinct phases. In the first phase, a Grover-based search was utilized to recover the secret key by iterating over possible inputs given a known plaintext, IV, and ciphertext. This demonstrated how Grover's algorithm can reduce brute-force key search complexity from $O(2^n)$ to $O(2^{n/2})$ for n-bit keys.

In the second phase, Simon's algorithm was applied to exploit structural periodicities within the cipher. The quantum circuit designed for this purpose produced a superposition of results that encode the hidden bit string. By conducting multiple quantum measurements and applying Gaussian elimination in the classical postprocessing phase, we successfully determined the hidden string.

Furthermore, detailed quantum resource estimates were provided for both the cipher and the Simon attack implementation. These estimates include the number of Clifford and T gates, T-depth, full depth, and qubit count. The results indicate that the simplified cipher and its quantum attack are feasible for simulation and potentially for execution on mid-scale fault-tolerant quantum computers. The minimal difference in resource usage between cipher construction and the Simon attack highlights the algorithm's power and its potential implications for stream cipher security in the post-quantum era.

Simon's algorithm stands out as an efficient quantum tool for solving hidden subgroup problems and has proven to offer exponential speedups over classical counterparts. The demonstrated quantum advantage underscores the urgent need for designing cryptographic primitives that are secure against both classical and quantum adversaries. As quantum hardware continues to evolve, such attacks may soon transition from theoretical models to practical threats.

REFERENCES

1. D. R. Simon, "On the power of quantum computation," *Proceedings 35th Annual Symposium on Foundations of Computer Science*, 1994, doi: 10.1109/sfcs.1994.365701.
2. B. M. Zhou and Z. Yuan, "Breaking symmetric cryptosystems using the offline distributed Grover-meets-Simon algorithm," *Quantum Information Processing*, vol. 22, no. 9, Sep. 2023, doi: 10.1007/s11128-023-04089-9.
3. F. Canale, G. Leander, and L. Stennes, "Simon's algorithm and symmetric crypto: generalizations and automatized applications," *Lecture Notes in Computer Science*, pp. 779–808, 2022, doi: 10.1007/978-3-031-15982-4˙26.

4. T. Santoli and C. Schaffner, "Using Simon's algorithm to attack symmetric key cryptographic primitives," *Quantum Information and Computation*, vol. 17, no. 1 & 2, pp. 65–78, Jan. 2017, doi: 10.26421/qic17.1-2-4.

5. P. Zhang, "Quantum related-key attack based on Simon's algorithm and its applications," *Symmetry*, vol. 15, no. 5, p. 972, Apr. 2023, doi: 10.3390/sym15050972.

6. H. Kuwakado and M. Morii, "Quantum distinguisher between the 3-round Feistel cipher and the random permutation," *2010 IEEE International Symposium on Information Theory*, Jun. 2010, doi: 10.1109/isit.2010.5513654.

7. H. Kuwakado and M. Morii, "Security on the quantum-type Even-Mansour cipher," *2012 International Symposium on Information Theory and Its Applications*. Honolulu, HI, USA, 2012, pp. 312–316.

8. A. Hosoyamada and K. Aoki, "On quantum related-key attacks on iterated Even-Mansour ciphers," *IEICE Transactions on Fundamentals of Electronics, Communications and Computer Sciences*, vol. E102.A, no. 1, pp. 27–34, Jan. 2019, doi: 10.1587/transfun.e102.a.27.

9. P. Zhang and Y. Luo, "Quantum key recovery attacks on tweakable Even–Mansour ciphers," *Quantum Information Processing*, vol. 22, no. 9, Sep. 2023, doi: 10.1007/s11128-023-04098-8.

10. X. Bonnetain, A. Schrottenloher, and F. Sibleyras, "Beyond quadratic speedups in quantum attacks on symmetric schemes," *Lecture Notes in Computer Science*, pp. 315–344, 2022, doi: 10.1007/978-3-031-07082-2˙12.

11. M. Kaplan, G. Leurent, A. Leverrier, and M. Naya-Plasencia, "Breaking symmetric cryptosystems using quantum period finding," *Lecture Notes in Computer Science*, pp. 207–237, 2016, doi: 10.1007/978-3-662-53008-5˙8.

12. M. V. Anand, E. E. Targhi, G. N. Tabia, and D. Unruh, "Post-quantum security of the CBC, CFB, OFB, CTR, and XTS modes of operation," *Lecture Notes in Computer Science*, pp. 44–63, 2016, doi: 10.1007/978-3-319-29360-8˙4.

13. G. Brassard, P. Høyer, and A. Tapp, "Quantum algorithm for the collision problem," *Encyclopedia of Algorithms*, pp. 1662–1664, 2016, doi: 10.1007/978-1-4939-2864-4˙304.

14. W. Liu, M. Wang, and Z. Li, "Quantum forgery attacks against OTR structures based on Simon's algorithm," *Modern Physics Letters A*, vol. 38, no. 18n19, Jun. 2023, doi: 10.1142/s021773232350092x.

15. S. Even and Y. Mansour, "A construction of a cipher from a single pseudorandom permutation," *Journal of Cryptology*, vol. 10, no. 3, pp. 151–161, Jun. 1997, doi: 10.1007/s001459900025.

16. E. Marsola do Nascimento and J. A. Moreira Xexeo, "A flexible authenticated lightweight cipher using Even-Mansour construction," *2017 IEEE International Conference on Communications (ICC)*, May 2017, doi: 10.1109/icc.2017.7996734.

17. P. Zhang and Q. Yuan, "Minimizing key materials: The Even–Mansour cipher revisited and its application to lightweight authenticated encryption," *Security and Communication Networks*, vol. 2020, pp. 1–6, Mar. 2020, doi: 10.1155/2020/4180139.

18. W. Liu, M. Wang, and Z. Li, "Quantum forgery attacks against OTR structures based on Simon's algorithm," *Modern Physics Letters A*, vol. 38, no. 18n19, Jun. 2023, doi: 10.1142/s021773232350092x.

19. M. Ågren, M. Hell, T. Johansson, and W. Meier, "Grain-128a: A new version of Grain-128 with optional authentication," *IACR Cryptology ePrint Archive*, Report 2011/600, 2011. Available: https://eprint.iacr.org/2011/600.

20. M. Hell, T. Johansson, and W. Meier, "Grain: A stream cipher for constrained environments," in *Selected Areas in Cryptography*, LNCS 3897, pp. 204–222, Springer, 2005.

21. Qiskit Community, *Qiskit Aer: Matrix Product State (MPS) Simulator Backend*, Qiskit Documentation, 2020. Available at: `https://qiskit.org/documentation/apidoc/aer_simulator.html#matrix-product-state-method`. Accessed: 2025-05-13.

22. T. Imamichi and S. Wörner, Matrix product state simulation of quantum circuits in Qiskit, in *Proceedings of the IEEE International Conference on Quantum Computing and Engineering (QCE)*, pp. 140–150, 2020. DOI: 10.1109/QCE49297.2020.00025.

23. R. Anand, A. Maitra, and S. Mukhopadhyay, "Grover on SIMON," *Quantum Information Processing*, vol. 19, no. 9, Sep. 2020, doi: 10.1007/s11128-020-02844-w.

24. J. Cui, J. Guo, and S. Ding, "Applications of Simon's algorithm in quantum attacks on Feistel variants," *Quantum Information Processing*, vol. 20, no. 3, Mar. 2021, doi: 10.1007/s11128-021-03027-x.

25. J. C. Garcia-Escartin and P. Chamorro-Posada, "A SWAP gate for qudits," *Quantum Information Processing*, vol. 12, no. 12, pp. 3625–3631, Aug. 2013, doi: 10.1007/s11128-013-0621-x.

Section VI

Cryptographic Implications of Quantum Computing

6 Cryptographic Implications of Quantum Computing

> "Quantum computing is not just a challenge for cryptography; it is a catalyst for the evolution of security."
>
> — Eleanor Rieffel

SUMMARY

The chapter explores the significant impact quantum computing will have on modern cryptographic systems. Cryptography is essential for maintaining confidentiality, integrity, and authenticity in digital communications, safeguarding critical infrastructure, and building trust in the digital economy. As quantum computing advances, traditional cryptographic systems will face new challenges. The chapter examines Shor's algorithm, which poses a major threat to Rivest-Shamir-Adleman (RSA) and Elliptic Curve Cryptography (ECC) by enabling quantum computers to efficiently solve the prime factorization and discrete logarithm problems, breaking these widely used public key cryptosystems. The potential of Grover's algorithm is also discussed, highlighting its ability to speed up brute-force attacks on symmetric encryption systems like AES, halving the security of traditional symmetric-key algorithms.

To mitigate these threats, the chapter suggests adopting AES-256 or longer key lengths, which are more resistant to quantum attacks, and recommends shifting to quantum-resistant algorithms for both symmetric and asymmetric encryption. However, practical considerations, such as increased computational overhead and the challenges of transitioning to new systems, are also explored. The vulnerabilities of classical cryptographic systems particularly public-key methods like RSA and ECC, and symmetric key algorithms like AES and DES are examined in light of the capabilities of quantum computers. As quantum computing progresses, it is crucial for organizations and governments to adapt and adopt post-quantum cryptography (PQC) to ensure data security in the quantum era. The chapter emphasizes the need for a proactive approach to protect sensitive information against the emerging quantum threats.

INTRODUCTION

Quantum computing has become a prominent topic in both theoretical and applied fields, significantly impacting modern cryptography. Quantum computing poses

DOI: 10.1201/9781003606338-6

significant implications for modern cryptography, particularly for asymmetric encryption schemes like RSA, ECC, and Diffie-Hellman, which rely on the computational difficulty of problems like integer factorization and discrete logarithms. Quantum algorithms, such as Shor's algorithm [1], could solve these problems exponentially faster than classical computers, rendering these encryption methods insecure.
Symmetric key encryption schemes, like AES, are less affected but would still require longer key lengths to maintain security, as Grover's algorithm [2] can reduce
the effective key search space. To address these challenges, the field of PQC is developing quantum-resistant algorithms based on hard mathematical problems, such
as lattice-based, code-based, and hash-based cryptographic approaches, which are
believed to remain secure against both classical and quantum attacks. The transition to quantum systems is complex and urgent, as encrypted data intercepted today
could be decrypted in the future when cryptographically relevant languages become
operational.

The most immediate implication is the vulnerability of asymmetric cryptographic
Quantum computing poses a profound threat to traditional cryptographic systems
due to its ability to perform certain calculations exponentially faster than classical
computers. However, algorithms specifically designed for quantum computers, such
as Shor's algorithm, can solve these problems in polynomial time, rendering these
encryption and digital signature systems effectively obsolete. The potential of quantum computing thus necessitates the reevaluation of current cryptographic practices
to ensure future-proof security.

The most immediate implication is the vulnerability of asymmetric cryptographic
systems that rely on public-key infrastructures (PKIs). RSA, for example, depends
on the difficulty of factoring large integers, a task infeasible for classical computers
given current computational limits. A sufficiently powerful quantum computer using
Shor's algorithm, however, could break RSA encryption by efficiently factoring the
key. Similarly, ECC, used in many secure communications, including SSL/TLS protocols, can be undermined by quantum computers capable of solving discrete logarithms in elliptic curve groups. This vulnerability has wide-reaching implications
for internet security, digital signatures, and secure communications across industries
[3].

Symmetric key cryptography is generally considered secure, but it is not completely safe from quantum computing threats. One such threat is Grover's algorithm,
a quantum algorithm that can significantly reduce the security of symmetric encryption by speeding up the search for the correct key. In a classical system, a 256-bit key
is considered very secure, but in a quantum context, Grover's algorithm would make
it as easy to break a 256-bit key as it would be to break a 128-bit key using classical methods. This doesn't mean symmetric encryption is completely broken, but it
does reduce the effective security. As a result, to maintain the same level of security
against quantum attacks, we would need to use longer keys. For instance, using a
512-bit key in a quantum environment would be necessary to ensure the same level
of security that a 256-bit key provides in classical systems [4].

The rise of quantum computing underscores the urgent need for quantum-resistant
cryptographic algorithms. The field of PQC is rapidly developing standards for

encryption methods that resist both classical and quantum attacks. Algorithms based on lattice-based' cryptography, hash-based cryptography, and multivariate polynomial problems are emerging as viable candidates for the post quantum era. These methods use mathematical problems believed to be intractable even for quantum computers. Institutions like the National Institute of Standards and Technology (NIST) are working to standardize PQC algorithms to ensure a smooth transition before large-scale quantum computers become practical. This effort is crucial for safeguarding sensitive data against future quantum attacks by developing encryption methods that remain secure even in the presence of quantum computing power. The NIST's ongoing process aims to identify and promote cryptographic algorithms that can withstand the capabilities of quantum computers, ensuring that secure communication, digital signatures, and key exchange protocols will remain safe as quantum technologies advance [5].

6.1 IMPORTANCE OF CRYPTOGRAPHY IN MODERN SECURITY

Cryptography is the foundation of security in the digital age, enabling the protection of sensitive information, ensuring secure communications, and verifying the authenticity of data and identities. It underpins various technologies and systems that modern society relies upon, from online banking and e-commerce to national defense systems. As digitalization becomes increasingly pervasive, the role of cryptography in safeguarding data, privacy, and trust continues to grow in importance [6, 7].

Data Confidentiality-One of the primary roles of cryptography is to ensure data confidentiality. Encryption techniques transform readable data into an unreadable format, accessible only to authorized parties with the corresponding decryption keys. This prevents unauthorized access to sensitive information, such as personal details, financial records, and intellectual property. Without cryptography, securing data transmitted over vulnerable networks, like the internet, would be nearly impossible.

Data Integrity and Authentication: Cryptography also ensures data integrity and authentication by verifying that information has not been altered in transit and confirming the identity of communicating parties. Digital signatures and hash functions are cryptographic tools used to detect tampering and establish trust between parties in online interactions. This is critical for preventing fraud, securing software updates, and enabling trusted transactions in an interconnected world.

Secure Communication: Cryptography facilitates secure communication, which is essential for both individuals and organizations. Protocols such as SSL/TLS rely on encryption to secure web traffic, ensuring that sensitive data exchanged between users and servers remains private and cannot be intercepted by attackers. Secure communication is vital for preserving privacy, conducting business securely, and maintaining the confidentiality of strategic information for governments and military operations.

Enabling Digital Economies: Modern cryptographic technologies enable the functionality of digital economies by powering secure payment systems, digital currencies, and blockchain networks. Cryptography ensures the safety of online transactions by protecting payment credentials and ensuring transactional integrity. For instance, public-key cryptography underpins the functioning of blockchain, guaranteeing the security of decentralized financial systems and protecting against forgery and unauthorized transactions [8].

Adapting to Emerging Threats: As cyber threats continue to evolve, the need for strong cryptographic systems becomes more important. Emerging technologies, like quantum computing, present risks to current cryptographic methods, making it essential to shift to quantum-resistant algorithms. Ongoing advancements in cryptographic research help ensure that security systems stay strong against both current and future threats, maintaining trust in the digital systems that are vital to societal and economic stability.

6.1.1 THE ROLE OF CRYPTOGRAPHY IN MODERN SECURITY

Cryptography underpins the systems and technologies that protect sensitive information, ensure privacy, and enable trust in digital environments. As society increasingly relies on digital interactions, the role of cryptography has expanded, safeguarding personal data, securing communications, and preparing for future technological challenges.

6.1.1.1 Protecting Confidentiality and Privacy

Cryptography transforms sensitive information into encrypted data accessible only to authorized parties. Key applications include:

Personal Data: Encryption plays a vital role in protecting sensitive personal details such as medical records, financial credentials, and private communications from unauthorized access or theft. For instance, the use of end-to-end encryption in messaging apps ensures that only the sender and recipient can read the messages, effectively preventing intermediaries from intercepting or accessing the content. Similarly, securing health records and protecting online transactions are critical applications of encryption in safeguarding personal data. With the increasing prevalence of digital threats, cryptographic methods and algorithms have evolved to provide robust protection for individuals' privacy, adapting to new challenges and technologies.

Business Information: Businesses rely heavily on cryptography to maintain their competitive edge by securing corporate secrets, contracts, and intellectual property. Protecting trade secrets, encrypting confidential business communications, and securing cloud storage are essential practices to ensure trust and prevent unauthorized access. Virtual Private Networks (VPNs) are a common cryptographic tool used by businesses to establish secure connections between remote employees and corporate networks, ensuring that sensitive information remains encrypted during transmission. By incorporating advanced encryption techniques, companies can safeguard their valuable information, maintain operational integrity, and build confidence among stakeholders.

Government Intelligence: The government uses cryptographic techniques to safeguard classified information and ensure national security. This includes securing military communications, protecting state secrets, and maintaining the integrity of critical infrastructure. Cryptography plays a key role in secure satellite communications, enabling the transmission of sensitive data without the risk of interception. By adopting advanced cryptographic methods, India can defend against evolving cyber threats, maintain secure communication channels, and protect national security.

6.1.1.2   Ensuring Data Integrity and Authenticity

Cryptography ensures that data remains unaltered during transmission or storage. Key mechanisms include:

Hash Functions: Hash functions are cryptographic algorithms that take an input (or "message") and produce a fixed-size string of characters, typically a sequence of numbers and letters, which is called a hash value or digest. This hash value acts as a unique fingerprint of the input data. One commonly used hash function is SHA-256 (Secure Hash Algorithm 256-bit), which generates a 256-bit (32-byte) hash value from any given input.
The main purpose of hash functions is to ensure data integrity. If even a small change is made to the input data, the hash value will drastically change, which helps in detecting any alterations or tampering. Hash functions are widely used in various applications such as data verification, digital signatures, and password hashing. They provide a unique, fixed-length representation of data, which plays a crucial role in maintaining the security and integrity of digital information by allowing the verification of data without revealing the original content.

Digital Signatures: Digital signatures are cryptographic tools used to verify the origin and authenticity of data, ensuring that it has not been altered and comes from a trusted source. They are commonly used to confirm the legitimacy of software updates, electronic documents, and secure communications. For example, when downloading software updates, digital signatures confirm that the update is genuine and hasn't been tampered with, protecting users from malicious software. Digital signatures combine hashing and asymmetric encryption techniques to create a unique signature for each piece of data. The recipient can verify the signature using the sender's public key, providing confidence that the data is both authentic and unchanged.

These mechanisms protect against fraud, counterfeiting, and manipulation in financial transactions, emails, and documents.

6.1.1.3 Securing Digital Communications

Cryptography secures communications in the digital age, preventing interception and unauthorized access [9]. Examples include:

SSL/TLS Protocols: SSL (Secure Sockets Layer) and its successor, TLS (Transport Layer Security), are cryptographic protocols designed to encrypt data transmitted between clients and servers. By establishing a secure connection, SSL/TLS ensures that sensitive information, such as login credentials, credit card details, and personal data, remains confidential during transmission. These protocols are fundamental to secure web browsing and online transactions, providing users with the assurance that their data is protected from eavesdropping and tampering. SSL/TLS uses a combination of asymmetric encryption for key exchange and symmetric encryption for data transfer, making it both secure and efficient. The implementation of SSL/TLS is visible through the "HTTPS" prefix in web addresses, indicating that the connection is secure and encrypted.

End-to-End Encryption (E2EE): End-to-End Encryption (E2EE) is a method of secure communication that ensures only the sender and receiver can access the messages being exchanged. Messaging platforms like WhatsApp and Signal implement E2EE to protect user privacy and prevent unauthorized access to the content of their conversations. With E2EE, the message is encrypted on the sender's device and can only be decrypted by the recipient's device, ensuring that intermediaries, including service providers, cannot read the message. This level of security is essential for maintaining user trust and protecting sensitive information in an increasingly digital world. E2EE is particularly valuable in contexts where privacy is paramount, such as in communications between journalists and their sources, human rights activists, and individuals living under repressive systems.

Virtual Private Networks (VPNs): Virtual Private Networks (VPNs) use encryption to secure communication over public networks, such as the internet. By creating a secure "tunnel" between the user's device and the VPN server, VPNs protect data from eavesdropping, interception, and tampering. This is particularly important for individuals accessing sensitive information from public Wi-Fi networks, as well as for remote employees connecting to corporate networks. VPNs provide anonymity and privacy by masking the user's IP address and encrypting their internet traffic, making it difficult for third parties to track online activities or steal data. Additionally, VPNs can bypass geographic restrictions, allowing users to access content and services that may be blocked or restricted in their location. This makes VPNs a valuable tool for ensuring both security and unrestricted access to information.

By securing interactions, cryptography enables trust in global commerce, remote work, and private communications.

6.1.1.4   Enabling Critical Infrastructures and Services

Modern critical systems rely on cryptography for secure operation:

Energy Grids: Cryptographic protocols are essential in securing communication between different components of energy grids. By encrypting the data exchanged between these components, cryptography mitigates the risks of cyberattacks that could disrupt the stability and functionality of the grid. Secure communication ensures that commands, status updates, and monitoring data remain confidential and unaltered, protecting the grid from malicious entities. Additionally, cryptographic techniques help to verify the authenticity of the data and the identity of communicating devices, enhancing the overall security of energy infrastructure and preventing potential threats to national energy supply systems. As smart grids become more prevalent, incorporating renewable energy sources and advanced metering infrastructure, the need for robust cryptographic solutions becomes even more critical to ensure the resilience and reliability of the energy supply.

Healthcare Systems: Encryption is crucial in safeguarding patient data, electronic medical records (EMRs), and connected medical devices within healthcare systems. By encrypting patient information, healthcare providers can ensure that sensitive data remains confidential and protected from unauthorized access. This is especially important as healthcare records often contain personal, financial, and medical information that, if compromised, could lead to severe consequences for patients. Encryption also protects data transmitted between medical devices and healthcare networks, ensuring that the integrity and confidentiality of the information are maintained. With the increasing integration of digital technologies in healthcare, robust encryption measures are vital to maintaining patient trust and ensuring compliance with privacy regulations. Furthermore, the advent of telemedicine and remote patient monitoring has amplified the need for secure data transmission, making encryption indispensable in modern healthcare practices.

Transportation and IoT devices: Cryptography plays a critical role in protecting autonomous vehicles, smart city infrastructures, and other Internet of Things (IoT) devices from cyber threats. Autonomous vehicles rely on secure communication to exchange data with other vehicles, traffic management systems, and cloud services. By encrypting this data, cryptography ensures that the vehicles' operational data remains secure and tamper-proof, reducing the risk of cyberattacks that could compromise safety. Similarly, smart city infrastructures, which encompass a wide range of connected systems such as traffic lights, surveillance cameras, and public transportation, depend on cryptographic protocols to safeguard the data exchanged between these devices. Encryption helps maintain the integrity and confidentiality of the data, preventing unauthorized access and ensuring the smooth functioning of the city's critical infrastructure. As the IoT ecosystem continues to expand, encompassing smart homes, wearable devices, and industrial IoT applications, the implementation of strong cryptographic measures becomes increasingly vital to protect against cyber threats and maintain user privacy.

These systems, often targeted due to their societal importance, require robust cryptographic measures for operational security.

6.1.1.5   Building Trust in the Digital Economy

Cryptography is the basis of digital commerce and trust-based systems:

Secure Payment Systems: Secure payment systems rely heavily on cryptographic protocols to protect transactions and ensure the integrity and confidentiality of financial data. Protocols like EMV (Europay, MasterCard, and Visa) chips are embedded in credit and debit cards to provide secure transaction processing. These chips use dynamic data authentication, making it difficult for fraudsters to clone or manipulate card information. Additionally, systems like PayPal use advanced encryption techniques to safeguard users' financial data during online transactions. By encrypting sensitive information, such as payment details and personal identification, secure payment systems prevent unauthorized access and ensure that transactions are completed safely and securely.

Blockchain Technology: Blockchain technology relies on cryptographic algorithms to ensure transaction integrity and security within decentralized networks. Each block in a blockchain contains a cryptographic hash of the previous block, creating an immutable chain of records. This ensures that any attempt to alter a transaction would be immediately detectable, as it would change the hash values of all subsequent blocks. Cryptographic algorithms also play a crucial role in enabling cryptocurrencies like Bitcoin, providing secure and transparent mechanisms for verifying and recording transactions. By utilizing public and private keys, blockchain technology ensures that only authorized parties can initiate and validate transactions, enhancing the overall security of the system [10].

E-Signatures and Contracts: Digital signatures enable legally binding agreements and streamline processes across various industries. By using cryptographic techniques, digital signatures verify the authenticity and integrity of electronic documents, ensuring that the signer is who they claim to be and that the document has not been tampered. E-signatures are widely used in sectors such as finance, real estate, and legal services, providing a secure and efficient way to execute contracts and agreements. The use of digital signatures eliminates the need for physical paperwork, reducing administrative overhead and enabling faster, more secure transactions. This technology is particularly valuable in remote and online environments, where traditional signature methods may be impractical.

This trust layer fosters confidence in online transactions and facilitates digital economic growth.

6.1.1.6   Adapting to Emerging Threats

Cryptography must evolve to address new challenges:

Advancing Cyber-Attacks: As cyber-attacks become more sophisticated, cryptography must continually adapt to counter these evolving threats. Advanced attacks such as side-channel attacks, which exploit information leaked during the physical implementation of cryptographic algorithms, and zero-day vulnerabilities, which target previously unknown software flaws, pose significant risks to digital security. To mitigate these threats, cryptographers are developing advanced techniques and countermeasures. This includes implementing secure hardware designs to protect against side-channel attacks and employing proactive vulnerability detection and patch management to address zero-day exploits. By staying ahead of attackers and anticipating new forms of cyber threats, cryptography continues to evolve to protect sensitive data and maintain the integrity of digital systems.

Proactive Regulation: Governments and organizations recognize the importance of staying ahead of emerging risks in the realm of cryptography. As a result, they invest in cryptographic research and establish standards to address potential vulnerabilities and ensure robust security measures. Regulatory bodies and industry groups work collaboratively to develop guidelines and best practices for implementing cryptographic solutions. This proactive approach includes funding research initiatives focused on PQC secure communication protocols, and advanced encryption techniques. Additionally, regulations such as the General Data Protection Regulation (GDPR) and other privacy laws mandate the use of strong encryption to protect personal and sensitive data. By investing in cryptographic research and establishing comprehensive standards, governments and organizations aim to create a secure and resilient digital infrastructure that can withstand the challenges of an ever-evolving threat landscape.

Continuous adaptation ensures the resilience and security of cryptographic systems in an evolving threat landscape. Cryptography is essential to securing the modern digital world. It protects personal privacy, ensures critical infrastructure security, and builds trust in economic systems and digital interactions. As technology evolves, so must cryptography, adapting to new challenges and opportunities. By ensuring confidentiality, integrity, authenticity, and resilience, cryptography provides a foundation for a secure and trustworthy digital future [11].

6.2 SHOR'S ALGORITHM AND ITS IMPACT ON RSA AND ECC

Shor's algorithm, proposed by Peter Shor in 1994, is a groundbreaking quantum algorithm that can efficiently factor large integers and solve discrete logarithms. These two problems form the mathematical backbone of many widely used public-key cryptographic systems, including RSA and ECC. Unlike classical computers, which solve these problems using exponentially time-consuming methods, quantum computers employing Shor's algorithm can perform these calculations in polynomial time, rendering these cryptographic schemes vulnerable to decryption [12].

6.2.1 IMPACT ON RSA

RSA encryption relies on the difficulty of factoring large composite numbers. Its security is tied to the assumption that factoring a product of two large prime numbers is computationally infeasible for classical computers. Shor's algorithm, however, bypasses this assumption by introducing quantum principles such as superposition and entanglement to find the prime factors of a given integer with exponential speedup. As a result, a sufficiently powerful quantum computer could efficiently decrypt RSA-encrypted data without access to the private key, considering the encryption reliability. This has significant consequences for secure communications, digital signatures, and data integrity, which are widely dependent on RSA.

The start of quantum computing poses a significant threat to the security of RSA encryption. If quantum computers reach the necessary level of computational power, they could render current RSA-based security measures obsolete. This would impact a wide range of applications, including secure communications, digital signatures, and data integrity. As RSA is widely used for securing web traffic, email encryption, and other sensitive data, the ability of quantum computers to break RSA encryption could have far-reaching implications for data privacy and security.

6.2.2 IMPACT ON ECC

ECC is widely regarded as more secure than RSA per bit length due to the complexity of solving the discrete logarithm problem in elliptic curve groups. This complexity allows ECC to provide strong security with smaller key sizes compared to RSA, making it efficient and effective for various cryptographic applications. However, the emergence of quantum computing, specifically Shor's algorithm, poses a significant threat to the security of ECC. Shor's algorithm extends to the discrete logarithm problem, meaning it can efficiently compute the private key associated with a public key in ECC systems. This capability renders elliptic curve-based protocols, such as ECDSA (Elliptic Curve Digital Signature Algorithm) and ECDH (Elliptic Curve Diffie–Hellman), equally susceptible to quantum attacks as RSA. The ability of quantum computers to break ECC encryption would have profound implications for secure communications and financial transactions, given the widespread use of ECC in modern cryptographic protocols.

ECC is heavily utilized in secure communication protocols, including SSL/TLS, which are fundamental to internet security. These protocols ensure that data transmitted over the internet remains confidential and protected from eavesdropping and tampering. If quantum computers can break ECC encryption, the integrity and confidentiality of internet communications would be compromised, leading to potential data breaches and loss of trust in digital security systems. Additionally, ECC is used in various financial systems to secure transactions and protect sensitive information. The compromise of ECC-based protocols would jeopardize the security of online banking, digital payments, and other financial activities, posing significant risks to individuals and organizations.

To address the threat posed by quantum computing, the field of post-quantum cryptography is developing new cryptographic algorithms that can withstand quantum attacks. Researchers are exploring various approaches, including lattice-based, hash-based, and code-based cryptography, to create algorithms that are resistant to the capabilities of quantum computers. These post-quantum algorithms aim to provide long-term security for digital systems, ensuring that cryptographic protocols remain robust in the face of emerging quantum threats. By transitioning to post-quantum cryptographic standards, we can protect sensitive data and maintain the integrity of secure communications and financial transactions in a future where quantum computing becomes widespread [13].

6.2.3 MAGNITUDE OF THE THREAT

The implementation of Shor's algorithm on a practical quantum computer represents a monumental threat to the security of existing cryptographic systems. Both RSA and ECC, which underpin much of today's secure communication infrastructure, would be rendered vulnerable. This includes not only current data but also previously intercepted communications that were encrypted using these systems. The retroactive vulnerability means that any data encrypted with RSA or ECC and stored or intercepted could be decrypted by a sufficiently powerful Cryptographically Relevant Large Quantum Computer (CRLQC). The potential for quantum computers to break RSA and ECC encryption with relative ease has profound implications. Secure internet communication, financial transactions, confidential government communications, and any other application relying on these cryptographic methods could be compromised. The threat is not just theoretical; it is an emerging challenge that could materialize as quantum computing power continues to grow.

Recognizing the gravity of the quantum threat, organizations and governments worldwide are proactively transitioning to quantum-safe cryptographic solutions. The field of PQC is focused on developing and standardizing algorithms that can withstand quantum attacks, ensuring that data remains secure even when quantum computing becomes more powerful. These new quantum-safe algorithms, such as lattice-based, hash-based, and code-based cryptography, are designed to protect sensitive data and maintain the integrity of digital communications.

In the context of symmetric key cryptography, although quantum computers can significantly speed up brute-force attacks using algorithms like Grover's, the overall structure of symmetric encryption remains more resistant to quantum threats compared to asymmetric methods. To address this, longer symmetric keys are being adopted to maintain the same security level in a quantum environment.

On the other hand, asymmetric key cryptography, which forms the basis of many encryption systems (such as RSA and ECC), is highly vulnerable to quantum attacks due to algorithms like Shor's algorithm that can break these systems in polynomial time. To mitigate this, quantum-safe alternatives, such as lattice-based public-key schemes, are being explored to replace current asymmetric encryption methods.

By adopting these new quantum-resistant algorithms across both symmetric and asymmetric encryption systems, we can ensure that our cryptographic systems remain secure, even as quantum computing continues to advance. This proactive approach is critical to preserving the confidentiality and integrity of our digital world, protecting it from the risks posed by quantum attacks [14].

6.3 GROVER'S ALGORITHM AND ITS IMPACT ON SYMMETRIC CRYPTOGRAPHY

Grover's algorithm, a pivotal quantum computing innovation, offers a quadratic speedup for searching unsorted databases or performing brute-force computations. The algorithm uses quantum principles such as superposition and interference to drastically enhance the efficiency of brute-force searches. Unlike classical algorithms, which require $O(N)$ operations to search through N possible solutions, Grover's algorithm can find the desired result in $O(\sqrt{N})$ operations, offering a significant speedup.

6.3.1 IMPLICATIONS FOR SYMMETRIC CRYPTOGRAPHY

Grover's algorithm poses a substantial threat to symmetric key cryptographic systems, such as those using block ciphers like AES (Advanced Encryption Standard). Classical brute-force search methods require 2^n operations to find an n-bit key, but Grover's algorithm can reduce this to $2^{n/2}$ operations. This effectively halves the effective key length, diminishing the security of symmetric key encryption. For example, a 128-bit key, which is considered secure against classical attacks, would be reduced to the security equivalent of a 64-bit key under Grover's algorithm. This reduction compels cryptographers to re-evaluate existing standards and consider increasing key lengths to maintain security in the quantum era. To ensure long-term data security, symmetric cryptographic systems must adopt quantum-resilient approaches, such as doubling key lengths or by doing structural change new quantum-resistant algorithms [15].

6.3.2 CLASSICAL VS. QUANTUM BRUTE FORCE

Classical Approach: Brute-forcing an n-bit key on a classical computer requires 2^n operations. This means that for a key of length n, a classical brute-force attack would need to try all possible 2^n combinations to find the correct key. The time required for this process grows exponentially with the length of the key, making it infeasible for sufficiently large key sizes. For example, a 128-bit key would require 2^{128} attempts, which is practically impossible to achieve with current classical computing resources.

Quantum Approach: Grover's algorithm, a breakthrough in quantum computing, reduces the complexity of brute-forcing an n-bit key to approximately $2^{n/2}$ operations. This represents a quadratic speedup compared to the classical approach. Grover's algorithm leverages quantum principles such as superposition and interference to search the key space more efficiently. For a 128-bit key, Grover's algorithm would only require 2^{64} attempts, which is significantly fewer than the classical approach and makes the brute-force search much more feasible for a quantum computer [16].

Implications for Symmetric Key Encryption Systems: The efficiency gain provided by Grover's algorithm poses significant challenges to symmetric key encryption systems, especially those utilizing shorter key lengths. The reduced security margin means that key lengths that were previously considered secure against classical attacks may no longer be sufficient in the quantum era. For instance, a 128-bit key, which is robust against classical brute-force attacks, would be reduced to the equivalent security of a 64-bit key under Grover's algorithm.

To address the threat posed by quantum computing, symmetric key encryption systems need to implement longer key lengths to maintain their security. A general guideline is to double the key length—for example, moving from 128 bits to 256 bits—to enhance resistance against quantum attacks, ensuring the continued integrity and confidentiality of encrypted data.

The rise of quantum computing requires a reassessment of cryptographic standards and a shift toward quantum-resilient methods to protect data from emerging quantum threats. By adopting longer key lengths and incorporating post-quantum cryptographic algorithms, we can safeguard symmetric encryption systems from the power of quantum computers, ensuring long-term security for sensitive information.

IMPACT ON SYMMETRIC KEY ENCRYPTION ALGORITHMS

The reduced computational effort offered by Grover's algorithm necessitates reconsideration of key lengths for symmetric key encryption systems. Here are the key examples:

AES-128

Classical brute-force complexity: $O(2^{128})$.
Grover-optimized complexity: $O(2^{64})$.
Implication: The quadratic speedup provided by Grover's algorithm significantly reduces the security of AES-128. While 2^{128} operations are infeasible for classical brute-force attacks, 2^{64} operations make AES-128 vulnerable to quantum attacks. As a result, AES-128 is considered insufficiently secure in the quantum era.

AES-256

Classical brute-force complexity: $O(2^{256})$.
Grover-optimized complexity: $O(2^{128})$.
Implication: Even with Grover's algorithm, 2^{128} operations remain infeasible for quantum computers. This helps maintain the high level of security offered by AES256, ensuring it remains resistant to quantum attacks. The effective key strength continues to be robust, making AES256 a secure encryption option in the quantum era. In addition to its key size, the design of AES itself plays a critical

role in its security. Its efficient structure and strong encryption mechanisms contribute to its resilience, making it a reliable choice for protecting sensitive data even as quantum computing advances..

To effectively counter quantum threats, organizations should consider a structural change by adopting AES-256 or equivalent encryption standards. By making this transition, organizations can maintain the confidentiality and integrity of their data in a quantum-enhanced landscape [17].

6.3.3   LIMITATIONS AND PRACTICAL CONSIDERATIONS

Despite its theoretical advantages, Grover's algorithm faces practical implementation challenges that currently limit its widespread applicability:

Quantum Hardware: Large-scale quantum computers with sufficient coherence time and low error rates are still under development. Building a quantum computer that can maintain quantum states long enough to perform complex computations without significant error rates remains a significant technical hurdle. The delicate nature of quantum states requires advanced error correction techniques and stable hardware environments, which are still being refined. The current generation of quantum computers is limited by the number of qubits they can coherently manage and the susceptibility of these qubits to decoherence and noise. Achieving fault-tolerant quantum computation, where errors can be detected and corrected without disrupting the quantum computation process, is essential for the practical implementation of Grover's algorithm.

Scalability: The resource requirements for Grover's algorithm grow substantially with problem size, limiting its immediate applicability. As the size of the problem increases, the number of qubits and the depth of quantum circuits required also increase. This scalability issue poses a challenge for implementing Grover's algorithm on practical quantum computers, as current quantum systems are limited in the number of qubits they can effectively manage and operate. Additionally, the complexity of creating and maintaining quantum entanglement across a large number of qubits presents a significant obstacle. As quantum computers grow in scale, the challenges associated with error rates, qubit coherence, and quantum gate fidelity will need to be addressed to make Grover's algorithm practically viable.

Quantum Algorithm Optimization: While Grover's algorithm provides a theoretical quadratic speedup, optimizing its implementation on real quantum hardware requires sophisticated techniques, such as designing efficient quantum oracles, minimizing circuit complexity, and implementing advanced error correction methods. Researchers are also exploring quantum algorithms that could offer advantages beyond Grover's algorithm. For instance, quantum walks, including continuous-time quantum walks, have been shown to outperform Grover's algorithm in certain search problems, achieving faster search results. The Quantum Approximate Optimization Algorithm (QAOA), designed for combinatorial optimization, has been proposed as a potential improvement over Grover's algorithm for finding optimal solutions in specific problem classes. Additionally, amplitude amplification, an extension of

Grover's algorithm, can improve search efficiency by refining the iterative process, offering faster performance in some cases. Another promising algorithm is the Harrow-Hassidim-Lloyd (HHL) algorithm, which solves linear systems of equations exponentially faster than classical methods, providing improvements for problems requiring substantial computational resources. These emerging algorithms represent significant strides toward bridging the gap between quantum computing's theoretical advantages and practical performance on near-term quantum devices, with researchers continuously refining them for real-world applications [18].

Regulatory and Standardization Efforts: Governments and international standardization organizations are crucial in leading the transition to quantum-resistant cryptographic systems. One key initiative is the NIST PQC project, which focuses on identifying, evaluating, and standardizing cryptographic algorithms that can withstand quantum attacks. For this transition to be successful, collaboration between academia, industry, and regulatory bodies is essential. Together, they can establish best practices, create guidelines, and ensure the widespread adoption of quantum-resistant cryptographic standards. These collective efforts will help build a secure and resilient cryptographic infrastructure that can effectively address the challenges posed by quantum computing.

6.4   VULNERABILITIES OF CLASSICAL CRYPTOGRAPHIC SYSTEMS

Cryptographic systems are fundamental to securing modern communication, but they are not invulnerable. Various cryptographic mechanisms face threats that exploit design flaws, implementation errors, or advances in computational power. Below, we examine some common vulnerabilities in public key cryptography, symmetric key cryptography, and related technologies like hash functions and digital signatures.

Public-key cryptography faces several vulnerabilities, including weak key generation, insecure key distribution, algorithmic weaknesses, and implementation flaws. Poorly generated keys can be predictable and vulnerable to attacks, while compromised key distribution channels can lead to man-in-the-middle attacks. Additionally, some algorithms have inherent weaknesses; for instance, RSA is vulnerable to quantum attacks, which can break the security of keys using Shor's algorithm. Implementation flaws in software or hardware can introduce vulnerabilities such as timing attacks or side-channel attacks that exploit information leakage during computation [19].

Symmetric key cryptography also has its share of vulnerabilities. Short key lengths reduce the security of symmetric key encryption algorithms, with Grover's algorithm in quantum computing potentially halving the effective security of key lengths. Weak encryption schemes may have design flaws that make them susceptible to cryptanalysis, such as differential or linear cryptanalysis. Implementation weaknesses, such as not using proper padding schemes, can introduce vulnerabilities. For example, the use of ECB (Electronic Codebook) mode in block ciphers can reveal patterns in encrypted data, compromising security.

To address these vulnerabilities, organizations should adopt proactive measures such as regular security audits, using strong algorithms, ensuring proper implementation, and providing education and training to developers and security professionals on best practices in cryptography. By understanding and addressing these vulnerabilities, we can strengthen the security of cryptographic systems and ensure the protection of sensitive data in an increasingly complex digital landscape.

6.4.1   PUBLIC KEY CRYPTOGRAPHY (RSA, ECC)

Cryptographic systems are essential for securing modern communication, but they face numerous threats that exploit design flaws, implementation errors, and advances in computational power. Below, we examine some common vulnerabilities in public-key cryptography [20].

Public Key Cryptography relies on the use of two mathematically related keys: a public key and a private key. These keys enable secure communication and digital signatures, ensuring data confidentiality, integrity, and authenticity. Here, we explore some common vulnerabilities associated with two widely used public-key cryptographic algorithms: RSA and ECC.

RSA (Rivest-Shamir-Adleman):
RSA is one of the most widely used public-key cryptographic algorithms. It relies on the mathematical difficulty of factoring large composite numbers. However, RSA faces several vulnerabilities:

Weak Key Generation: Poorly generated RSA keys can be predictable and vulnerable to attacks. Using strong random number generators is critical for secure key generation.

Quantum Vulnerability: RSA is susceptible to quantum attacks. Shor's algorithm can efficiently factor large numbers, breaking the security of RSA by revealing the private key. This makes RSA vulnerable to future quantum computers.

Key Distribution: Secure key distribution is essential. Compromised key distribution channels can lead to man-in-the-middle attacks, where an attacker intercepts and alters communication.

Implementation Flaws: Software and hardware implementations of RSA can introduce vulnerabilities. Timing attacks and side-channel attacks exploit information leakage during computation to deduce the private key.

Understanding and addressing these vulnerabilities is crucial to maintaining the integrity, confidentiality, and authenticity of data. As quantum computing advances, the cryptographic community must prioritize the development and adoption of quantum-resistant algorithms to ensure long-term security [21].

6.4.2   SYMMETRIC KEY CRYPTOGRAPHY (DES, AES)

Cryptographic systems are essential for securing modern communication, but they face numerous threats that exploit design flaws, implementation errors, and advances in computational power. Below, we examine some common vulnerabilities in symmetric-key cryptography. **Symmetric-Key Cryptography** uses the same key for both encryption and decryption, making it essential to keep the key secure. Here, we explore some common vulnerabilities associated with two widely used symmetric-key cryptographic algorithms: DES (Data Encryption Standard) and AES (Advanced Encryption Standard).

DES (Data Encryption Standard):
DES was widely used before being superseded by AES. It relies on a 56-bit key, making it vulnerable to brute-force attacks [22]. Here are some key vulnerabilities:

Short Key Length: The 56-bit key length of DES is insufficient to withstand brute-force attacks, as modern computational power can exhaustively search the key space relatively quickly. This limitation makes DES unsuitable for protecting sensitive data in today's security landscape.

Weaknesses in Key Scheduling: DES has specific weaknesses in its key scheduling algorithm that can lead to certain keys being less secure. For example, certain keys, known as weak keys, produce the same subkeys in multiple rounds of encryption, reducing the algorithm's overall security.

Susceptibility to Differential and Linear Cryptanalysis: DES is vulnerable to cryptanalysis techniques that exploit patterns in the encryption process. Differential cryptanalysis examines how differences in plaintext affect differences in ciphertext, while linear cryptanalysis uses linear approximations to describe the behavior of the block cipher. These techniques can significantly reduce the effort required to break DES encryption.

Triple DES (3DES): In an attempt to increase security, Triple DES (3DES) was introduced, which applies the DES algorithm three times with two or three different keys. However, even 3DES is now considered less secure compared to modern algorithms like AES, especially given the advances in computational power and cryptanalysis techniques. The effective key length of 3DES, although longer than DES, still makes it less desirable for high-security applications.

AES (Advanced Encryption Standard):
AES is one of the most widely used symmetric-key encryption algorithms, known for its security and efficiency [23]. However, it faces some vulnerabilities:

Short Key Lengths: While AES-128 is considered secure against classical attacks, Grover's algorithm in quantum computing can reduce the effective security to that of a 64-bit key. To counteract this, longer key lengths like AES-256 are recommended.

Side-Channel Attacks: AES implementations can be vulnerable to side-channel attacks that exploit information leakage during computation. Techniques like Differential Power Analysis (DPA) can deduce the encryption key by analyzing power consumption patterns. Other side-channel attacks include electromagnetic analysis and cache-timing attacks, which can also reveal critical information about the encryption process.

Fault Attacks: By inducing faults in the hardware during encryption, attackers can clean information about the secret key. This requires robust error detection and correction mechanisms to mitigate. Fault attacks can be performed using techniques such as voltage manipulation, clock glitches, or temperature variations to introduce errors in the cryptographic computation.

Implementation Challenges:
Symmetric-key cryptography must also contend with various implementation challenges that can introduce vulnerabilities. These include:

Proper Use of Modes of Operation: Choosing the correct mode of operation for block ciphers is critical. Modes like ECB (Electronic Codebook) are insecure as they reveal patterns in the plaintext. Secure modes such as CBC (Cipher Block Chaining), GCM (Galois/Counter Mode), and others should be used to ensure data confidentiality and integrity.

Secure Key Management: Ensuring the secure generation, distribution, storage, and disposal of keys is essential. Poor key management practices can lead to unauthorized access and compromise of encrypted data.

Understanding and addressing the vulnerabilities in symmetric-key cryptography is crucial to maintaining the confidentiality and integrity of data. While AES remains a robust choice, it must be implemented with longer key lengths and protected against side-channel and fault attacks. DES, on the other hand, is largely obsolete and should be replaced with more secure algorithms like AES. As quantum computing advances, the cryptographic community must continue to develop and adopt quantum-resistant algorithms to ensure long-term security.

REFERENCES

1. P. W. Shor, "Algorithms for quantum computation: discrete logarithms and factoring," Proceedings 35th Annual Symposium on Foundations of Computer Science, pp. 124–134, 1994, doi: 10.1109/SFCS.1994.365700.
2. L. K. Grover, "A fast quantum mechanical algorithm for database search," Proceedings of the 28th Annual ACM Symposium on Theory of Computing, pp. 212–219, 1996, doi: 10.1145/237814.237866.
3. L. K. Grover, "A Fast Quantum Mechanical Algorithm for Database Search," Proceedings of the 28th Annual ACM Symposium on Theory of Computing, 1996, pp. 212–219, doi: 10.1145/237814.237866.
4. Michael A. Nielsen and Isaac L. Chuang, Quantum Computation and Quantum Information, Cambridge University Press, 2002.
5. D. J. Bernstein and T. Lange, Post-Quantum Cryptography, Springer, 2019, ISBN: 978-3-030-22081-3.

6. National Institute of Standards and Technology (NIST), "Post-Quantum Cryptography Standardization," NIST Special Publication 800-203, 2016, [Online]. Available: https://csrc.nist.gov/publications/detail/sp/800-203/final.

7. C. Liu, M. Xie, Z. Xu, and L. Zhang, "Quantum Algorithms and Cryptography," Journal of Quantum Computing, vol. 5, no. 3, pp. 85–101, 2016, doi: 10.1016/j.jqc.2016.02.007.

8. M. Petersen, "Blockchain Technology in Cryptocurrencies and Digital Transactions," Journal of Computer Security, vol. 26, no. 3, pp. 333–356, 2018, doi: 10.3233/JCS-170748.

9. W. Stallings, Cryptography and Network Security: Principles and Practice, 7th ed., Pearson, 2016.

10. D. Larkin, "Blockchain Technology: Principles and Applications," International Journal of Advanced Research in Computer Science and Software Engineering, vol. 8, no. 4, pp. 1–9, 2018.

11. N. Koblitz, Advances in Cryptology—Proceedings of CRYPTO '87, Springer, 1987, doi: 10.1007/3-540-48184-2.

12. J. Hoffstein, J. Pipher, and J. H. Silverman, An Introduction to Mathematical Cryptography, 2nd ed., Springer, 2008.

13. N. Koblitz and A. Menezes, "Elliptic Curve Cryptography: The New Era of Public-Key Cryptosystems," IEEE Security & Privacy, vol. 10, no. 3, pp. 56–63, 2012, doi: 10.1109/MSP.2012.25.

14. A. J. Menezes, P. C. van Oorschot, and S. A. Vanstone, Handbook of Applied Cryptography, CRC Press, 1996.

15. W. Diffie and M. E. Hellman, "New Directions in Cryptography," IEEE Transactions on Information Theory, vol. IT-22, no. 6, pp. 644–654, Nov. 1976, doi: 10.1109/TIT.1976.1055638.

16. D. J. Bernstein, Introduction to Post-Quantum Cryptography, Springer, 2017.

17. A. Benenson, "Privacy-Preserving Cryptography in E-Commerce and Communication Systems," Computer Science and Communications, vol. 9, no. 4, pp. 45–50, 2004.

18. J. Katz and Y. Lindell, Introduction to Modern Cryptography, 2nd ed., Springer, 2014.

19. A. Reid, "Security and Cryptography for Secure Communications in the Modern Internet Age," Journal of Applied Cryptography, vol. 10, no. 1, pp. 22–35, 2012.

20. Peter W. Shor and John Preskill, "An Overview of Quantum Computing," Nature, vol. 449, no. 7150, 2007, pp. 618–625, doi: 10.1038/nature06274.

21. S. Baker, "The Role of Cryptography in Ensuring Healthcare Data Security and Patient Privacy," Journal of Healthcare Information Management, vol. 32, no. 2, pp. 77–83, 2018.

22. National Institute of Standards and Technology (NIST), Data Encryption Standard (DES), Federal Information Processing Standards Publication 46-3, 1995, available at https://nvlpubs.nist.gov/nistpubs/FIPS/NIST.FIPS.46-3.pdf.

23. National Institute of Standards and Technology (NIST), Advanced Encryption Standard (AES), FIPS Publication 197, 2001, available at https://nvlpubs.nist.gov/nistpubs/FIPS/NIST.FIPS.197.pdf.

Section VII

Future Trends and Applications

7 Future Trends and Applications

"Quantum computing is not a distant dream. It's a fast-approaching reality that will redefine what's computationally possible."

— Arvind Krishna

SUMMARY

This chapter outlines the emerging need for quantum-safe cryptography in light of advances in quantum computing. It introduces Mosca's Theorem as a strategic forecasting tool to assess when quantum threats may compromise current cryptographic systems. The discussion emphasizes differentiating between vulnerable asymmetric primitives (like RSA (Rivest-Shamir-Adleman) and ECC (Elliptic Curve Cryptography)) and more resilient symmetric primitives, which, although more secure, still require enhancements such as increased key lengths and modified algorithms. The chapter categorizes post-quantum security levels and proposes general countermeasures, including algorithmic modifications, improved key management, and strong randomization practices to protect against quantum attacks like Grover's and Simon's algorithms.

Looking forward, the chapter highlights several key research and implementation trends, such as Quantum Key Distribution (QKD), the development of quantum-resistant symmetric ciphers, and quantum-secure cryptographic protocols. It stresses the importance of standardization and interoperability in achieving global readiness for the quantum era. Emerging areas like quantum networking and the application of quantum cryptography beyond key distribution are also explored. The chapter concludes by reinforcing the urgency of proactive preparedness to ensure robust cryptographic security in the coming age of quantum computing.

As technology evolves, the field of cryptography continues to adapt to emerging challenges and opportunities. Future trends and applications in cryptography reflect the growing complexity of security requirements and the advancing threat landscape. Below is an exploration of key directions in cryptographic development.

DOI: 10.1201/9781003606338-7

7.1 INTRODUCTION TO QUANTUM-SAFE CRYPTOGRAPHY

Quantum-safe cryptography, also known as post-quantum cryptography, refers to cryptographic algorithms that are designed to be secure against the potential threats posed by quantum computers. Unlike classical computers, which use bits to represent data as either 0s or 1s, quantum computers leverage quantum bits or qubits, which can exist in multiple states simultaneously. This unique property enables quantum computers to solve certain mathematical problems much more efficiently than classical computers.

One of the key implications of quantum computing is its ability to break widely-used cryptographic schemes that rely on the difficulty of problems such as integer factorization and discrete logarithms. Algorithms like RSA, DSA (Digital Signature Algorithm), and ECC are particularly vulnerable to quantum attacks. Shor's algorithm, for instance, can efficiently factor large numbers and compute discrete logarithms, rendering these cryptographic schemes insecure in the presence of a sufficiently powerful quantum computer. This has significant implications for the security of digital communication, financial transactions, and data storage [1].

7.1.1 MOSCA'S THEOREM: A QUANTUM RISK FORECASTING FRAMEWORK

As the era of quantum computing rapidly approaches, evaluating cryptographic readiness becomes not just an academic concern but a practical imperative. **Mosca's Theorem** offers a powerful risk evaluation framework by assessing how long data must remain secure, how long migration will take, and how soon quantum threats may materialize [2].

KEY PARAMETERS

x: Number of years your data must remain confidential (*cover time*).
y: Number of years it will take to transition to a post-quantum cryptographic infrastructure (*migration time*).
z: Number of years remaining until a large-scale quantum computer becomes viable or other advances threaten current cryptosystems (*collapse time*).

7.1.2 MOSCA'S THEOREM AND QUANTUM THREAT PREPAREDNESS

In the evolving landscape of quantum computing, the security of classical cryptographic systems is under serious scrutiny. With advances in quantum algorithms such as Shor's factoring algorithm and Grover's search, traditional encryption methods especially those relying on factoring or discrete logarithm problems are at risk of becoming obsolete. One of the most widely referenced frameworks for assessing the urgency of migrating to quantum-safe cryptographic systems is **Mosca's Theorem**, introduced by Michele Mosca [3].

MOSCA'S THEOREM

Mosca's Theorem addresses the fundamental trade-offs between three key time-based variables shown in Figure 7.1:

x: The number of years your information must remain secure (cover time).
y: The time required to migrate existing systems to a quantum-resistant infrastructure (migration time).
z: The estimated time remaining until a large-scale quantum computer is built (collapse time).

Mosca's inequality is expressed as:

$$\text{If } x+y > z, \textbf{ then worry.} \quad \text{If } x > z \text{ or } y > z, \textbf{ big trouble!}$$

This simple but powerful inequality enables decision-makers to quantify their risk based on how these parameters interact.

DETAILED INTERPRETATION

Case 1: $x+y > z$
Even if the current cryptographic systems seem adequate, if the time it takes to transition to quantum-safe algorithms plus the time for which information must remain secure exceeds the time until quantum capabilities arrive, there is an impending risk. Preparations must begin immediately.
Case 2: $x > z$
If the required security lifespan of the data exceeds the collapse time, then even perfect encryption today cannot safeguard the data through its intended lifetime. Adversaries could store encrypted data today and decrypt it once a quantum computer becomes available.
Case 3: $y > z$
If the infrastructure migration will take longer than the time until quantum computers arrive, then existing systems will collapse before post-quantum alternatives can be deployed. This scenario represents a systemic failure.

PRACTICAL INSIGHTS

While Mosca's theorem offers a theoretical framework for anticipating quantum threats, its practical implications are profound and require careful analysis. One of the main challenges is the uncertainty surrounding the value of z, the time remaining

(Case 1:) $x + y > z$

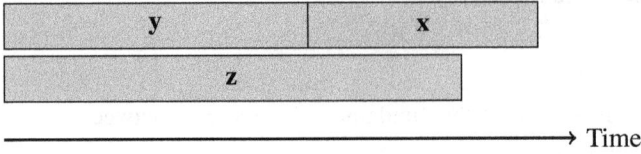

(Case 2:) $x > z$

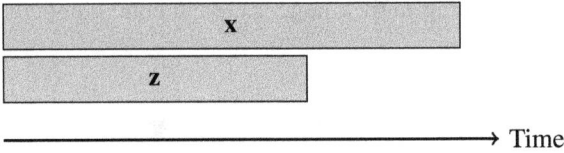

(Case 3:) $y > z$

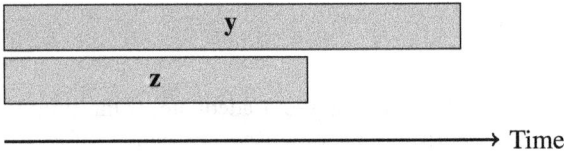

Figure 7.1 Illustrative cases derived from Mosca's Theorem. Each scenario demonstrates a time-based relationship among required security lifespan (x), migration time (y), and quantum readiness collapse point (z)

until a large-scale quantum computer is built. Estimates vary, but it is generally believed to fall somewhere between 10 and 30 years. This uncertainty makes planning for quantum-safe migration a difficult but necessary task [3].

In sectors that manage highly sensitive data such as defense, healthcare, and finance the value of x, the number of years that data must remain secure, is often quite large, frequently ranging from 10 to over 50 years. This long security requirement places significant pressure on organizations to begin transitioning now to ensure data confidentiality in the quantum future.

The time required for this transition, denoted as y, involves far more than simply adopting new cryptographic algorithms. Migration encompasses a comprehensive overhaul of existing infrastructure, including software reengineering, cryptographic key management changes, hardware replacement or updates, adherence to new regulatory standards, and staff retraining. These are time-intensive and resource-heavy tasks.

Attempting to rush the migration process to shorten y without thorough planning and validation can lead to insecure and error-prone implementations. Such shortcuts can undermine the very security goals the transition aims to achieve. Therefore, the migration strategy must strike a balance between the urgency imposed by the looming quantum threat and the diligence required for secure and resilient system upgrades.

7.1.3   QUANTUM SECURITY LEVELS AND PQC STRENGTH CATEGORIES

The transition to quantum-safe cryptography requires rigorous standards to classify and compare the security of Post-Quantum Cryptography (PQC) algorithms. In light of the anticipated threats posed by large-scale quantum computers, the National Institute of Standards and Technology (NIST) has proposed a structured framework to categorize cryptographic security.

UNCERTAINTY IN SECURITY STRENGTH ESTIMATES

There are inherent uncertainties in estimating the quantum security strength of cryptographic algorithms. These arise from two main sources:

Quantum Algorithmic Advances: Future discoveries may introduce new quantum algorithms that significantly reduce the complexity of cryptanalytic attacks.
Quantum Hardware Development: The practical characteristics of future quantum computers, such as speed, coherence time, error rates, and architectural limitations, remain difficult to predict.

To mitigate these challenges, NIST advocates for a classification system that uses broad security categories rather than precise bit-level estimates. These categories serve to align both symmetric and asymmetric primitives under a unified model.

NIST PQC SECURITY STRENGTH CATEGORIES

Each level corresponds to the estimated cost of defeating a symmetric cryptographic primitive using the best-known quantum or classical techniques.

Level 1 (NIST-L1): Resistance equivalent to brute-force key search on AES-128.
Level 2 (NIST-L2): Resistance equivalent to collision search on SHA-256 or SHA3-256.
Level 3 (NIST-L3): Resistance equivalent to brute-force key search on AES-192.
Level 4 (NIST-L4): Resistance equivalent to collision search on SHA-384 or SHA3-384.

Level 5 (NIST-L5): Resistance equivalent to brute-force key search on AES-256.
Level 6 (NIST-L6): is also known as paranoid security.

RESOURCE ESTIMATES FOR CRYPTANALYTIC ATTACKS

Table 7.1 outlines the estimated resources needed to attack symmetric primitives, under both quantum and classical models (2016 estimates) [4].

Table 7.1
Resource estimates for attacks (call for proposal 2016)

S.No.	Algorithms	Resource estimates
1	AES-128	2^{170}/MAXDEPTH quantum gates or 2^{143} classical gates
2	SHA3-256	2^{146} classical gates
3	AES-192	2^{233}/MAXDEPTH quantum gates or 2^{207} classical gates
4	SHA3-384	2^{210} classical gates
5	AES-256	2^{298}/MAXDEPTH quantum gates or 2^{272} classical gates
6	SHA3-512	2^{274} classical gates

INTERPRETING MAXDEPTH PARAMETERS

The MAXDEPTH term reflects assumptions about serial gate execution limits:

MAXDEPTH = 2^{40}: Current yearly limit for logical quantum gate operations.
MAXDEPTH = 2^{64}: Decade-long limit for classical serial computation.
MAXDEPTH = 2^{96}: Millennium-long limit with idealized atomic-scale qubits.

This classification guides the selection and standardization of PQC algorithms that must operate securely under the threat of emerging quantum capabilities.

UPDATED RESOURCE ESTIMATES FOR CRYPTANALYTIC ATTACKS (2022)

In the 2022 Call for Proposals [5], NIST released revised estimates for the resources required to break symmetric cryptographic primitives using classical and quantum methods. These updated values provide more conservative and realistic expectations based on advances in quantum algorithm cost analysis and circuit depth assumptions.

These revised benchmarks reinforce the need for robust quantum-resistant algorithms that can provide long-term security assurances even in the face of improved quantum algorithms and computing hardware. The slight reduction in quantum cost estimates (e.g., from 2^{170} to 2^{157} for AES-128) emphasizes the dynamic nature of cryptanalytic modeling and the importance of conservative design margins in PQC standards (Table 7.2).

Table 7.2

Resource estimates for attacks (call for proposal 2022)

S.No.	Algorithms	Resource estimates
1	AES-128	2^{157}/MAXDEPTH quantum gates or 2^{143} classical gates
2	SHA3-256	2^{146} classical gates
3	AES-192	2^{221}/MAXDEPTH quantum gates or 2^{207} classical gates
4	SHA3-384	2^{210} classical gates
5	AES-256	2^{285}/MAXDEPTH quantum gates or 2^{272} classical gates
6	SHA3-512	2^{274} classical gates

7.1.4 ASYMMETRIC KEY CRYPTOGRAPHIC PRIMITIVES

The researchers are developing quantum-safe cryptographic algorithms that can withstand quantum attacks. These quantum-resistant algorithms are based on mathematical problems that are believed to be hard for both classical and quantum computers. There have been several interesting approaches to post-quantum cryptography that have been investigated in recent years. These include the following:

Lattice-based cryptography
Code-based cryptography
Multivariate cryptography
Hash-based cryptography
Supersingular Isogeny-based cryptography

LATTICE-BASED CRYPTOGRAPHY

Lattice-based cryptography is one of the most promising and well-studied approaches in the realm of post-quantum cryptography. This approach relies on the hardness of well-known lattice problems, such as the *Learning With Errors* (LWE) problem and the *Shortest Vector Problem* (SVP). These problems are believed to be computationally intractable even for quantum computers, making lattice-based schemes strong candidates for securing communications in a post-quantum world.

The LWE problem, in particular, has gained significant attention because it offers strong security guarantees and is versatile enough to be the foundation for constructing a wide variety of cryptographic primitives. Its hardness has been shown to be reducible from worst-case lattice problems, which means that breaking a cryptographic scheme based on LWE would be as hard as solving the hardest instances of certain lattice problems. This property, known as *worst-case to average-case reduction*, is one of the key reasons why lattice-based schemes are considered highly secure [6].

Another fundamental lattice problem is the SVP, which asks for the shortest non-zero vector in a high-dimensional lattice. This problem is believed to be extremely difficult, and many cryptographic constructions rely on its assumed hardness. Importantly, these underlying problems remain hard not only for classical computers but also for quantum algorithms, including those that generalize Shor's and Grover's algorithms.

In addition to their strong theoretical security guarantees, lattice-based cryptographic schemes are often efficient and scalable. They are well-suited for modern computing environments, as they typically involve simple mathematical operations like modular addition and multiplication. This makes them attractive for implementation on constrained devices, such as those found in IoT networks and mobile systems.

One notable example of a lattice-based cryptographic scheme is **NTRUEncrypt**, which is based on problems related to polynomial rings and lattice structures. NTRUEncrypt was one of the earliest practical lattice-based encryption schemes and has been extensively studied and refined over the years. It offers strong security guarantees while maintaining high performance and low computational overhead. NTRUEncrypt is particularly appealing because of its small key sizes and fast encryption/decryption times, which make it suitable for resource-constrained environments. Its design is resistant to known quantum attacks, and its security relies on the hardness of finding short vectors in certain structured lattices. NTRUEncrypt was selected as one of the finalists in the NIST Post-Quantum Cryptography standardization process under the category of public-key encryption and key encapsulation mechanisms [7].

Beyond encryption and digital signatures, lattice-based cryptography also supports a wide range of advanced cryptographic functionalities. Notably, it enables the construction of **fully homomorphic encryption** (FHE) schemes, which allow arbitrary computations to be performed on encrypted data without needing to decrypt it first. This opens up transformative possibilities for secure cloud computing and privacy-preserving data analytics. Furthermore, lattice-based schemes can support **functional encryption**, where access to encrypted data can be finely controlled based on specific functions or policies [8].

Given these advantages—strong security rooted in worst-case hardness, practical efficiency, resistance to quantum attacks, and support for advanced features—lattice-based cryptography is widely regarded as a foundational pillar of future cryptographic systems [9].

CODE-BASED CRYPTOGRAPHY

Code-based cryptography is one of the oldest forms of post-quantum cryptographic schemes, dating back to the late 1970s. These algorithms rely on the computational hardness of decoding a general linear code, a problem that has been shown to be NP-hard. The most well-known example is the **McEliece cryptosystem**, which was introduced in 1978. It is based on the difficulty of decoding random linear error-correcting codes, specifically Goppa codes. Despite its long history, the McEliece cryptosystem has withstood decades of cryptanalytic scrutiny and remains unbroken by both classical and quantum algorithms.

The McEliece cryptosystem is notable for its speed and robustness. It allows for very fast encryption and decryption operations, making it suitable for high-throughput applications. However, one of its primary drawbacks is the large size of its public keys, which can range from several hundred kilobytes to even megabytes, depending on the parameter set. Nevertheless, the trade-off is considered acceptable given the strong security assurances it provides. Importantly, McEliece is one of the few cryptosystems that remain secure in the face of quantum adversaries, as the best known quantum attacks offer only polynomial speedups over classical ones, which are still computationally infeasible [10].

A closely related scheme is the **Niederreiter cryptosystem**, which is also based on error-correcting codes but uses a different mathematical formulation. The Niederreiter variant typically offers the same level of security as McEliece, with some optimizations in terms of ciphertext size and implementation efficiency. Both schemes form the foundation of ongoing research in code-based cryptography and are among the strong contenders in the NIST post-quantum cryptography standardization process [11].

In parallel with code-based approaches, some cryptographic schemes explore hardness assumptions based on **NP-complete problems**. These schemes derive their security from the assumption that certain decision or optimization problems—known to be NP-complete—remain hard to solve even for quantum computers. Examples include the subset-sum (knapsack) problem, graph coloring, and satisfiability (SAT). While theoretically appealing, many early schemes based on NP-complete problems were broken or shown to have structural weaknesses, often due to hidden algebraic properties or poorly chosen parameters [12].

Nonetheless, ongoing research aims to construct practical and secure cryptographic primitives grounded in NP-completeness. The main appeal of such approaches lies in the broad range of problems available and the general belief that NP-complete problems are inherently hard to solve in all cases, even with quantum resources. If successfully realized, cryptosystems based on NP-complete problems could offer new directions for post-quantum security with diverse applications across different platforms [13].

MULTIVARIATE CRYPTOGRAPHY

Multivariate cryptography is a class of post-quantum cryptographic schemes based on the hardness of solving systems of multivariate polynomial equations over finite fields. Solving such systems is known to be an NP-hard problem, and there are currently no efficient algorithms—classical or quantum—that can solve them in general, particularly when the equations are constructed with certain structures to resist attacks [14].

This approach is particularly attractive for its potential to provide efficient and secure digital signature schemes. In contrast to many lattice-based or code-based encryption systems, multivariate schemes can offer relatively small signature sizes and fast verification times, making them suitable for applications requiring lightweight cryptography, such as embedded systems, smart cards, and IoT devices [15].

A prominent example is the **Rainbow signature scheme**, which is a layered generalization of the Unbalanced Oil and Vinegar (UOV) signature scheme. Rainbow has been a leading candidate in the NIST post-quantum cryptography standardization project due to its strong security assumptions and performance characteristics.

The scheme constructs a trapdoor function based on a structured set of multivariate quadratic equations, which allows for fast signature generation and efficient verification [16].

Another important multivariate scheme is the **Unbalanced Oil and Vinegar (UOV)** scheme, which simplifies the construction of secure multivariate equations by dividing variables into "oil" and "vinegar" categories. This separation helps to prevent attacks that exploit algebraic structures, making UOV one of the more resilient multivariate approaches [17].

Despite their advantages, multivariate schemes must be carefully parameterized to avoid algebraic attacks that exploit patterns in the underlying polynomial systems. Ongoing research continues to refine the balance between security, efficiency, and practicality, making multivariate cryptography an active and promising area for post-quantum digital signatures [18].

HASH-BASED CRYPTOGRAPHIC SCHEMES

Hash-based cryptographic schemes are a class of post-quantum cryptography that rely on the security of cryptographic hash functions, which are well-known for their resistance to preimage, second-preimage, and collision attacks. These schemes are particularly well-suited for digital signatures because they do not depend on hard mathematical problems such as integer factorization or discrete logarithms. Instead, hash-based signatures leverage the fundamental property of cryptographic hash functions, namely their *collision resistance*—the difficulty of finding two distinct inputs that produce the same hash output.

The most notable example of a hash-based cryptosystem is the **Merkle signature scheme**, proposed by Ralph Merkle in 1979. The Merkle scheme builds digital signatures by using a tree structure of hash functions, where each node in the tree is a hash of its children, and the root of the tree serves as the public key. Merkle's approach allows for the efficient verification of signatures and provides strong security guarantees based on the hardness of finding collisions in hash functions [19].

One of the most important advancements in hash-based cryptography is the **eXtended Merkle Signature Scheme (XMSS)**. XMSS is a stateful hash-based signature scheme designed to resist quantum attacks. Unlike earlier Merkle-based schemes, XMSS provides a secure method for generating multiple signatures without reusing keys. Its efficiency and security have made it one of the leading candidates in the NIST post-quantum cryptography standardization project [20].

Another notable hash-based scheme is the **Leighton-Micali Signature Scheme (LMS)**, which is designed to offer secure digital signatures with a small signature size and fast signing and verification times. Like XMSS, LMS is based on a tree structure, but it is optimized for high-speed signature generation, making it suitable for applications that require frequent signing, such as secure communications and software updates [21].

Both XMSS and LMS are quantum-resistant due to their reliance on the collision resistance of hash functions, ensuring that they remain secure even against adversaries armed with quantum computers [22].

SUPERSINGULAR ISOGENY-BASED CRYPTOGRAPHY

Supersingular isogeny-based cryptography is a promising post-quantum crypto-graphic technique that relies on the hardness of finding isogenies between super-singular elliptic curves. An isogeny is a special type of morphism between ellip-tic curves that preserves their group structure. In the context of cryptography, an isogeny-based approach involves mapping one elliptic curve to another using an isogeny, with the computational difficulty of finding these isogenies serving as the foundation of security. Supersingular elliptic curves are particularly well-suited for this purpose because they have special properties that make certain computational problems associated with isogenies difficult to solve, even for quantum computers.

The security of supersingular isogeny-based cryptosystems is based on the con-jectured hardness of the *supersingular isogeny problem*, which involves computing isogenies between supersingular elliptic curves. While classical algorithms struggle to solve this problem in polynomial time, no efficient quantum algorithms have been discovered to date, making isogeny-based schemes resistant to quantum attacks. This is in stark contrast to traditional schemes like RSA or ECC, which are vulnerable to quantum algorithms like Shor's algorithm.

Supersingular isogeny-based cryptographic schemes offer several attractive prop-erties, such as *compact key sizes*, which make them suitable for constrained envi-ronments, such as embedded systems and IoT devices. Additionally, these schemes are versatile and can be used for a variety of cryptographic purposes, including key exchange and digital signatures. A notable example of a scheme based on supersin-gular isogenies is the **Supersingular Isogeny Diffie-Hellman (SIDH)** protocol [23], which allows two parties to securely exchange cryptographic keys. Another exam-ple is the **Supersingular Isogeny Key Encapsulation (SIKE)** scheme [24], which provides a secure key exchange mechanism in the post-quantum era.

Both SIDH and SIKE have been recognized as strong candidates for quantum-resistant cryptography, with ongoing research focused on improving their efficiency and scalability [25].

By proactively transitioning to quantum-resistant algorithms, sensitive informa-tion can be safeguarded, ensuring the continued trust in digital infrastructure amid evolving technological threats. The adoption of quantum-safe cryptographic solu-tions is essential for maintaining the long-term security of digital communication and data. Through collaboration, research, and standardization, a secure and resilient cryptographic ecosystem can be built to withstand the challenges posed by quan-tum computing. The ongoing development and implementation of quantum-resistant algorithms will play a crucial role in protecting the confidentiality, integrity, and au-thenticity of digital information in the quantum era.

7.1.5 SYMMETRIC KEY CRYPTOGRAPHIC PRIMITIVES

In symmetric cryptography, doubling the sizes of keys is often assumed to be a suf-ficient protection against quantum adversaries. This is because Grover's quantum search algorithm, which can be used for generically recovering the key, is limited to a quadratic speedup. However, this oversimplified assumption may not be sufficient always.

In this direction, let us take an example from the classical paradigm. After the attacks were reported on the Data Encryption Standard (DES), which uses a 56-bit key to encrypt any plaintext, Double-DES was proposed with the motivation of increasing the security to 112 bits. However, due to the attack called *Man-in-the-Middle*, the security of Double-DES remains 56 bits instead of the expected 112 bits.

In the quantum domain, in the paper entitled *Beyond Quadratic Speedups in Quantum Attacks on Symmetric Schemes* by Xavier Bonnetain et al. (CoRR, Vol. abs/2110.02836, 2021, https://arxiv.org/abs/2110.02836), the authors reported a symmetric block cipher design with:

a security bound of $2.5n$ against classical adversaries,
a quantum attack in time roughly 2^n, using classical queries only.

This gives, for the first time, a proven 2.5 speedup on a quantum attack in the classical query model.

In this regard, one may consider the paper titled *Grover on Chosen IV Related Key Attack Against GRAIN-128a* by Samanta et al. (INDOCRYPT 2023). In the paper, the authors showed that exploiting Grover's algorithm as a tool followed by classical processing, the query complexity of a chosen IV-related key attack considered by Banik et al. in ACISP 2013, can be reduced to $O(2^{32})$ from $O(2^{64})$, which is actually far beyond the quadratic limit of 2^{128}. Thus, doubling the key might not be the only viable strategy to confirm the security of symmetric ciphers in the post-quantum era.

Additionally, doubling the key size may increase the round number. For example, AES-128 is designed for 10 rounds whereas AES-256 is designed for 14 rounds. This affects a large number of parameters such as speed, weight, and cost of the resources.

Finally, it might not be a wise assumption that only Grover's Search Algorithm warrants the security of symmetric key cryptology. Simon's Period Finding Algorithm may also pose a threat to the same. In this regard, one may refer to the paper *Breaking Symmetric Cryptosystems using Quantum Period Finding* by Marc Kaplan et al. (CRYPTO 2016). In the paper, the authors showed how Feistel construction becomes vulnerable to a distinguishing attack on a three-round scheme.

QUANTUM ATTACK STRATEGY USING GROVER'S ALGORITHM

Quantum cryptanalysis using Grover's algorithm presents a structured approach to attacking symmetric key ciphers. The overall methodology involves circuit construction, oracle formulation, and iterative amplitude amplification shown in Figure 7.2. The following flowchart outlines the decision-making and operational steps in executing a Grover-based quantum attack against a block cipher:

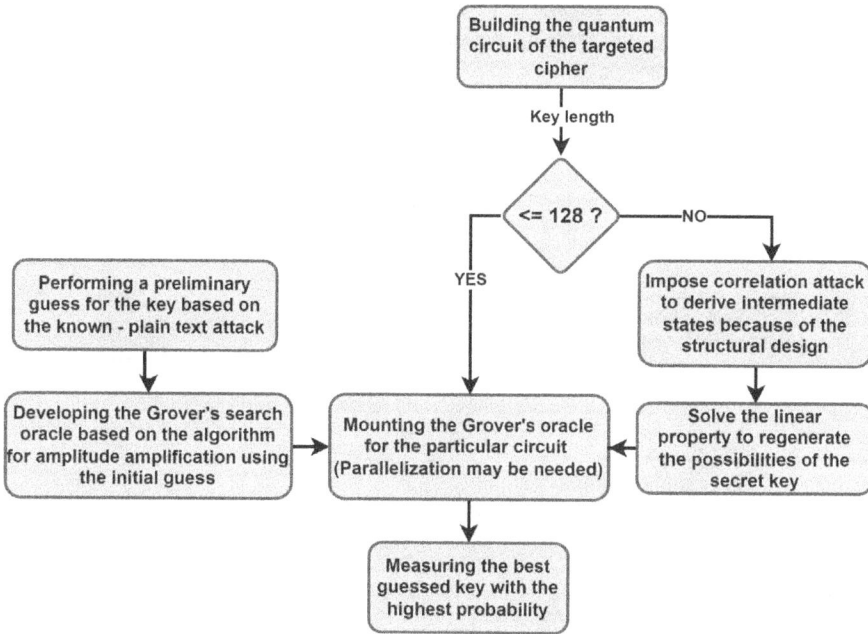

Figure 7.2   Flowchart of a quantum Grover-based attack strategy on symmetric-key ciphers

EXPLANATION OF FLOWCHART COMPONENTS

Building the quantum circuit: The process begins by encoding the encryption function as a quantum circuit, which serves as the basis for the oracle.

Key Length Decision: Depending on the cipher's key size, different strategies are employed. If the key length is 128 bits or less, Grover's algorithm is considered viable.

Preliminary Key Guess: In the YES path, the attacker can exploit known plaintext-ciphertext pairs to initialize a promising guess and reduce the search space.

Grover Oracle Development: An oracle is constructed to reflect correct guesses of the key. Amplitude amplification is used to increase the probability of measuring the correct result.

Mounting and Executing Grover's Algorithm: The oracle is embedded into the Grover iteration loop. Depending on the complexity, parallelization may improve efficiency.

Measurement Phase: After the required $O(\sqrt{N})$ iterations, the quantum register is measured to reveal the most likely key candidate.

Structural Cryptanalysis (NO path): For keys longer than 128 bits, direct Grover search becomes infeasible. Instead, structural attacks such as correlation attacks are employed.

Intermediate State Analysis: These attacks exploit cipher properties to derive partial state information, which is then used to infer the secret key via algebraic analysis.

This flowchart reflects a hybridized quantum-classical approach tailored to cipher design and key length. The method adapts between brute-force amplification and structure-based inference to maximize the effectiveness of quantum adversaries.

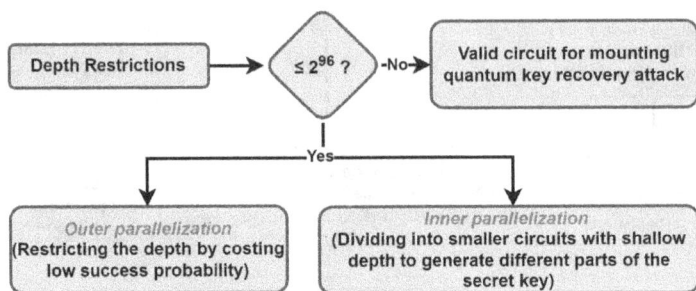

Figure 7.3 Flowchart representing quantum attack feasibility under depth restrictions

DEPTH CONSTRAINTS IN QUANTUM KEY RECOVERY ATTACKS

Quantum circuits used for cryptanalytic attacks are limited by physical constraints such as coherence time and gate fidelity. These limitations impose restrictions on the maximum allowable depth of a quantum circuit—quantified by a parameter commonly referred to as **MAXDEPTH**. A typical reference depth used in feasibility analysis is 2^{40} logical gate operations.

Figure 7.3 outlines a decision framework used to assess whether a quantum key recovery attack can be realistically executed under such depth constraints.

Depth Restrictions: The attack is initially assessed based on the required depth of the quantum circuit implementation.
Decision Node ($\leq 2^{40}$): If the required circuit depth is within 2^{40} gates, it is considered feasible to mount a practical quantum key recovery attack. In this case, amplitude amplification and measurement (such as in Grover's algorithm) can proceed within realistic hardware capabilities.
If the Depth Exceeds the Limit: When the circuit depth requirement exceeds 2^{40}, the quantum attack must be adapted using one of the following parallelization strategies:

Outer Parallelization: This approach restricts depth by trading off success probability. Multiple low-depth circuits are executed independently, each with a low chance of success. The key is eventually recovered by combining results from several runs.

Inner Parallelization: The quantum circuit is divided into smaller sub-circuits, each responsible for a portion of the key search. These sub-circuits are designed with reduced depth, allowing them to operate under the imposed hardware constraints. This technique often requires the cipher to support decomposition of its key space or internal structure.

This analysis plays a critical role in determining whether a theoretical quantum attack is viable in practice and guides cryptanalysts in designing hardware-aware attack strategies.

Symmetric key cryptography is a fundamental component of modern cryptographic systems, where the same secret key is used for both encryption and decryption. With the emergence of quantum computing, the security landscape for symmetric cryptographic primitives is also shifting. Although symmetric cryptography is generally more resistant to quantum attacks compared to asymmetric cryptography, quantum algorithms still impose new constraints and performance requirements [26].

Symmetric key cryptography relies on the shared knowledge of a secret key between communicating parties. The two primary categories of symmetric primitives are:

Block ciphers: These encrypt data in fixed-size blocks. Examples include AES (Advanced Encryption Standard), DES (Data Encryption Standard), and 3DES.

Stream ciphers: These encrypt data one bit or byte at a time. Examples include RC4 and Salsa20.

Other important primitives include:

Message Authentication Codes (MACs): Used for verifying data integrity and authenticity, such as HMAC.

Authenticated Encryption (AE): Combines encryption and authentication, with schemes like AES-GCM.

7.1.6   GENERAL COUNTERMEASURES

Stream ciphers are vulnerable to quantum algorithms such as Grover's and Simon's. Effective countermeasures focus on key management, cipher design, and protocol-level enhancements to improve resistance against quantum threats.

7.1.6.1   Increasing Key Length

Grover's algorithm reduces the complexity of brute-force key search from 2^n to approximately $2^{n/2}$, effectively halving the security level of symmetric ciphers. For instance, a 128-bit key provides only 64-bit security against a quantum adversary.

To restore robust security, increasing the key length is a common strategy. A 256-bit key would require around 2^{128} operations even with Grover's algorithm, thus maintaining an adequate security margin.

However, longer keys introduce practical challenges, such as increased memory usage, reduced throughput, and greater computational overhead. As such, key length extension should be carefully balanced with performance requirements and considered alongside other quantum-resistant strategies to ensure comprehensive protection.

7.1.6.2   Algorithm Modifications

Modifying cryptographic algorithms is a key strategy to improve resilience against quantum attacks. These modifications focus on enhancing non-linearity, adapting cipher modes, and incorporating advanced key and randomness techniques.

Incorporating Non-linearity

Increasing the non-linearity in cipher design reduces predictability and improves resistance to quantum analysis. This includes using complex S-boxes, generalized Feistel structures, and replacing LFSRs with Non-linear Feedback Shift Registers (NLFSRs). Techniques like chaotic maps can further enhance unpredictability but must be weighed against implementation costs.

Mode of Operation Adjustments

Adopting secure modes such as Authenticated Encryption with Associated Data (AEAD) provides encryption and integrity protection. Modes like Galois/Counter Mode (GCM) and Encrypt-then-MAC (EtM) hinder quantum-aided forgery and ciphertext manipulation. Additionally, nonce-based encryption helps prevent replay and adaptive attacks by ensuring ciphertext uniqueness, enhancing overall quantum resistance.

7.1.6.3   Key Management Enhancements

Enhancing key management through frequent key rotation and robust key derivation functions is essential to mitigate quantum threats.

Frequent Key Rotation

Frequent key rotation reduces the duration a key remains in use, limiting the time quantum adversaries have to perform brute-force attacks like Grover's. Although it introduces additional management overhead, this strategy significantly improves overall cryptographic resilience.

Key Derivation Functions

Quantum-resistant Key Derivation Functions (KDFs) generate secure keys from initial keying material using high-entropy inputs and memory-hard techniques. Functions such as Argon2 and PBKDF2 can be strengthened with higher iteration counts and secure hash functions like SHA-3. Incorporating HMAC-based expansion further prevents key prediction or compromise, ensuring robust protection even against quantum adversaries.

7.1.6.4   Randomization Techniques

Randomization enhances the quantum resistance of symmetric ciphers by reducing structural predictability.

Random Initialization Vectors (IVs)

Using cryptographically secure pseudo-random number generators (CSPRNGs) for IVs ensures that each encryption session produces a unique ciphertext, even with the same key. For nonce-based modes, uniqueness is essential, but combining it with randomness adds further protection.

Random Key Generation

Keys should be derived from high-entropy sources to resist quantum brute-force techniques like Grover's algorithm. Regular key refreshment and secure management protocols further limit an adversary's ability to exploit key reuse.

Integration with Cipher Modes

Cipher modes such as CTR and GCM rely on random or pseudo-random IVs to prevent keystream repetition. This integration ensures added robustness against quantum-enabled pattern recognition.

Defense Against Replay Attacks

Randomized IVs protect against quantum replay attacks by ensuring ciphertext uniqueness, thereby preventing adversaries from gaining statistical advantages through message repetition.

7.1.7   FUTURE DIRECTIONS

Quantum cryptography promises to reshape secure communication by leveraging the fundamental principles of quantum mechanics. As both quantum technologies and quantum attacks continue to evolve, the research and development of quantum cryptography is expected to expand in multiple directions. This section outlines key future directions for the field [27].

7.1.7.1 Advancement of Quantum Key Distribution (QKD)

QKD remains one of the most mature applications of quantum cryptography. QKD is expected to evolve significantly in the coming years. A major focus will be on scalability and integration, aiming to develop QKD networks that can be deployed on a global scale and integrated with existing fiber-optic and satellite communication infrastructures. Cost reduction is another critical area, with efforts directed toward creating affordable and compact QKD devices suitable for widespread commercial and consumer use. Additionally, enhancing key generation and data transmission rates is essential to meet the demands of high-speed communication networks. A particularly important research direction is Device-Independent QKD (DI-QKD), which seeks to eliminate the need for trust in the internal workings of quantum devices, thereby protecting against side-channel attacks and implementation flaws [28].

7.1.7.2 Quantum-Resistant Symmetric Key Systems

Although symmetric key cryptography is relatively resistant to quantum attacks, future research will focus on enhancing its resilience and efficiency in the quantum era. One key direction is the optimization of key sizes and algorithms, where cryptographic parameters are adjusted to ensure adequate security against Grover's algorithm while preserving computational performance. Another important area involves designing quantum-resistant modes of operation, which includes innovating block cipher modes and authenticated encryption schemes capable of withstanding quantum adversaries. Furthermore, the development of lightweight post-quantum ciphers is essential, particularly for embedded systems and IoT devices that require efficient yet secure cryptographic primitives in resource-constrained environments.

7.1.7.3 Quantum-Secure Cryptographic Protocols

Beyond individual cryptographic algorithms, entire cryptographic protocols must be reassessed in light of emerging quantum threats. One significant area of focus is the design of quantum-secure Multi-Party Computation (MPC) protocols that can operate securely even when adversaries possess quantum computational capabilities. In addition, there is a need to develop quantum-secure zero-knowledge proofs that maintain both their soundness and zero-knowledge properties when subjected to quantum attacks. Another promising direction is the integration of quantum-resistant algorithms into blockchain technologies, ensuring the long-term security of consensus mechanisms and cryptographic primitives used within decentralized systems [29].

7.1.7.4 Standardization and Interoperability

With growing international efforts in post-quantum cryptography, such as NIST's PQC standardization initiative, future research will emphasize the establishment of comprehensive frameworks and guidelines. A key direction is the development of global standards for quantum cryptography, promoting collaboration on protocols, key lengths, and implementations to ensure consistency and interoperability across nations and systems. Additionally, hybrid cryptographic systems that combine classical and quantum-resistant algorithms are expected to play a critical role in maintaining security during the transitional period toward fully quantum-secure infrastructures. Equally important is the creation of regulatory frameworks that provide governance, compliance guidelines, and certification procedures for the safe and effective deployment of quantum cryptographic technologies.

7.1.7.5 Quantum Cryptography Beyond Key Distribution

Future quantum cryptographic protocols are expected to extend well beyond QKD, opening new possibilities for secure communication and digital trust. One such direction is the development of quantum digital signatures, which aim to provide secure and unforgeable authentication mechanisms grounded in quantum principles. Another promising area is the creation of quantum money and tokens—quantum-secure monetary systems that leverage the no-cloning theorem to prevent duplication and counterfeiting. Additionally, foundational cryptographic tools such as quantum oblivious transfer and bit commitment are being explored as essential components for constructing more complex and robust quantum-secure protocols [30].

7.1.7.6 Quantum Network Infrastructure

Building a full-scale quantum internet will be essential for realizing many of the cryptographic advancements enabled by quantum technologies. Research directions in this area include the development of quantum repeaters and entanglement swapping techniques, which are crucial for enabling long-distance quantum communication. Additionally, the creation of quantum internet protocols is a key focus, aiming to design network layers and communication protocols specifically tailored for quantum data transmission. Furthermore, exploring entanglement-based communication models is an exciting frontier, as it offers the potential to leverage quantum entanglement as a resource for novel cryptographic capabilities and secure communication systems [31].

7.1.8 CONCLUSION

Quantum cryptography is still in its early stages but holds immense potential. Its future development hinges on both theoretical advancements and technological breakthroughs. As quantum computing matures, proactive investment in quantum-safe and quantum-enabled cryptographic systems is imperative to ensure long-term security and privacy in the digital age.

Cryptography is a dynamic and ever-evolving field, continually adapting to meet the security demands of the digital age. By staying informed about advancements in cryptographic research and adopting innovative solutions, we can ensure the long-term security and privacy of digital communication and data. The collaboration between researchers, industry, and government will be essential in developing and implementing the next generation of cryptographic technologies, safeguarding our digital future. By addressing current challenges and anticipating future developments, the field of cryptography will continue to provide the foundation for secure communication, data protection, and trust in the digital world.

REFERENCES

1. Brassard, G., & Crépeau, C. (2025). Quantum cryptography. In *Encyclopedia of Cryptography, Security and Privacy* (pp. 2032–2032). Springer Nature Switzerland.
2. M. Mosca. (2015). Cybersecurity in an era with quantum computers: Will we be ready?, *Proceedings of the 5th Conference on Quantum Cryptography (QCrypt).* Available at: `https://eprint.iacr.org/2015/1075`
3. M. Mosca. (2018). Timeframes for quantum security, *White Paper, Global Risk Institute*, 2018. Available at: `https://globalriskinstitute.org/publications/timeframes-for-quantum-security/`
4. National Institute of Standards and Technology (NIST). (2016). *Call for Proposals for Post-Quantum Cryptography.* Retrieved from `https://csrc.nist.gov/CSRC/media/Projects/Post-Quantum-Cryptography/documents/call-for-proposals-final-dec-2016.pdf`
5. National Institute of Standards and Technology (NIST). (2022). *Call for Proposals for Post-Quantum Digital Signature Algorithms.* Retrieved from `https://csrc.nist.gov/csrc/media/Projects/pqc-dig-sig/documents/call-for-proposals-dig-sig-sept-2022.pdf`
6. National Institute of Standards and Technology (NIST). (2024). *Module-Lattice-Based Digital Signature Standard.* Retrieved from `https://www.nist.gov/`
7. Hoffstein, J., Pipher, J., & Silverman, J. H. (1998). NTRU: A ring-based public key cryptosystem. In *Algorithmic Number Theory* (pp. 267–288). Lecture Notes in Computer Science, Vol. 1423.
8. Marcolla, C., Sucasas, V., Manzano, M., Bassoli, R., Fitzek, F. H., & Aaraj, N. (2022). Survey on fully homomorphic encryption, theory, and applications. *Proceedings of the IEEE*, 110(10), 1572–1609.
9. Hieta-aho, E., Rautell, M., & Lintulampi, A. (2025, January). Security of lattice-based cryptography. In *Quantum Software Day 2025*.
10. Overbeck, R., & Sendrier, N. (2009). Code-based cryptography. In *Post-quantum cryptography* (pp. 95–145). Springer Berlin Heidelberg.
11. Niederreiter, H. (1986). A public-key cryptosystem based on shift register sequences. *In Advances in Cryptology—EUROCRYPT'85: Proceedings of a Workshop on the Theory and Application of Cryptographic Techniques* (pp. 35–39). Springer Berlin Heidelberg.
12. Garey, M. R., Johnson, D. S., & Stockmeyer, L. (1974). Some simplified NP-complete problems. In *Proceedings of the Sixth Annual ACM Symposium on Theory of Computing* (pp. 47–63).
13. Biasse, J. F., & Micheli, G. (2025). The code equivalence problem and its applications to cryptography. *La Matematica*, 1–27.
14. Ding, J., & Petzoldt, A. (2017). Current state of multivariate cryptography. *IEEE Security & Privacy*, 15(4), 28–36.
15. Dey, J., & Dutta, R. (2023). Progress in multivariate cryptography: Systematic review, challenges, and research directions. *ACM Computing Surveys*, 55(12), 1–34.

16. Ding, J., & Schmidt, D. (2005). Rainbow, a new multivariable polynomial signature scheme. In *International Conference on Applied Cryptography and Network Security* (pp. 164–175). Springer Berlin Heidelberg.
17. Kipnis, A., Patarin, J., & Goubin, L. (1999). Unbalanced oil and vinegar signature schemes. In *Advances in Cryptology—EUROCRYPT '99: International Conference on the Theory and Application of Cryptographic Techniques* (pp. 206–222). Springer Berlin Heidelberg.
18. Ustimenko, V. (2025). On symbolic computations over arbitrary commutative rings and cryptography with the temporal Jordan-Gauss graphs. *Cryptology* ePrint Archive.
19. Buchmann, J., García, L. C. C., Dahmen, E., Döring, M., & Klintsevich, E. (2006). CMSS—an improved Merkle signature scheme. In *Progress in Cryptology-INDOCRYPT 2006: 7th International Conference on Cryptology in India* (pp. 349–363). Springer Berlin Heidelberg.
20. Hülsing, A., Butin, D., Gazdag, S., Rijneveld, J., & Mohaisen, A. (2018). *XMSS: eXtended Merkle signature scheme (No. RFC8391).*
21. Cao, Y., Wu, Y., Wang, W., Lu, X., Chen, S., Ye, J., & Chang, C. H. (2021). An efficient full hardware implementation of extended Merkle signature scheme. *IEEE Transactions on Circuits and Systems I: Regular Papers*, 69(2), 682–693.
22. Dolev, S., Yagudaev, A., & Yung, M. (2025). HBSS: (Simple) hash-based stateless signatures–hash all the way to the rescue! *Cryptography and Communications*, 1–18.
23. Costello, C., Longa, P., & Naehrig, M. (2016). Efficient algorithms for supersingular isogeny Diffie-Hellman. In *Advances in Cryptology—CRYPTO 2016: 36th Annual International Cryptology Conference* (pp. 572–601). Springer Berlin Heidelberg.
24. Seo, H., Anastasova, M., Jalali, A., & Azarderakhsh, R. (2020). Supersingular isogeny key encapsulation (SIKE) round 2 on ARM Cortex-M4. *IEEE Transactions on Computers*, 70(10), 1705–1718.
25. Mishra, S., Mondal, B., & Jha, R. K. (2025). A survey on isogeny-based cryptographic protocols. *Wireless Networks*, 31(3), 2993–3024.
26. Baseri, Y., Chouhan, V., Ghorbani, A., & Chow, A. (2025). Evaluation framework for quantum security risk assessment: A comprehensive strategy for quantum-safe transition. *Computers & Security*, 150, 104272.
27. Chahar, S. (2025). Guardians of privacy: Unravelling public key cryptography. In *Next Generation Mechanisms for Data Encryption* (pp. 14–34). CRC Press.
28. Singh, S. K., Kumar, S., Chhabra, A., Sharma, A., Arya, V., Srinivasan, M., & Gupta, B. B. (2025). Advancements in secure quantum communication and robust key distribution techniques for cybersecurity applications. *Cyber Security and Applications*, 100089.
29. Xiong, J., Shen, L., Liu, Y., & Fang, X. (2025). Enhancing IoT security in smart grids with quantum-resistant hybrid encryption. *Scientific Reports*, 15(1), 3.
30. Subramani, S., & Svn, S. K. (2025). Review of security methods based on classical cryptography and quantum cryptography. *Cybernetics and Systems*, 56(3), 302–320.
31. Sihare, S. R. (2025). Guided and unguided approaches for quantum key distribution for secure quantum communication. *Security and Privacy*, 8(1), e453.

For Product Safety Concerns and Information please contact our EU
representative GPSR@taylorandfrancis.com
Taylor & Francis Verlag GmbH, Kaufingerstraße 24, 80331 München, Germany

www.ingramcontent.com/pod-product-compliance
Lightning Source LLC
Chambersburg PA
CBHW060343220326
41598CB00023B/2791

9 781032 998527